Memories and Monsters

Memories and Monsters explores the nature of the monstrous or uncanny, and the way in which psychological trauma relates to memory and narration. This interdisciplinary book works on the borderland between psychology and philosophy, drawing from scholars in both fields who have helped mould the bourgeoning field of relational psychoanalysis and phenomenological and existential psychology. The editors have sought out contributions to this field that speak to the pressing question: how are we to attend to and contend with our monsters?

The authors in this volume examine the ways in which we might best relate to our monsters, and how the legacies of ancient traumas and anxieties continue to affect our current stories, memories, and everyday practices. Covering such manifestations of the monstrous as racism, crimes against humanity, trauma as portrayed in music and art, and the Holocaust, this book explores the impact the uncanny has on our individual and collective psyches.

By focusing on a very specific theme, and one that excites the imagination, *Memories and Monsters* stokes the flames of an important current movement in relational psychoanalysis. It will appeal to psychoanalysts and psychoanalytic psychotherapists, as well as professionals in psychology and graduate-school students and tutors in the fields of both psychology and philosophy.

Eric R. Severson is a philosopher specializing in the work of Emmanuel Levinas. He is the author of the books *Levinas's Philosophy of Time* (Duquesne University Press, 2013) and *Scandalous Obligation* (Beacon Hill Press, 2011), and editor of several volumes on ethics, the philosophy of religion, and psychology. He currently teaches philosophy at Seattle University.

David M. Goodman is a licensed clinical psychologist, Associate Dean of Academic Affairs and Advising at the Woods College of Advancing Studies at Boston College, Director of the Psychology and the Other Institute, and a teaching associate at Harvard Medical School/Cambridge Hospital.

Relational Perspectives Book Series

Lewis Aron & Adrienne Harris
Series Co-Editors

Steven Kuchuck & Eyal Rozmarin
Associate Editors

The Relational Perspectives Book Series (RPBS) publishes books that grow out of or contribute to the relational tradition in contemporary psychoanalysis. The term *relational psychoanalysis* was first used by Greenberg and Mitchell[1] to bridge the traditions of interpersonal relations, as developed within interpersonal psychoanalysis and object relations, as developed within contemporary British theory. But, under the seminal work of the late Stephen A. Mitchell, the term *relational psychoanalysis* grew and began to accrue to itself many other influences and developments. Various tributaries—interpersonal psychoanalysis, object relations theory, self psychology, empirical infancy research, and elements of contemporary Freudian and Kleinian thought—flow into this tradition, which understands relational configurations between self and others, both real and fantasied, as the primary subject of psychoanalytic investigation.

We refer to the relational tradition, rather than to a relational school, to highlight that we are identifying a trend, a tendency within contemporary psychoanalysis, not a more formally organized or coherent school or system of beliefs. Our use of the term *relational* signifies a dimension of theory and practice that has become salient across the wide spectrum of contemporary psychoanalysis. Now under the editorial supervision of Lewis Aron and Adrienne Harris, with the assistance of Associate Editors Steven Kuchuck and Eyal Rozmarin, the Relational Perspectives Book Series originated in 1990 under the editorial eye of the late Stephen A. Mitchell. Mitchell was the most prolific and influential of the originators of the relational tradition. Committed to dialogue among psychoanalysts, he abhorred the authoritarianism that dictated adherence to a rigid set of beliefs or technical restrictions. He championed open discussion, comparative and integrative approaches, and promoted new voices across the generations.

Included in the Relational Perspectives Book Series are authors and works that come from within the relational tradition, extend and develop that tradition, as well as works that critique relational approaches or compare and contrast it with alternative points of view. The series includes our most distinguished senior psychoanalysts, along with younger contributors who bring fresh vision. A full list of titles in this series is available at https://www.routledge.com/series/LEARPBS.

1 Greenberg, J. & Mitchell, S. (1983). *Object Relations in Psychoanalytic Theory.* Cambridge, MA: Harvard University Press.

Memories and Monsters

Psychology, Trauma, and Narrative

Edited by Eric R. Severson
and David M. Goodman

Routledge
Taylor & Francis Group
LONDON AND NEW YORK

First published 2018
by Routledge
2 Park Square, Milton Park, Abingdon, Oxon OX14 4RN

and by Routledge
711 Third Avenue, New York, NY 10017

Routledge is an imprint of the Taylor & Francis Group, an informa business

British Library Cataloguing in Publication Data
A catalogue record for this book is available from the British Library

Library of Congress Cataloging in Publication Data
A catalog record for this book has been requested

ISBN: 978-1-138-06544-4 (hbk)
ISBN: 978-1-138-06545-1 (pbk)
ISBN: 978-1-315-15971-3 (ebk)

Typeset in Times New Roman
by Keystroke, Neville Lodge, Tettenhall, Wolverhampton

To George Kunz, a dear friend, mentor, and pioneer in existential and phenomenological psychology.

Contents

Contributors

Doris Brothers is a co-founder of the Training and Research in Intersubjective Self Psychology Foundation and co-editor with Roger Frie of the journal *Psychoanalysis, Self and Context*. Her latest book is *Toward a Psychology of Uncertainty: Trauma-Centered Psychoanalysis* (Analytic Press, 2008). She is in private practice in Manhattan.

Paul Cantz is a licensed and board-certified clinical psychologist, Associate Professor and Associate Director of Training at Adler University, Chicago, on faculty at the University of Illinois at Chicago College of Medicine and the Spertus Institute for Jewish Learning & Leadership, and a staff/supervising psychologist at Hartgrove Hospital, Chicago. He and co-author Kalman J. Kaplan have a forthcoming book titled *Biblical Psychotherapy: Reclaiming Scripture for Positive Psychology and Suicide Prevention* (Lexington).

Peter Capretto is a fellow in Theology and Practice at Vanderbilt University in the area of religion, psychology, and culture. His publications on trauma, psychoanalysis, and the philosophy of religion have appeared in the *Journal of the American Academy of Religion*, *The Heythrop Journal*, and the *Journal of Religion and Health*, and with Eric Boynton he is the editor of *Trauma and Transcendence: Limits of Theory and Prospects in Thinking*, which will be published by Fordham University Press in early 2018. His writings are informed by his clinical work as a hospice chaplain, crisis counselor, and pastoral psychotherapist.

Philip Cushman holds graduate degrees in American Studies (M.A.) and Family Therapy (M.A.), and a Ph.D. in psychology. He also was enrolled in Hebrew Union College in the graduate Rabbinic Program (1967–1971). He served as core faculty in the doctoral psychology department at California School of Professional Psychology, Alameda (1994–2002) and core faculty in the doctoral psychology program at Antioch University Seattle. He has also taught at the University of Washington Tacoma, Evergreen State College, and Seattle University. He has been in private practice since 1978 in California and in Washington since 2002, and has authored *Constructing the Self, Constructing America: A Cultural History of Psychotherapy* (Addison-Wesley, 1996), and articles about psychotherapy and psychoanalysis in several journals including *American Psychologist, Contemporary Psychoanalysis, Psychoanalytic Dialogues*, and *Psychohistory Review*.

Roger Frie is Professor of Education at Simon Fraser University, Affiliate Professor of Psychiatry at the University of British Columbia, Vancouver, and Psychoanalytic Faculty and Supervisor at the William Alanson White Institute, New York. He is a historian, philosopher, and psychoanalyst who has published numerous books on human interaction, memory, and responsibility, most recently *Not in My Family: German Memory and Responsibility After the Holocaust* (Oxford University Press, 2017).

David M. Goodman is a licensed clinical psychologist, Associate Dean of Academic Affairs and Advising at the Woods College of Advancing Studies at Boston College, Director of the Psychology and the Other Institute, and a teaching associate at Harvard Medical School/Cambridge Hospital.

George Horton is a licensed clinical psychologist in Oklahoma City. He provides psychotherapy, consultation, and clinical supervision at the VA Hospital and in private practice. He is a clinical faculty member of the Department of Psychiatry and Behavioral Sciences at the University of Oklahoma School of Medicine.

Steven Huett is staff psychologist as well as a supervising and teaching faculty at Denver Health Medical Center. He is also an affiliate faculty through the University of Colorado School of Medicine at Anschutz Medical Campus. He completed a Ph.D. in clinical psychology and an M.A. in theology at Fuller Theological Seminary in Pasadena, California.

Jerome A. Miller, Emeritus Professor of Philosophy at Salisbury University, is the author of *The Way of Suffering* (Georgetown University Press, 1989), and *In the Throe of Wonder* (SUNY Press, 1992), as well as a contributor to and co-editor of *Sobering Wisdom: Philosophical*

Explorations of Twelve Step Spirituality (University of Virginia Press, 2014). He is currently completing work on a book about the evolutionary significance of human intentionality.

Diana Souza Pinto is a researcher and professor at the Social Memory Graduate Program at the Federal University of the Rio de Janeiro State (UNIRIO). She has an M.A. in Applied Linguistics and a Ph.D. in Mental Health at the Federal University of Rio de Janeiro (UFRJ). Her research activities have focused on the development of an interdisciplinary approach to the study of psychiatric inmates' discourse.

Branca Telles Ribeiro is Distinguished Professor at Lesley University (Cambridge, MA) and Researcher at the Institute of Psychiatry at the Federal University of Rio de Janeiro (UFRJ). Her research examines communication between health care providers and patients in clinical settings, particularly in psychiatry and mental health. She leads a project in communication and access to health for Brazilian immigrant women in the Boston area.

Joel Rosenberg is Director of the Program in Judaic Studies at Tufts University, and a member of the core faculty in the Tufts Program in International Literary and Visual Studies, and, more recently, the Program in Film and Media Studies. Originally a scholar of biblical literature, he wrote *King and Kin: Political Allegory in the Hebrew Bible* (Indiana University Press, 1986). Since the mid-1990s, following a 1995 grant by the National Endowment for the Humanities, he has been immersed in film studies, beginning with a groundbreaking essay "Jewish Experience on Film: An American Overview" (*American Jewish Year Book*, 1996), and he has recently completed a book titled *Navigating Catastrophe: A Judeo-Cinematic Trajectory—Five Studies in Mass Media and Mass Destruction*, which examines six films of Jewish experience made between 1920 and 1947.

Orin Segal is an Israeli rehabilitation neuropsychologist, practicing as a senior psychologist in the pediatric rehabilitation unit in Safra Children's Hospital, and running a private clinic. He obtained his Ph.D. in the Psychoanalysis and Hermeneutics Track at Bar-Ilan University in Israel.

Eric R. Severson is a philosopher specializing in the work of Emmanuel Levinas. He is the author of the books *Levinas's Philosophy of Time* (Duquesne University Press, 2013) and *Scandalous Obligation* (Beacon

Hill Press, 2011), and editor of several volumes on ethics, the philosophy of religion, and psychology. He teaches philosophy at Seattle University.

Peter Shabad is a Clinical Associate Professor of Psychology at Northwestern University Medical School. He is on the faculty of the Institute for Psychoanalysis and the Teaching and Supervisory Faculty of the Chicago Center for Psychoanalysis. He is the co-editor of *The Problem of Loss and Mourning: Psychoanalytic Perspectives* (IUP, 1989) and the author of *Despair and the Return of Hope: Echoes of Mourning in Psychotherapy* (Rowman & Littlefield/Aronson, 2001). He is currently writing a new book entitled *Seizing the Vital Moment: Passion, Shame, and Mourning* to be published by Routledge. He is in private practice in Chicago.

Amira Simha-Alpern is a clinical psychologist, a certified psychoanalyst, and a clinical supervisor. She is the past Executive Director of the Suffolk Institute for Psychotherapy and Psychoanalysis; faculty at the Derner Institute, Adelphi University; and Clinical Assistant Professor of Psychiatry at Stony Brook University. She maintains private practice in Smithtown, NY.

Malcolm Owen Slavin, Ph.D., is a founder, faculty, and supervisor at the Massachusetts Institute for Psychoanalysis (MIP) and an associate editor of the journals *Psychoanalytic Dialogues, Contemporary Psychoanalysis*, and *Psychoanalysis, Self and Context.* His first book, co-written with Daniel Kriegman, was *The Adaptive Design of the Human Psyche: Psychoanalysis, Evolutionary Biology and the Therapeutic Process* (Guilford Press, 1992). His forthcoming book, *Original Loss: Grieving Existential Trauma in Art and the Art of Psychoanalysis* (Routledge), combines existential, evolutionary, and psychoanalytic perspectives.

Jerome Veith specializes in hermeneutic and phenomenological approaches to subjectivity, history, and temporality. He is the author of *Gadamer and the Transmission of History* (Indiana University Press, 2015), and has also translated the *Heidegger Reader* (Indiana University Press, 2009) and Günter Figal's *Aesthetics as Phenomenology* (Indiana University Press, 2015). He teaches philosophy at Seattle University.

Acknowledgments

This book is part of a groundswell of interest in the intersection between psychology and philosophy, a movement supported by a broad range of talented and dedicated people. The development of this book is the culmination of one strand of this movement, a daring experiment in the liminal space where memories, myths, and trauma invade and inhabit human lives and communities. The academic and practical work performed at this boundary requires patience and daring. First and foremost, then, we express our gratitude to the authors of these chapters, who are able to articulate at such edges and exemplify a type of academic moral imperative to do so. It has been a pleasure learning from your journeys—both personal and intellectual.

It is also crucial that we acknowledge some of the hardworking participants in this collaborative undertaking. Many of the ideas in this volume were first generated for a conference, the 2015 meeting of *Psychology and the Other*, a biannual gathering of clinicians, philosophers, and psychologists. The ideas shared at these meetings have a dynamic energy that is the byproduct of interdisciplinary work and concern for human identity, suffering, and potential.

Such events are labor intensive, requiring extensive work undertaken by speakers, students, mentors, editors, steering committee members, scholars, and administrators. Although there are too many such contributors to mention here, it is important that we underscore our gratitude to the diverse members of the hardworking community that generates ideas and conversations like the ones readers will find in this book. Though we cannot name them all, a number of friends and colleagues have played crucial roles in the development of the conference and this volume. First, Brian Becker and Heather Macdonald, amidst all of the demands of full-time jobs and intense lives, have been incredible partners in creating this space of welcome. Words simply escape. Also, we must express particular gratitude to a small team of colleagues and students who met weekly for two years in preparation for an event that gathered nearly 500 people from 42 countries. This group included Ben Arcangeli, Sam Arcangeli, Jacqueline Aug, Abigail Collins, Adeline Dettor, Samuel Gable, Katie Goodman, David House, Cacky Mellor, Danielle Moreno, Tyler Rubin, and Kimm Topping. This group donated incalculable time and creative energy to the conference and the profound interdisciplinary work that resulted. In addition to his role as the technical director of the conference, David House went above and beyond in helping to record and transcribe conference proceedings in a manner that allows a much larger audience to benefit (see Malcolm Slavin's chapter as an example). Furthermore, each chapter in this book has been very carefully read and analyzed by Tyler Rubin and Adeline Dettor, who bring a fresh and earnest perspective to this project. These young scholars spent many hours analyzing, editing, and formatting the material—creating a better volume with their investment.

For his leadership of and vision for the *Relational Perspectives Book Series*, we are ever appreciative of Steven Kuchuck's generosity and enriching involvement throughout the life of this manuscript preparation process. Charles Bath's steady hand has helped us navigate the editorial waters in such an inviting and interested manner. It makes an otherwise laborious process a meaningful experience.

Several institutions have provided virtual and physical venues for this burgeoning conversation. For the formation of this particular volume, we would like to express gratitude to Brent Slife, the Richard L. Evans Chair of Religious Understanding at Brigham Young University. Brent has been a generous benefactor and a beautiful being who exemplifies this form of scholarly exchange. Lesley University has been committed from the start, devoting space and resources for meetings and publications. We wish to thank Provost Selase Williams and Elizabeth Chambers for sharing in this vision and being early investors in this undertaking. The *Psychology and the Other* conferences also provide an opportunity for clinicians to expand their understanding and enliven their practice. The Danielsen Institute at Boston University, with Lauren Kehoe and George Stavros supervising, oversees the Continuing Education process for these gatherings. We wish to express profound gratitude to Boston College (BC), and specifically its Woods College of Advancing Studies. BC's Woods College, under the leadership of the Dean, Father James Burns, has made a deep and lasting investment in providing a home for this dynamic community.

Our deepest gratitude flows toward our spouses and our children. They have inspired us, profoundly, and been patient with the long hours we spend tending to the movement we call "Psychology and the Other."

Introduction

Listening to monsters

Eric R. Severson and David M. Goodman

Sigmund Freud recounts a story about a young, married couple who moved into a furnished apartment and came to believe that the place was haunted. The dining-room table was carved with frightening crocodiles, and in the shifting shadows of the night these monstrous creatures sprung to life, haunting the flat with foul smells and ghostly movements (Freud, 1919/1966). These experiences, which are sometimes silly and sometimes quite serious, are connected to what Freud called the experience of the *uncanny*. Monsters are everywhere. They move out of the imaginations of our storytellers and lurk in the dark corners of our dreams. Monsters are never just monsters; ghosts never merely ghosts. They are specters, and Freud calls them uncanny because they are interwoven with memories, experiences, or events that have been (mostly) forgotten. The uncanny is the experience of something once familiar but now repressed or no longer available to thought. The monsters of our nightmares, of our fictions, are not unarmed. They know our weaknesses, our fears, and the layers of personal and trans-generational trauma that we struggle to name or understand. Our monsters may sometimes know us better than we know ourselves. Monsters are not scary because they are unfamiliar; they are often frightening because they are *too* familiar.

Nearly a century after Freud's landmark essay, *The Uncanny* (1919/1966), psychologists and philosophers continue to ponder the nature of the monstrous, the uncanny, and the way psychological trauma relates to memory and narration. This is a book about the monstrous and its impact on our psyches, about the realm of the sublime and its relationship to individuals and communities. The authors in this volume take up this intersection directly, asking in a variety of ways how we might best relate to our monsters, about the legacies of ancient anxieties and traumas that reverberate in our stories, memories, and everyday practices. In some cases, they point us to how monsters are beasts intentionally forged, as in the case of the Jewish Golem, discussed in fascinating detail in this volume by Philip Cushman and Joel Rosenberg. But even our carefully crafted monsters are liable to get away from us, as many of the Golem legends warn. The *Terminator* franchise and the *Matrix* trilogy (to name only two) narrate this story in more modern terms—we create machines that turn on us and the result is apocalyptic and monstrous.

We must learn from our monsters. They reflect and reinforce our fantasies and histories. They speak vividly, albeit with screens and exceptional amounts of emotional noise. But, what if we learn to listen to the fantasy behind the monster? For instance, our fascination with zombies, in *The Walking Dead* or numerous other movies and shows, may speak to some potential fantasies we have about our present predicament. Is the world we are creating in late-stage capitalism and present-day consumerism dulling us into mostly dead but still ambulating flesh eaters? Or, do we, perhaps, identify with the violent, monstrous, and insatiable hunger that we see in these undead characters as we abide by liberal and progressive kindnesses with one another? What might it mean for us to turn to our monsters and ask them to teach us? Such a project would require that we learn to listen and better understand the way monsters are called into being. Some monsters emerge from the depths of our fears, from the dark regions of anxiety, from the fear of the unknown. Other monsters are friendlier, called into being to protect, comfort, and battle on our behalf—serving as a talisman or performing actions unavailable to us. We have even turned our monsters into reality, training animals and machines to bring our fantasies and hauntings to life. Sometimes monsters remain firmly attached to their history, to their rootedness in the situation that called them into being. But often they tear away from their chains, released into the world. This book wagers that our monsters have a tremendous amount to teach us, particularly if we can learn to listen to them.

To learn from our monsters, we must learn to sit with stories, and listen with attentiveness to narratives fragmented by trauma, forgetfulness, and the passage of time. In a series of chapters by leading thinkers in psychology and philosophy, this book investigates the way memory and the monstrous appear in a host of contemporary manifestations, such as racism, crimes against humanity, music and art, and the Holocaust. None of these authors attempts a systematic philosophy of the uncanny, if such a study would even be possible. Each of them understands that, when it comes to this relevant frontier in psychology, we must work with fragments and stories, with dreams and incomplete memories. The study of trauma, after all, should not be approached like a jigsaw puzzle, as though the purpose of treating and studying trauma is to put the pieces of a shattered "whole" back together. The realm of the uncanny, the domain of monsters, is full of gaps and chasms. These are sometimes sacred spaces, not mysteries to be solved or potholes to be paved over. In this regard, we must be gentle with our monsters; they can only tell their stories if we resist the urge to banish them or ignore their existence.

Of course, there are times when we must shine a flashlight beneath the bed. Monsters can reinforce our fears, deepen our prejudices, and give longevity to wounds that continue to haunt our lives and communities. Racism and sexism are often said to *haunt* human societies, beasts that manage to feed even when we strive to starve them. Some of our monsters are distortions of the other person, as Amira Simha-Alpern argues in Chapter 11. By idealizing the other person, we both distort the other and rob ourselves of any genuine experience of that relation. Attending to monsters is sometimes not about starving them but nourishing them with our attention. Of course, at other times, their mangling and inhibiting power must be contained and their influence restrained. But how do we do this without re-energizing it?

This volume takes particular interest in the complicated impact our memories and monsters have on psychological formation, and the ways they shape our relations to other persons. The following chapters work on the borderland between psychology and philosophy, drawing from scholars in both fields who have helped mold the bourgeoning fields of relational psychoanalysis and phenomenological and existential psychology. An intriguing movement is underway, particularly among clinicians and academic psychologists who are dissatisfied with reductive or medical approaches. Each author's work collected in this volume demonstrates an eagerness to explore the particularity of the other person, the uniqueness of each lived experience, and the need for psychology to better attend to the radical otherness of the other person.

Some of the clearest appearances of monsters are in our dystopian myths. In the first chapter, Paul Cantz begins with an investigation of the way mortality and death anxiety manifests itself in our mythology. The inherent incapacity to fully comprehend one's mortality, as Freud (1913/1953) famously observed, represents an intractably stubborn dynamic of the human condition since, "in the unconscious, every one of us is convinced of his own immortality" (pp. 304–305). Although Freud understood death anxiety as merely a projection of more superficial instinctual conflicts, typically related to castration anxiety, other thinkers, such as Otto Rank, Ernest Becker, and Robert J. Lifton, among others, preferred to view the terror of death as ontologically formative in the development of the individual psyche and, on a broader scale, the formation and orientation of culture. Cantz focuses on the various ways death anxiety underwrites dystopian myths and the quest for immortality, on the one hand, and how the heroes that these myths produce paradoxically function as both a defense against death anxiety as well as an adaptive model for personal resiliency, on the other.

The second and third chapters of this collection are companion pieces, both concerning the fascinating myth of the Jewish Golem. Philip Cushman, whose work has been seminal in the field of psychoanalysis, turns his attention to the peculiar and culturally informed concept of the self. He argues that the current self is reflected and produced by the hegemony of electronic machines and communication processes and the demands of a competitive, exhausting neoliberal economy. The result, Cushman suggests, is that we are moving toward a flat, multiple self, which suffers less from a twentieth century "emptiness" than from a twenty-first-century fear of social relations and a desperate search for entertainment. It is a self populated with a multitude of identities clustering around the outside of the individual, waiting to be called to center stage, depending on the needs of the moment to hide or escape. Ills are thought to be highly behavioral and concrete, such as anxiety, depression, and identity confusion. Healers are technicians who draw from behavioral techniques that patch up and make functional. Of particular interest is the connection between electronic living and the grip that outcome studies, manualized treatments, and academic competencies have on the clinical professions. We either identify with or try to turn ourselves into cyborg-like, robotic Golems. Cushman turns our attention to an alternative, hermeneutic approach to psychotherapy, one built on an encounter with difference, moral discourse, and reparative moments of Gadamerian dialogue.

In the next chapter, Joel Rosenberg focuses more closely on the Jewish legend of the Golem, the "Clay Man" called into being to protect oppressed and threatened Jewish communities. This richly suggestive myth, originally tied to mystical meditation and to reflection on the human being as both creator and creature, eventually became the fount of folktales that began to flourish in late medieval and early modern times, and has familiar analogues in the popular culture of many societies in modern times. Rosenberg traces the Golem theme, and the closely associated reflection of Jewish sources on technology and magic, from its origins in biblical sources through apocalyptic, Judeo-Pythagorean, pietistic, and folkloric sources from antiquity to the modern era, making particular use of Walter Benjamin's 1933 essay "Experience and Poverty" on the decline of experience under forces of technology and war (Benjamin 1933/1999). These sources are read in the context of Cushman's argument that psychologists have come to serve a "dominationist" ideology while ignoring the real needs of patients by feeding their grief, trauma, or depression through clinical categories invented by the profession for its own convenience (serving even the practice of torture). Particular attention is devoted to the Jewish mystical theme of the Hebrew letter "Aleph," which Kabbalah and early Hasidism made the basis of meditative practice, and which Cushman uses to symbolize the double potential of psychologists to either enhance or undermine patient recovery.

The fourth and fifth chapters are also companions, featuring a conversation about loyalty, passion, and vulnerability. Peter Shabad explores the way we can develop a frightening and unhealthy loyalty to our monsters. He wonders: is loyalty really a virtue? What then are we to make of the fact that the very same steadfastness of honoring a commitment to family, friends, nation, or God is also intrinsic to the robot-like loyalty that fuels the "Heil Hitler" salute to the Führer? Shabad argues that a blind loyalty that becomes a rule precisely because of its moral virtue preempts an organic commitment that emerges from love and the freedom of choice on which love is based. Rather than viewing loyalty as an automatic obedience to an unchanging oath, Shabad uses Kierkegaard's ideas to describe a passion-fueled process, in which one makes repetitive "leaps of faith" through the transitions of self-dying toward a continually renewed commitment to relationship with the other person.

Responding to Shabad's thesis, Jerome Miller focuses on the primal passion that leads us to such problematic manifestations of loyalty. Passion, Miller points out, is not reducible to or explainable by something more basic than it. Picking up Shabad's emphasis on the nature of passion as not just immanent in but constitutive of the self, Miller discusses how impassioned self-donation moves one beyond oneself. Even for the very young child, it involves exposing and entrusting oneself to the other as other. Miller suggests that this means that, because of the self-donative movement of passion, the future does not belong to one's own story. This alterity of the future contributes to a transcendence of oneself as it makes one primordially vulnerable and liable to rejection.

In the sixth chapter, Roger Frie wonders if it is possible, after the Holocaust, to talk about "German suffering?" The controversial discourse of German wartime suffering has gained traction over the past decade. But when Germans focus on their own traumas, how do they account for the unimaginable suffering their nation caused others? When does talk of suffering become a way of avoiding guilt and responsibility for the Holocaust? The questions posed in this chapter go to the very core of German struggles with memory. Frie uses his own inherited memories as a third-generation German, whose parents were children during the war and whose grandparents were active in the war. He suggests that German wartime experience tends to be remembered in isolation from its historical circumstances. As a result, intergenerational memory in German families easily gives way to talk of victimization. The kind of moral slippage the author describes creates narratives in which the Nazi past and the role of family members as perpetrators and bystanders are kept at bay. Frie's aim is to address the moral contexts of trauma using his inherited memories as a starting point for reflection and exploration. The author juxtaposes his family's experience of the bombings of Hannover with the simultaneous annihilation of Hannover's German-Jewish community, and the experience of a single German-Jewish family. The observations drawn can be applied to other historical traumas in which contexts of perpetration and moral responsibility are neglected, particularly among past perpetrator groups.

Hauntings find their way into our mythologies, our literature, and our histories. In the seventh chapter, Jerome Veith argues that a proper grasp of haunting demands a reconceptualization of human memory and temporality and that the concepts for this revision are available to us in philosophical hermeneutics. Veith moves deftly between history, philosophy, and psychology to develop a richer understanding of our hauntings and their significance. He draws on two works of literature that exemplify both the experience of haunting and our possible responses to it: W. G. Sebald's *Austerlitz* and Toni Morrison's *Beloved.* Extreme experiences of suffering and trauma reverberate throughout human memory and identity, whether or not they are recollected. Veith argues that on a collective level, historical hauntings demand to be recognized, but these demands require a new accounting for the way we relate to the complexities of our wounded histories. We must come to terms with the way our memories are not merely incomplete records of the past; our haunts, ghosts and monsters are both relevant and intractably ambivalent.

Doris Brothers then takes a close look at the way societal narratives are formed and mutated. She contends that it is often when our survival is gravely threatened that our experience of being human may be lost or weakened. Brothers examines the societal narratives that have imperiled our survival by fueling practices that have generated unprecedented environmental catastrophes, increased economic disparity between the rich and the poor, and perpetuated oppression based on race, religion, class, ethnicity, gender, sexual orientation, and political affiliation. These practices, she asserts, constitute "crimes against humanity" in the sense that they threaten human connectedness and degrade a sense of agency. She attempts to show how the use of "public narrative" developed by Marshall Ganz, which involves developing a "story of self," a "story of us," and a "story of now," may work to combat these crimes.

In Chapter 9, Branca Telles Ribeiro and Diana Souza Pinto discuss how psychiatric patients and inmates construct discursively their relationship to psychiatric institutions. Their investigation is rich, filled with clinical illustrations of the powerful dynamics of the way selfhood is configured among people who are institutionalized together. Specifically, they focus on recurrent themes that emerge in patients' and inmates' narratives as they relate to location. Their narratives and perceptions of self and other are shaped and changed according to their environments and the people with whom they interact. The authors' key question examines how participants perform different personal and institutional roles related to a specific location in the construction of meaning in face-to-face interactions. Ribiero and Pinto investigate the way human beings both haunt and help one another.

Orin Segal, in his chapter, explores some very practical concerns for the psychotherapist. Drawing on a series of clinical examples, Segal explores the dynamics of "self-dissolution," particularly as it emerges from acquired chronic medical conditions, such as chronic illnesses and physical injuries. These experiences are described in psychological research literature as traumatic, emphasizing subjective loss of control over one's own body and world. These experiences often lead to prolonged mourning processes over the loss of a sense of self, an experience sometimes called self-dissolution or a "shattered self." This is an "unheimilich" feeling of estrangement from oneself, of regarding oneself as an unknown other, which is amplified by the awareness of one's own injured body. Focusing on this subjective self-perception, of being one and an-other for oneself, Segal presents a comprehensive narrative framework for clinical and theoretical understanding. Segal helps us better understand how we become strangers to ourselves.

In the following chapter, Amira Simha-Alpern explores how we can turn friends into strangers. She considers the powerful need for an idealized other, a need that leads to a significant distortion of reality. This need is driven, argues Simha-Alpern, by a desire to preserve the self and its need for security. Taking the maternal, caretaking mother as her principal example, she suggests that the drive to idealize is powerful enough to sacrifice the actual experience of a nurturing figure in our real-life relationships. Instead, we invent her in our minds or distort her real attributes. Because the most convenient way of heightening feelings of safety is through the modification and control of perception, the real rejecting, abandoning, or unavailable mother is neglected in favor of a phantasmic, idealized mother whose image is colored by wish fulfillment. She becomes an omnipotent and omniscient figure who provides unconditional, everlasting care and gives comfort. To illustrate this thesis, the chapter reviews the universal portrayal of maternal archetypes in Greco-Roman and Judeo-Christian myths depicting maternal feminine imagoes.

Might psychology contribute to the estrangement of self and the other person, to rendering oneself or one's neighbor into a monster? In Chapter 12, Peter Capretto guides us into Foucault's controversial critique of psychoanalysis, particularly as it relates to madness and sexuality. For Foucault, there is a dangerous and subversive power invoked by a psychoanalytic approach to culture, politics, and religion. Despite their profound influences on late-twentieth-century and contemporary theories of identity, psychoanalytic and Foucauldian perspectives differ on a rather central issue: when it comes to understanding human sexuality and experiences of madness, does the concept or logic of psychic interiority help philosophical and psychological theory in thinking identity's relation to sexuality and madness? Looking primarily to Jacques Derrida as a contemporary of Foucault and as a complex apologist of psychoanalytic theories of sex and madness, this chapter argues that the dispute between Foucault and psychoanalysis on sex, madness, and interiority is best understood as a difference and disagreement on the methodological limits of philosophy and psychology alike. Capretto outlines Foucault's concern, but utilizes the work of Jacques Derrida to critique Foucault's choice to eschew the limitations of psychic interiority. Foucault misses the ways that psychoanalysis critiques discourse on madness and sex through interiority itself, which in turn resists the ideological silencing of madness and sexuality.

Like Capretto, Steven Huett and George Horton take up a strident challenge to psychoanalysis, exploring the appearance of the monstrosity of the self within literature. Huett and Horton draw from a critique of psychology that emerges from a character in Nabokov's *Lolita*. The book opens with the 37-year-old Humbert Humbert's confession of his love affair with the 12-year-old Lolita. Nabokov knows that readers will be tempted to psychoanalyze Humbert, so he confronts the reader with a jeering, literary challenge to the psychoanalytic tradition. Nabokov, after all, called psychoanalysis voodooism and Freud "the Viennese witch doctor." The authors argue that the folly of a psychoanalytic reading of *Lolita* inheres in the paradox of Nabokov's prose, which overtly tempts the literary psychoanalyst with the putative confession of the eloquent and loquacious pedohebephile, Humbert. This confession simultaneously leaves the reader enthralled by his storytelling and disturbed at deriving subjective pleasure from a story with such manifestly deplorable content. Huett and Horton propose a potential meaning behind *Lolita*, located in what they call "the troubling cavern of alterity within oneself." It is not possible to honestly analyze or access *Lolita* without, ironically, confessing as the reader the multiplicity of stirrings aroused by the book. These authors draw upon intersubjective theories to perform this reader-response approach, to express our own ambivalence, to better approach Humbert, and to explore the delicate and often problematic terrain between aesthetic enjoyment and moral complicity.

The book concludes with a visceral chapter by Malcolm Slavin who wonders: what is the origin of the vital human need for art? And what are the connections between our capacity to imagine, to create, and the therapeutic process? Slavin points back in time, to the visual images, music, and storytelling that allowed human beings to create "sacred spaces" and rites. Since the dawn of our species, these spaces have enabled us to grieve our loss of embeddedness in nature—to bear the newly emerged existential anxieties we faced when we became human. We evolved the capacity to use the visceral power of imagination within a relational context to create a sense of meaning and agency that potentially transcends the limits of language. Slavin explores art and treatment in light of how both patient and therapist may use "potential" or "transitional" space to experience, share, and transform the personal and existential dilemmas that haunt the human condition. We encourage readers to watch a video performance of Slavin's aesthetic presentation, linked at the beginning of his chapter.

Our hope is that this book will help us better listen to and discern the ways we are haunted. History, after all, is not a chronicling of past events but the very event of folding ourselves into a lived understanding of the richly historical world that we together inhabit. This world we share is full of wandering ghosts, monsters, and fantastic beasts that, for better or worse, help us understand our selves, our cultures, and our communities. This volume offers no complete compendium to these dynamics, nor does it attempt to be comprehensive in its exploration of history or trauma. Instead, this collection starts a series of conversations about how psychologists and philosophers can wrestle with the forces that wound and heal our shared world.

References

Benjamin, W. (1999). "Experience and Poverty," in *Selected Writings: Vol. 2 (1927–1934)*, pp. 731–736. Cambridge: Cambridge University Press. (Original work published 1933.)

Freud, S. (1953). "Thoughts for the Times on War and Death," in J. Strachey (Ed. and Trans.), *The Standard Edition of the Complete Psychological Works of Sigmund Freud, Volume IV*, pp. 304–305. London: Hogarth Press. (Original work published 1913.)

Freud, S. (1966). *The Uncanny*, in J. Strachey (Ed. and Trans.), *The Standard Edition of the Complete Psychological Works of Sigmund Freud, Volume XVII*, pp. 217–256. London: Hogarth Press. (Original work published 1919.)

Chapter 1

Apocalyptic exceptionalism and existential particularity

The rise in popularity of dystopian myths and our immortal "other"

Paul Cantz

> *I believe that men are generally still a little afraid of the dark, though the witches are all hung, and Christianity and candles have been introduced.*
>
> (Henry David Thoreau, *Walden*)

Introduction

The innate incapacity to fully comprehend one's mortality, as Freud (1913/1966) famously observed, represents an intractably stubborn dynamic of the human condition since, "in the unconscious, every one of us is convinced of his own immortality" (pp. 304–305). Although Freud understood death anxiety as merely a projection of more superficial instinctual conflicts, typically related to castration anxiety, other thinkers – thinkers who have infused a strong existential inflection into psychoanalytic theory, such as Otto Rank, Ernest Becker, and Robert J. Lifton, among others – have preferred to view the terror of death as ontologically formative in the development of the individual psyche and, on a broader scale, the formation and orientation of culture as a whole.

In this chapter, I focus on exploring how death anxiety underwrites dystopian media, which in likelihood gives expression to the archetypal mythopoeic duality of our mortal and immortal senses of self. I further suggest that these media can function as both a defense against as well as a remedy for death anxiety. This is premised on the idea that distinctive cultural pressures will encourage in-kind mythopoeic expressions of archetypal impulses, resulting in psychological symmetry with a person's experience and understanding of reality – what Jung referred to as "synchronicity," commonly defined as an acausal connecting principle. To this end, two questions figure prominently: (1) What significant variables in contemporary society have motivated this notable spike in dystopian myths? (2) With what elements are consumers of these myths primarily identifying?

Background

Although dystopian myths have been a ubiquitous, cross-cultural preoccupation throughout the course of recorded human history (e.g. the Epic of Gilgamesh, the Norse Ragnarok, the Book of Revelations, etc.), in our post-nuclear, post-9/11 age we have witnessed a substantive increase in apocalyptic media (namely literature, television, video games, and film). Borg (2003), in writing about the clinical relevance of Paul Virilio and Sylvere Lotringer's (1997) concept of "Pure War" (which refers to the psychological sequelae of existing in a world in which humankind has developed the potential to completely annihilate itself), offers an explanation for why these types of horrific events have led to an increase in personal traumas: "disasters may highlight the massive insecurities that lie beneath the surface of an otherwise well-protected cultural exterior" (p. 58). In tandem with what ostensibly seems to be an ever increasing rate of terrorist attacks across the globe, the automatic impulse to dissociate our conscious awareness of death in any sustainable fashion has become progressively futile. Mortimer Ostow (1986) likewise suggested a relationship between apocalyptic fantasies and psychopathology, chiefly schizophrenia, explaining that people too deeply entrenched in this mindset "treasure the illusion that they and the world will be reborn into a messianic age" (p. 278) – a particularly dangerous attitude since in this context rebirth necessarily follows mass destruction. In the time since Ostow made these observations, however, these apocalyptic and messianic worldviews have not only intensified, but, like the decapitated Lernean Hydra, have manifested in a multiplicity of directions, impacting contemporary theological, secular, and socio-political myths about the current 'fallen' state of society and the utopian promises that await us right on the horizon of our illusions.

This rise in contemporary expressions of dystopian myths has been paced by an increased preoccupation in the biotechnology community with the project of achieving physical immortality. The desire to transcend the constraints of mortality and temporality has, until relatively recently, been the pursuit of mystics and alchemists. With the burgeoning field of nanotechnology accompanied by ambitious biogenetic advancements, the prospect of achieving embodied immortality seems closer to fulfillment with the passing of each news cycle. Prominent figures in the anti-aging movement, chief among them gerontologist Aubrey de Grey and futurist Ray Kurzweil, can largely be credited for establishing and propagating the contemporary scientific infatuation with achieving immortality. They and others have increasingly been shifting the bio-medical zeitgeist in a direction that implicitly privileges youth while 'disease-ifying' the aging process, and consequently pathologizing death.

This parallel between the increased interest in dystopian myths and the growing acceptance of anti-aging research within the medical community and popular culture points to a conceptual relationship that remains primed for theoretical elaboration. In numerous cases, dystopian myths serve as a catalytic holding environment for expressing and identifying latent strivings for various archetypal impulses, notable among them the primordial wish to achieve immortality. These expressions manifest in both embodied and disembodied forms that correlate to one's metaphysical proclivities. Examples of disembodied forms correspond to the ephemeral, supernatural realm (e.g. the immortal soul, reincarnation, etc.), and typically manifest within the context of organized religious traditions, while embodied forms of immortality are often portrayed in more materialistic, often supernatural or science-fiction terms (e.g. super-humans, vampires, zombies, cyborgs, etc.). As the prospect of achieving embodied immortality has become more of a scientifically palatable enterprise, this seems to have ushered in what could be considered the leading edge of the sub-genre of dystopian films that do not rely on purely supernatural explanations (i.e. are more "reality based," most commonly as viral outbreaks, though more recently by various technological means).

Film, as a consequence of its visual elements, has acted as an especially potent vehicle to express archetypal, mythopoeic impulses in the service of promoting what Irving Singer (2008) has termed "aesthetic truthfulness." Better suited and more quickly produced than other mediums, especially compared to literature, television offers viewers the experience of developing meaningfully emotional investments and subsequent psychological identifications with the characters on the screen. It is for this reason that I have chosen to utilize the contemporary popular TV series *The Walking Dead*, produced by the American cable channel AMC, as an exemplar to explicate how prominent themes of death anxiety and death denial as well as the corresponding desire to achieve immortality psychically translates into specific styles of myth identification. This personalized type of myth identification amplifies and gives expression to an uncanny fusion of 'I-ness' and 'otherness' that flirts with the boundaries between our mortal and immortal senses of self.

The evolution of the zombie genre

Neo-liberal scholars such as Hall (2011) have chosen to interpret the zombie genre in particular as a metaphor for the seemingly unavoidable political, economic, and cultural breakdown of Western capitalistic society, which Hall compares to an epidemic not unlike that of a viral zombie outbreak, and as such capitalism "relentlessly expands, and it will collapse once there is no one else to infect" (p. 15). Films such as *Dawn of the Dead* and the *Resident Evil* franchise are of this type. Similarly, Paul Cantor (2013) has suggested that zombies have often been used to symbolize "the force of globalization" (p. 29). Other scholars have likewise identified racism, class warfare, deindustrialization, the specter of nuclear warfare, genetic modifications, and even space exploration as subtexts for the upsurge of zombie media, several of which have been portrayed in George Romero's iconic series of zombie films.

Indeed, I find many of these explanations compelling insomuch as there have obviously been deliberate efforts made on the production side to co-opt zombie folklore in the service of illuminating sociological dynamics. Kaleidoscopic in function as well as in expression, the zombie genre really is not at all a 'genre' in the conventional sense, but rather it functions as an ever-evolving metaphorical vehicle that promotes a mythopoeic frame for artists to address any myriad of cultural anxieties.[1]

The Walking Dead employs the dystopian backdrop of a zombie apocalypse, though this show pivots the genre from focusing solely on constructing meta-commentary on the social, political, and economic domains of culture to one that functions on a more individual plane of foundational myth identification, namely addressing the psycho-moral dualities of good and evil, tyranny and freedom, and mortality and immortality.[2] It is this latter domain that I wish to focus on since I think it represents both the symptom of a growing cultural anxiety around aging and death as well as potentially offering a psychological antidote for such death anxiety. The dualities expressed in *The Walking Dead* naturally resonate with the elemental dualities that paradoxically gel to form our experience of self, and therefore we can discern a process of dual identification linked with competing mythopoeic impulses, in varying ratios in accordance with one's degree of psychological maturity.

When we focus our explanation away from the perspective of the standard group or collectivistic psychological analyses and the corresponding identificatory processes that these films facilitate, I believe that we can uncover compelling psychological dynamics that also operate on the individual level (cf. Arlow, 1961; cf. Cantz, 2012; Cantz & Castle, 2013). To this end, the eminent mythologist William Doty (2000) considered one of the functions of myth to be "the primal, foundational accounts of aspects of the real, experienced world and humankind's roles and relative statuses within it" (p. 31), which in turn illuminates "the political and moral values of culture and provides systems of interpreting individual experience within a universal perspective" (p. 33). The dystopian, post-apocalyptic mythscape, with its necessarily fantastical elements, seems to provide a fertile space to explore and perhaps even play with concepts that are unconsciously unpalatable in their pure state, namely the reality of death. As Otto Rank (1936) reminds us, "the idea of death appears so much more clearly in religion, mythology and folklore than in the individual who apparently can bear the idea of death only collectively" (p. 120).

It is important to analyze these cinematic dynamics with the understanding that 'death' often serves as a metaphor that can hold multiple meanings depending on the manner in which consumers of these contemporary expressions of myths identify. 'Death' is the common designation for the absence of something that had once been alive; it is a privileged idea of non-being – a special label for posthumous categorization that can only be conceptualized by a living being who necessarily[3] projects their phantasies of being dead onto the unfathomability of no longer being. In a way, this is a motivated confabulation to explain the unexplainable. Therefore, to psychically accommodate for zombies, and perhaps more aptly their moniker (the 'un-dead') requires the creation of an artificial third category of being that personifies death. This absurd third category allows for a socially sanctioned expression of our fears of death and of losing our sense of selves. The manner in which individuals identify with these zombie characters will either lead to an emboldening of existing neurotic defenses or, more ambitiously, assuage death anxiety in the service of living a fulfilling life.[4]

Two modes of myth identification

The allure of dystopian myths in general, perhaps more strongly expressed in *The Walking Dead* in particular, facilitates a process of dual identification for the individual viewer. Consumers of these dystopian myths happily allow themselves to be transported by the illusion of surviving improbable (not to mention impossible!) 'what if' apocalyptic scenarios, whilst being able to concurrently psychically accommodate the demise of the majority of humanity. This produces, or perhaps uncovers, an important psychic space where contradictory forms of myth identifications can co-exist in a manner that is emotionally tolerable – a psychic field where one can engage with the terror of alterity by proxy.

Otto Rank's (1926/1971) theoretical elaboration on the theme of *der Doppelgänger* (the double) may be more instructive in conceptualizing the living characters in *The Walking Dead* than in previous zombie media since, distinctive to this series, the audience quickly learns that regardless of whether one becomes 'zombified' by an actual zombie (which is the conventional method by which zombie transformation occurs), one inevitably transitions into a zombie upon death, natural or otherwise. Rank contended that the double originally functioned as a type of psychic defense, serving to insure against the destruction of their ego, or, as Freud put it in his essay *The Uncanny* (1919/1966, p. 217), the double functioned as an "energetic denial of the power of death." It is likely that the 'immortal' soul acted as the first 'double' of the body, facilitating a sense of immortalized otherness that was simultaneously experienced as being both similar to and distinctive from oneself. It is worth noting that this concept continues to carry theological currency in the Judeo-Christian tradition, as for example: "For this perishable body must put on the imperishable, and this mortal body must put on immortality" (1 Corinthians 15:53).

In an elaboration of Rank's ideas on the double, Freud (1919/1966) observed that once "this stage [of primary narcissism] has been surmounted, the 'double' reverses its aspect. From having been an assurance of immortality, it becomes the uncanny harbinger of death … The 'double' has become a thing of terror" (pp. 234–235). Following this line of thought, it is tempting to understand zombies as representing a materialistic approximation of the mythopoeic desire of possessing an immortal soul, though heavily accented by the conscious awareness of death.

It is therefore striking that in *The Walking Dead*, the mythopoeic duality of mortality/immortality is dealt with in a manner that is the inverse of how we customarily find it; the cultural preoccupation around anxieties connected to the prospect of aging and dying makes primarily identifying with our "immortal" shadow selves – our "soul selves," as it were – psychologically appealing, though not necessarily comforting. The zombies in *The Walking Dead* potentially then serve as a projection of our mortal selves – a visually gruesome reminder of our corporeality, which in turn mobilizes death anxiety by compelling us to externalize and escape the grips of aging and death in our phantasy lives, lest it overcomes us first; the moral charge becomes: 'destroy death before death destroys me.' This type of myth identification, however, becomes activated with viewers who maintain an elevated measure of death anxiety, and therefore it functions to reinforce the comforting illusion of immortality – survival against all odds – which also aligns with increasingly socially acceptable trends based on the scientific fetishization of 'curing' aging and solving the 'problem' of death. The mortal characters – those who are not zombies – then function as a projection of the viewer's wish to remain immortal.

Thus we can discern two main modes of myth identification as it relates to *The Walking Dead*. The first is the externalized type, where the double is represented by a zombie and psychically corresponds to the mythopoeic impulse to alienate the concept of death from our sense of selves in order to maintain the illusion of immortality. The second mode, the internalized type, transcends death denial and links with the decidedly more psychologically mature way of metabolizing death anxiety through the psychic integration of the eventuality of our non-being into our core sense of self.

The externalized type: our immortal selves

To survive a zombie outbreak or any dystopian scenario corresponds to what I refer to as the illusion of "apocalyptic exceptionalism," which fittingly echoes one's denial of death and aligns with a type of individual psychology that has not yet successfully come to grips with the eventuality of one's mortal demise.

If we can indulge our imaginations and concede that a dystopian/apocalyptic scenario is possible in the order of magnitude portrayed on television and in other media, the reasonable individual will conclude that they, like most people, will likely perish in the ensuing destruction of life and civilization as we know it. However, I do not think that consumers of these contemporary myths tune in every week for an existential reality check, *per se*, though undoubtedly for some that is indeed what happens. Instead, and understandably so, most viewers first identify with the living characters struggling to survive against incredible odds, corresponding to a mythopoeic hero identification that resonates with our immortal sense of self – that is to say, our wish that we are immortal. If the process of hero identification remained within these psychic limits, providing the consumers of these media an enhanced sense of personal resiliency and courage, then we could be confident that these myths simply promote the maturation of the ego in the service of reinforcing a multitude of societal values, such as individual agency, sacrifice, and responsibility, to name only a few prominent examples. However, the identificatory process extends past or, presumably for some, leapfrogs what is psychically helpful, instead strengthening deep-seated anxieties around death.

Deserving of closer analysis is also the very notion that within a zombie dystopia one can actually 'kill' death, or, going one step further, that an agentic 'death' exists in our phantasy life. When living characters in *The Walking Dead* destroy zombies out of a visceral fear of dying, they are cinematically expressing a denial of the reality of their own mortality. For instance, it seems that characters annihilating the so-called 'un-dead' (which can operationally be translated as 'the spectre of mortality') forcefully deny their eventual non-being through eradicating the possibility of dying, which ultimately, if not paradoxically, strengthens their existing fear and subsequent denial of death. The irony in this scenario is that death wins either way: either by annihilating the living person entirely (death without an 'encore' life, as it were), or by turning them into an 'un-dead' zombie – a fate that promotes an anxiety-riddled phantasy that encourages the viewer into imagining their own decaying corpse.[5] It is this feature that Mitchel (2007) identified as representing the critical distinction between vampires – another mythic figure that has likewise received a surge of popularity in the media – and zombies:

> as vampires have become increasingly attractive and acceptable as romantic partners [in media], zombies, in contrast, have remained emphatically monstrous. The vampire body is preserved, if chilly; the zombie body decomposes, marking by its increasing decay the time since death: the vampire is a fantasy of immortality, the zombie a *memento mori*.
>
> (p. 392)

This jarring reminder that our prized human physicality remains hopelessly vulnerable to the ravages of decomposition can understandably pose enough of a psychic threat that a retreat into the convenient defense of death denial represents perhaps the best form of psychological adaptation for some people.

The internalized type: our mortal selves

On the other side of the coin, when a character in *The Walking Dead* destroys a zombie as a willful choice, devoid of the insecurities inherent in death anxiety – that is, when a screen persona is portrayed as having chosen to accept the eventuality of dying – we can surmise that those viewers who identify in this manner are experiencing an in-kind acceptance of their own mortality, and so they end up neutralizing their fear of death and refocusing their energies on living a meaningful life, not despite death, but *because* death exists. This theme has become central in several plot arcs in *The Walking Dead*, with some characters being portrayed as oscillating between these two positions of the externalized and internalized types, even at times holding both types in psychic tension.

Underscoring the existential sense of urgency in claiming one's utter humanity in spite of, if not because of, one's own mortality, according to Kierkegaard (1843/1959) every individual must endeavor throughout their lives to continue choosing themselves in action. Kierkegaard explains that establishing an ethical self can only be achieved following the full experiencing and ultimate acceptance of the despair of our limitations, namely the limitations of our lifespan. It follows that Kierkegaard illuminates an inescapable ethical dilemma for immortalists: live forever in a state of existential and moral stagnation, or embrace one's eventual demise and strive for the possibility of attaining the ultimate 'good' of experiencing an ethical life – a life saturated with meaning created from the crucible of the mourning and acceptance of one's temporality on this earth. Despair becomes the prerequisite experience for existential fulfillment; dystopia the road to navigate in order to arrive at one's personal utopia.

By confronting death *qua* zombie, the internalized type of consumer of *The Walking Dead* and similar media grapples with the most ominous existential truism, but not out of a fear of dying, but rather out of the will to live. This is an important existential and psychological distinction since, as Rank (1936) theorized, the fear of death derives from the fear of losing one's individuality, of "being dissolved again into the whole" (p. 124), which in this case would be a horde of depersonalized zombies. Therefore, by identifying with the characters who eradicate their inner zombies – characters who successfully traverse that collective expression of de-individuated others that represents the fate of every being composed of flesh and blood – the consumer of these myths finds a potent exemplar in assuaging their own fear of death with the consequence of focusing on leading a fulfilling life (… all in the comfort of their living room!).

Conclusion

In a later elaboration on the subject of 'the double', Rank (1941) traces the evolution of this motif in a direction that nicely encapsulates the function of the aforementioned existential brand of zombies:

> Originally, the double was an identical self (shadow, reflection), promising personal survival in the *future*; later, the double retained together with the individual's life his personal *past*; ultimately he became an opposing self, appearing in the form of evil which represents the perishable and mortal part of the personality repudiated by the social self.
>
> (pp. 81–82, italics in original)

Acceptance that death remains embedded within us, like an unexpressed virus,[6] and that to live a fulfilled life free from an overwhelming fear of death requires the willful acceptance of, if not enthusiasm for, our temporal nature. As for Shakespeare's Claudio, who says, "Striving for life, I seek death; seeking death, I find life" (Shakespeare, Taylor, & Wells, 1991: *Measure for Measure*, Act III, Scene 1), it remains our lifelong project to endeavor to accept our inner zombie and eradicate our immortal 'other' in order to exist in a psychologically mature existential singularity.

Notes

1 It is notable that in 2004 *Shaun of the Dead* came out and ushered in a sub-genre of zombie comedies (zombedies?), partially sanitizing the horrors of death with humor. Films such as *Zombieland* (2009), *Fido* (2006), and others have followed, along with numerous zombie drama-dies, such as *Life after Beth* (2014) and *Warm Bodies* (2013), that, while each utilizing the genre in creative

ways – even sometimes humanizing zombies – nevertheless maintain more of a sociological rather than a psychological emphasis to their commentary on the human condition.

2 The serialized format of television dramas is perhaps uniquely suited to facilitate more ambitious dynamics of myth identification and, arguably, psychological maturation.

3 'Necessarily' since we have no special, verifiable knowledge of what, if anything, occurs after life.

4 Of course, we must acknowledge that a good number of people choose to avoid consuming zombie media of any type, which could sometimes, though not always, indicate an even stronger defensive stance against grappling with one's mortality, even if only by proxy.

5 AMC actually produced an app for smartphones which allowed users to zombify profile photographs of themselves or others.

6 I am here acutely aware that I am appropriating a medical concept to metaphorically illustrate my point, which may seem as if it contradicts my expressed distaste for framing death in the language of disease. Nevertheless, while I have borrowed from the medical model in order to metaphorically illustrate an idea, others have done so in a way that is irresponsibly literal.

References

Arlow, J. (1961). Ego psychology and the study of mythology. *Journal of the American Psychoanalytic Association, 9*, 371–393.

Bible, The New Revised Standard Version (NRSV).

Borg, M. B. (2003). Psychoanalytic Pure War: Interactions with the post-apocalyptic unconscious. *Journal for the Psychoanalysis of Culture & Society, 8*, 55–67.

Cantor, P. A. (2013). The apocalyptic strain in popular culture: The American nightmare becomes the American dream. *The Hedgehog Review (Summer)*, 23–33.

Cantz, P. (2012). Towards a biblical psychoanalysis: A second look at the first book. *Mental Health, Religion & Culture, 15*, 779–797.

Cantz, P. & Castle, M. (2013). A psycho-biblical response to death anxiety: Separation and individuation dynamics in the Babel narrative. *Journal of Psychology & Theology, 41*, 327–339.

Doty, W. G. (2000). *Mythography: The study of myths and rituals*. Tuscaloosa, AL: University of Alabama Press.

Freud, S. (1913/1966). *Totem and taboo*, in J. Strachey (Ed. and Trans.), *The standard edition of the complete psychological works of Sigmund Freud, Volume XIII*, 1–161. London: Hogarth Press.

Freud, S. (1919/1966). *The Uncanny*, in J. Strachey (Ed. and Trans.), *The standard edition of the complete psychological works of Sigmund Freud, Volume XVII*, 217–256. London: Hogarth Press.

Hall, D. (2011). Varieties of zombieism: Approaching comparative political economy through *28 Days Later* and *Wild Zero*. *International Studies Perspective, 12*, 1–17.

Kierkegaard, S. (1843/1959). *Either/Or, Vol I.* New York, NY: Doubleday.
Mitchel, F. (2007). Life and death and something in between: Reviewing recent horror cinema. *Psychoanalysis, Culture & Society, 12*, 390–397.
Ostow, M. (1986). The psychodynamics of apocalyptic: Discussion of papers on identification and the Nazi phenomenon. *International Journal of Psychoanalysis, 67*, 277–285.
Rank, O. (1926/1971). *The double: A psychoanalytic study*. Chapel Hill, NC: UNC Press Books.
Rank, O. (1936/1978). *Will therapy*. New York, NY: Norton.
Rank, O. (1941/1956). *Beyond psychology*. New York, NY: Dover Publications, Inc.
Shakespeare, W., Taylor, G., & Wells, S. W. (1991). *The complete Oxford Shakespeare*. Oxford: Oxford University Press.
Singer, I. (2008). *Cinematic mythmaking: Philosophy in film*. Cambridge, MA: The MIT Press.
Virilio, P. & Lotringer, S. (1997). *Pure War*. New York, NY: Semiotext.

Chapter 2

The Golem must live, the Golem must die

On the moral imperative of writing critical cultural histories of psychology

Philip Cushman

> *Why keep learning?*
> *Because an avatar might be the next you.*
> (Continuing Education Department, University of Washington)

In the course of the past 30 years, powerful health care corporations and some federal agencies have been engaged in executing a neoliberal strategy of medicalizing psychotherapeutic practices, quantifying outcomes, creating consumer desire, and controlling labor (Marecek & Gillham, 2006); this is what critics refer to as the industrialization of health care. In response, many schools of psychotherapy have capitulated to this campaign by relying increasingly on a model of care that is highly technicist and behavioral, deemphasizes social context and interactive process, utilizes unilateral rather than collaborative approaches, and privileges quantified outcomes research that produces what is wrongly called "evidence-based practices." Psychology now proudly proclaims itself to be a STEM (i.e., science, technology, engineering, and math) discipline (Churchill, 2012). All of this has led to an authoritarian management of the labor force by means of a hierarchical – and highly procedural – administrative structure. Clinicians and professional associations such as the American Psychological Association (APA) at first cautiously complied with and then enthusiastically endorsed these controls on therapeutic and academic practices. Psychology and corporate America have joined forces to offer psychotherapy treatment in what is claimed to be the briefest, most rational, most cost-efficient manner possible (Austad & Berman, 1991).

However, amid this burst of self-congratulatory fervor, some concerns arise. It is one thing to comply when compromise is necessary for survival. For instance, therapy must be made understandable and reasonable to patients and billing organizations, an approach that could lead to mutuality and fairness in decision making and create a modicum of economic safety for therapists. But when the search for financial security and social status become the only goals, other values are lost from sight. Then the search for safety and recognition can degenerate into continuing fearfulness and ambition and finally the wish to dominate patients and control symptoms as ends in themselves.

This is particularly dangerous when competitiveness and domination are omnipresent features of the overall culture; when the predominant way of being is shaped in such a way as to discourage critical thought, historical awareness, interpersonal cooperation, and self-reflection. I believe that is the predicament in which we in psychology find ourselves today. Throughout Western psychology's history, psychologists have laid claim to the legitimacy accorded the physical sciences by presenting their practices as scientistic;[1] but alternative visions of psychology, while not warmly welcomed, were tolerated. As time has passed, however, the profession has come to desire more and more: more legitimacy, more wealth, more influence, more power. As a result, the field now demands near total submission to scientistic ideology. These desires and the abuses they produce threaten to destroy us. As I will explain below, they are our Golem.

Fortunately, there are also theories and values available that could offer an alternative vision for psychology. They are visions drawn from hermeneutics, historical study, relational theory, critical thought, and, for me, also from a particular confluence of Jewish traditions. In my mind, these traditions combine to encourage political resistance to the militarism, scientism, and proceduralism of our time. Many who will read this chapter are engaged in such resistance, although we do so in different ways; one way I attempt resistance, and encourage my students to attempt it, is through studying and writing the critical cultural history of psychology.

The *aleph* and the Golem

In the late 1960s, I first studied midrash – that is, Jewish biblical commentary from late antiquity (starting approximately at the beginning of the Common Era), which are stories about stories. From midrash, I learned about the importance of paradox and the value of playfulness, contextuality, intertextuality, and relationality in Jewish tradition. I learned about the presence–absence dialectic: out of the apparent absence of direct Divine intervention, the rabbis of long ago and their students created a new kind of presence: a relational presence, located in the space between study partners (Aron, 2007; Cushman, 2007; Stern, 1996). I learned about the concept of bringing on the Messiah. I learned that, in the words of Rabbi Tarfon, "you are not required to complete the task [that is, the bringing on of the Messiah], but neither are you free to desist from it." "The struggle to survive," Elie Wiesel wrote in 1966,

> will begin here, in this room, where we are sitting. Whether or not the Messiah comes doesn't matter; we'll manage without him. It is because it is too late that we are commanded to hope. We shall be honest and humble and strong, and then he will come, he will come every day, thousands of times every day. He will have no face, because he will have a thousand faces. The Messiah isn't one man … he's all men. As long as there are men there will be a Messiah. One day you'll sing, and he will sing in you.
>
> (Wiesel, 1966, p. 225)

This interpretative, relational, anti-fundamentalist, story-telling stream of Jewish tradition demonstrates some of the moral understandings that can help us oppose contemporary trends in mainstream psychology and can be applied in order to offer alternative theory and practices.

The Immense *Aleph*

Once, sometime probably in the first centuries of the Common Era, the midrashic rabbis tried to decide what in the entire body of Judaic literature was the direct word of God and what was only human interpretation (Scholem, 1965, pp. 29–31). Many ideas, over many weeks, were offered and debated. They got close to agreement many times, only to be disappointed repeatedly. One rabbi suggested the entire Hebrew Bible, then another argued for the Five Books of Moses, then another the Ten Commandments, then the First Commandment, then the first word of the First Commandment, then the first letter of the first word of the First Commandment. Finally, miraculously, everyone agreed with that. That letter is an *aleph*, and in this story it is referred to as the Immense *Aleph*, because the rabbis thought it was the only direct sound of God's voice. All of God's love and care and wisdom, all that he hoped to give to humans, is contained in that one letter. The sound of the Immense *Aleph*, awe-inspiring and terrible, pregnant with a meaning beyond human comprehension, must have been filled to the breaking point with the overwhelming intensity of the direct experience of God. All the rest, except for that one sound, is interpretation.

Now, that's amazing: midrash has been going on now for over 2000 years and the main justification for it is that every mark, letter, and word in the Hebrew Bible is meant by God to communicate something to humans, and it is our job to interpret them.

So, if only one letter is the direct word of God, that is a remarkably paradoxical and playful statement. But there is more: the letter *aleph* is a silent letter. There is an immensity that the world offers, but it makes no sound until humans interpret it. Even God's voice was unhearable, the rabbis realized, until generations of poor, anonymous Jewish scholars in Mediterranean academies and later in tiny European *shtetls* put pen to paper and interpreted God's silences through their particular and quite varied cultural understandings. It is only through our imaginative interpretive insights that God's voice speaks – an important aspect of the partnership, the covenant, between the Jews and God. And our insights, of course, are always imperfect: uncertain, as the hermeneuticists like to say, and incomplete. Not knowing, or not knowing perfectly, is not easy to tolerate, but we must in order to live a fully human life.

Life would be so much easier if there were only one truth and we could know it perfectly. The Immense *Aleph* is without end, pregnant with what is possible, but vulnerable to all the fears and flaws of the human heart. Interpretation – creative responses that draw from the wisdom of cultural traditions – is that important: it is all we have, and yet it is enough. But it is not easy.

The Golem

Let us now travel forward in time to 1580. In Prague, so the story goes, the Chief Rabbi Judah Loew was faced with rumors about a looming pogrom (a semi-organized, vicious attack on person and property) against the Jews, one in an endless history of violent, bloody attacks on defenseless minority

Jewish communities throughout Europe and the Middle East over the last 1500 years (Margolis & Marx, 1973). The Jews were legally unable to mount an army or even carry weapons, and denied legal protections in feudal, medieval Europe, so Rabbi Loew tried to save his people by turning to mystical Jewish practices. Out of the clay of the Vlatava River he fashioned a giant, human-shaped figure, called the Golem (Idel, 1989). Through secret incantations, and by writing the word *emet*, meaning truth, on the forehead of the giant, he brought the Golem to life. The Golem's job was to protect the Jews from marauding, anti-Semitic mobs, and he did so brilliantly over many months. The Golem would magically increase in size and strength in proportion to the strength of the enemy so that he could protect the Jews no matter how fierce the attack, and the threat was temporarily extinguished.

But the longer the Golem remained alive, the more he began to enjoy life. The legend tells us he came to love the sunsets over the river; he would sit and quietly watch the colors of evening. He also loved to wander in the forest, a lonely, hulking figure at home with the woodland animals. But then trouble began: the enormous Golem frightened the townspeople, and indeed, due to his great strength, he did cause trouble from time to time, which led to complaints. Rabbi Loew came to realize the problem and face the truth: he had to act for the good of all, even those who had previously done his people harm. Although the Golem pleaded with the rabbi to let him live on, and although the rabbi had grown fond of the giant, he could not allow the Golem to harm others. With much sadness, he erased from the giant's forehead the first letter of *emet*; the word then became *met*, which means "death," and the Golem ceased living.

Now, the first letter of the word *emet* is *aleph.* So a few years ago it occurred to me that perhaps the letter that the rabbi erased was not just any old *aleph*, but was indeed the Immense *Aleph*! This makes sense, because it is precisely the capacity to interpret that makes us fully human. If the value of interpretation, symbolized by the *aleph,* is removed from us, then we just follow orders: we can't question, we can't think critically, we can only be robotic true believers, accepting the pronouncements of those in power, believing that there is only one truth in the text and those in control know what it is. In other words, without interpretation we become fundamentalists or mindless conformists, tools of authoritarian leaders and rigid ideologies. Or we become proponents of scientism, unwilling to see the value of nuanced philosophical thought about matters of the heart.

Initially, the Golem had to live in order to protect a small, defenseless minority. And although his presence brought security to the Jews, he had to cease living because his great strength had begun to cause harm to others. The rabbi realized that although the power that the Golem brought to the community was greatly satisfying and brought a sense of security rarely experienced by Jews in what was then their 1500-year Diaspora, the Golem's power ultimately violated the rabbi's most deeply held moral principles.

Within the corporate structure of medieval society, Jewish communities were allowed into a particular duchy or principality only when specifically invited in order to start or enhance the territory's capitalist economy. Jews were not granted rights and protections except under specific circumstances determined by particular rulers, protections that could be – and eventually always were – revoked for economic gain or political leverage. Jews, as resident aliens, usually were prohibited from farming or joining an artisan guild, restricted to lending money, and occasionally allowed to be involved in commerce, activities the Church declared sinful and prohibited Christian believers from engaging in. Jews were forced to live in geographically restricted areas, often in walled-in areas that came to be called ghettos. And they were routinely humiliated, for instance forced to wear identifying clothing such as a yellow star. Later, inevitably, they would be outrageously taxed or extorted, forcibly converted to Christianity or left to the mob, and either expelled or prevented from leaving, depending on the ruler's momentary financial and political situation. They were not allowed to establish their own state or organize a military. The Jews were a despised and defenseless minority, continually vulnerable to and tortured through specific laws (Marcus, 1983), religious crusades, or pogroms (Margolis & Marx, 1973; Sachar, 1979).

However, over time Jewish communities developed a creative response to their legal restrictions, a response Rabbi Loew embodied in his decisions about the Golem. Without the legal ability to protect themselves, Jews developed a culture based on values such as communalism, compassion, and pacifism. They developed religious customs and communal practices that required the protection of the stranger and the poor, aided widows and orphans, and justified those practices through complex textual interpretations attributed to God's commands. Of course, medieval Jews weren't saints, they were entirely human, and with that comes the potential for hypocrisy, greed, cruelty, and the wish for revenge. Still, culture does constitute the self, and given the inescapable situation the Jews lived in for many centuries, it seems clear that they made a virtue out of a necessity. The values of nonviolence, compassion, textual study, critical historical interpretation, and relationality were central to Jewish communal life for the better part of the last 2000 years (Cushman, 2007; Stern, 1996). The moral commitments that moved Rabbi Loew to end the Golem's life and the manner in which he did so were an enactment of some of the central values of Jewish medieval culture.

Today, military power and corporate influences in health care are indeed seductive, but ultimately the indiscriminate and unnecessary exercise of power is wrong and must be stopped, even if that means a community or a profession must live with less money and security. Great strength can cause harm even unintentionally, and sadly, especially when combined with current neoliberal instrumentalism (Fowers, 2010; Sugarman, 2015) or what has been called a "doer–done to" relation (Benjamin, 1990), it tends to degenerate into the wish to dominate. Then we interpret all problems as military or financial and can only conceive of coercive solutions.

The wish to dominate, however, does not appear out of nowhere. It is the embodiment of the way of being in the modern era, writ large. The centrality of domination is what made the Cartesian split a driving force in Western imperialism (that is, the domination of non-Christians and people of color, labor, and women). One way of explaining the current popularity of mean-spirited political domination is by drawing on recent theory about "social" narcissism, which is not dependent on theory that focuses solely on psychological wounding from the early years of life. In this explanation, a charismatic demagogue manifesting domination as a way of being is understood to be living in a narcissistic inflation, a defensive way of being meant to cover up unconscious guilt or shame from, among other things, racism or the increasing economic inequality in the U.S. Neoliberal theory about both the rightness and effectiveness of unrestricted capitalism serves to (1) justify oppression, (2) avoid the awareness of the complicity of the affluent and the privileged, and (3) cover over what precedes the wish to dominate, which is the wounding and self-blame experienced in a neoliberal, racist world. Similarly, supporters of such policies or leaders are drawn by the vicarious triumphalism and personal inflation engendered by neoliberalism's justifications and blame, even if its policies are ultimately politically and/or economically damaging to the same supporters.

In such ways, the doer–done to dynamic thrives and continues to be reproduced in both interpersonal interactions and larger social structures such as institutional racism or militaristic foreign policy.

When strength is combined with the wish to dominate, exploitation and abuse multiply; national defense shifts into aggression, borders are seen as colonial opportunities, and, tragically, republics transmogrify into empires. Empires, inevitably, destroy democracy and degrade and defile their own citizens. Rabbi Loew had to remove life from the Golem not only to protect the non-Jews but also to maintain the moral integrity of his own people.

Critical cultural histories of psychology

Hasidism (a Jewish sect originating in the eighteenth century) has taught that in order to make a better world we must begin here, where we stand (Buber, 1958). If this is true, what are we to do today, here, where we stand, in universities and/or psychotherapy offices? From my point of view, it is our responsibility to interpret and critique our field, to put into question our most cherished theories, to notice, study, and comment on the relationship our theories have to the larger cultural frame and the more detailed political arrangements of our time and place. It is not enough for us only to carry on philosophical and theoretical elaborations and debates as if philosophy and clinical theory are removed from the larger events and forces of the social world around us. It is our responsibility to make a better world by studying the connections between our professional practices and the politics of our world.

Hermeneutic contributions to this project have been extremely important. Martin Heidegger (1962), Hans-Georg Gadamer (1989), and Charles Taylor (1989) have explained why textual criticism is always, necessarily, a moral enterprise. This is because interpretations are framed by understandings of the good, whether acknowledged or disguised. As a result, hermeneutic cultural history cannot claim that it is an objective practice; all research in the human sciences, all research into what matters to humans, is necessarily a type of moral discourse. Critical cultural historians cannot claim what is called "a view from nowhere"; they are responsible for describing the moral commitments that motivate and frame their work.

For that reason, I have featured the *aleph* and Golem stories; my commitments are grounded in a combination of Jewish interpretive traditions, philosophical hermeneutics, and critical theory. This might seem an unlikely combination, but to me it makes sense. Jewish midrashic tradition embodies qualities such as the importance of interpretive processes over objectivist claims, contextualization as a way of study, intertextuality as a way of understanding human literature, and compassionate relationality as a way of being (Cushman, 2007). Altogether, these four qualities could be thought of as comprising important elements of resistance to a fundamentalist and idolatrous way of being, and the development of a respectful, engaged, diverse, democratic way of life. These qualities are fundamental to philosophical hermeneutics.

Critical and postmodern theories could be interpreted as an attempt to apply Heidegger's focus on historicity in order to research the humanities and social sciences. But unfortunately, they are absent Gadamer's and Taylor's awareness of the inescapably moral nature of historical traditions, and therefore need Gadamer's concept of dialogue in order to contribute constructively to our current dilemmas (Cushman, 2005; Richardson, Fowers, & Guignon, 1999). So this combination of midrashic, hermeneutic, and critical traditions gives me a way of interpreting historical events, a way of understanding their larger political contexts, a motivation for undertaking and enduring the difficulties of textual study, and then a commitment to communicating its results.

Starting in 1990, I wrote about the empty self and its fit with the politics of the post-World War II era (Cushman, 1990). These days, we are confronted with a new configuration of the self, new arrangements of power and privilege, new ways our clinical theories fit with the political status quo. So now we need new cultural histories of our field, new research that identifies how our practices either resist or collude with the destructive elements of our time and place, and new ways of developing alternative practices that could shape a different social world.

Early twenty-first-century America: virtual worlds, multiple selves

I believe the predominant self of our time is now reflected and produced in part by the growing hegemony of electronic machines, gadgets, activities, games, and communication processes; the overall frame of consumerism; and a socioeconomic climate and psychological way of being created by neoliberal theory and practice. It began to shift from an empty self to what Peter Gilford and I (Cushman & Gilford, 1999, 2000) now call a shallower, flatter self. This new self suffers less from being empty of meaning and initiative than from anxiety about interpersonal relations, a psychological reaction caused by an ongoing traumatizing social world, an edgy, competitive desire to dominate and exploit, and a compulsion to search, always, for opportunities to consume and be entertained. It is populated with a multitude of identities developed over time by living in an electronic, computerized world, identities that focus on avoiding and controlling aversive social interactions and purchasing various consumer products. These multiple identities cluster around the outside of the person, waiting to be called to center stage, depending on the social needs of the moment.

At present, I am particularly concerned with the connection between two kinds of phenomena in our contemporary social world. One is the way the flattened, multiple self functions: for instance, how people live, interact, and especially perform or use identity when on Facebook, online dating services, and massively multiplayer online role-playing games (MMORPGs) like Second Life, Farmville, or Piercing Blow. The second is the iron grip that behavioral tools such as quantitative outcome studies (Hoffman, 2009; Stern, 2013), manualized psychotherapy treatments (Lord, 2014), and academic competencies in graduate education in psychology (Cushman, 2012) currently have on the profession, including the shape and spirit of the APA code of ethics.

In other words, the cultural terrain of our contemporary social world is one that brings to light both an obsession with electronic communication and entertainment, and an ever-growing, increasingly taken-for-granted reliance on a quantifiable, bureaucratic proceduralism. It seems counterintuitive that these two seemingly opposite types of phenomena are linked. But I believe they have certain qualities and functions in common. We either make electronic Golems to aid and protect us, or we try to turn ourselves into Golems: non-interpretive, deadened worker bees or heroic war machines.

Electronic living and the multiple self

There is a type of popular film that portrays the idea that Golem-like machines are simply better versions of humans, or that humans need to become more effective by being infused with machine parts. For instance, there is a television commercial in which a young man is in a business meeting, populated by several well-dressed people, all sitting around a large conference table. He takes out a new smartphone, called a Droid, and begins to search for information, calculate some problem, or key in some data. His fingers punch the screen at an ever-faster rate, almost as if the phone itself has taken over his actions. And then, as his fingers work faster still, they begin turning into a robot's fingers, and then his hands and wrists and arms all turn into metal parts of a machine. The voice-over states that the Droid, in order to hook "you up to everything you need to do," will turn "you into an instrument of efficiency." The man's fingers are now almost a blur, racing at superhuman speed. His Droid has turned him into an android.

What happens to the self and our understandings of the good when our model is an information-processing machine? When humans become just another flashing image, a virtual persona, then what is to stop us not only from inventing and living through avatars but also from thinking of ourselves as avatars? A person comes to light now as a multiple self, composed of a cluster of images – perhaps some of them virtual images – from which one chooses at any one time, depending on who one needs to impress or attract or sell something to or protect oneself from. These various images might well be attractive, flashy, even beautiful, but they are flattened: they have little substance or depth, no reason for being except to perform a specific purpose in a larger, fictive game – they are entirely instrumental.

This relation between alternative selves and our current social world is portrayed artistically in the 2009 film *Avatar* (Cameron, 2009). Jake Sully's life before being scientifically transformed into an avatar is crass, superficial, cruel. He is marked, in fact disabled, by it. But through scientific advances he is transformed into an avatar, and then the avatar is transported to a radically different physical and social world, one that is beautiful, spiritual, proud. Jake comes to embody new values, and tries to convince those in control of his old world that the path they are on is wrong, but to no avail. By the end of the film (no surprise here), he chooses to remain permanently in his avatar and live in that new world. His only hope is to leave his old self and escape into his avatar and the world to which his avatar belongs – escape is the only option. In the new, electronic world of today, we seem to be developing a new kind of healing technology: a virtual therapeutic for a multiple, flattened self.

Electronic living and managed care

There are obvious reasons related to the accumulation of capital and the exercise of political control that bureaucratic forms, actuarial tables, and financial calculations are prominent in the decision-making processes and public relations campaigns of the corporations and federal agencies that now control health care. In turn, those in control have come to insist that therapists submit scientized, behavioral conceptualizations and evaluations of therapy in order for their practices to be reimbursed. Complying with those procedures has effected profound changes in the ways therapists now define and evaluate mental ills, their therapeutic practices, their own roles, capacities, and limits, and thus the ways they conceive of, enact, and teach therapeutic theory and practice.

For instance, 100 percent of evidence-based treatments for trauma are manualized (Lord, 2014). In a second example, on July 21, 2014, Magellan Health Inc. announced that it "will soon offer expanded computerized cognitive behavioral treatment programs." It will do so in order to "address common concerns in the behavioral health community . . . [such as] a lack of access to clinicians" (Magellan, 2014, p. 2). Evidently, the way to address the shortage of therapists is to do away with them entirely. Here we see proceduralism, in the form of manuals and computer programming, as a substitute for human meeting, for those precious moments when, together, we make presence and meaning out of absence and grief. If quantitative measures determine outcome, then only practices that can be reduced to numbers – and thus rendered countable – will be thought of as proper data that could be used to determine worthwhile outcomes. Similarly, only those ills that can be reduced to numbers and countable problems, those identified in Axis I of the *Diagnostic and Statistical Manual of Mental Disorders* (DSMs) III and IV, will come to be understood as proper – and reimbursable – diagnoses.

Often, contemporary psychological explanations of the human mind such as cognitive theory are modeled on computer processes. In our time, human mentation is described in computer language, the distinction between machines and humans narrows (and in some pop culture venues becomes nonexistent), and the superiority of war machinery such as cyborgs or terminators is often taken for granted. When U.S. society's criteria for what is valuable are based primarily on efficiency, computational speed, and physical strength, computers and war machines will of course be superior to slower, weaker, more vulnerable humans.

In the shadow of managed care and in sync with the larger electronic and neoliberal consumer culture, psychologists have been influenced by, and in turn have given voice to, increasingly quantified and cognitivist understandings of the human being. As a result, we have quietly and perhaps even willingly acceded to a hyperconcrete, mechanistic, instrumental understanding of psychotherapy practices and then have structured graduate degree programs accordingly. It is a structure based on market values and a semi-magical belief in the effectiveness of pre-established behavioral procedures for every interpersonal interaction, psychotherapy event, and academic learning situation. Michael Sandel (1984) once described the U.S. as a procedural republic, but now it seems increasingly clear that the U.S. isn't really a republic anymore. We are an empire now – a procedural empire.

Electronic living, proceduralism, and psychotherapy

Both computers and scientistic therapeutics depend on quantification and procedural rules. They may seem to be radically different phenomena, but in fact their origins and functions are similar. A computer is a machine that simply follows orders – orders programmed into it through what is called a procedure code. So computers, in a way, are all procedure; they do not, cannot, interpret. Heidegger (1977) argued that technology is not a neutral tool; it is a frame of reference that affects every aspect of social life. In that framework, most everything shows up as either a resource to be used (what he called "standing reserve") or the machine that uses it. The modern, technological world, in combination with neoliberal political ideology, transforms all interactions, including human relating, into a doer–done to relation.

What happens to psychotherapy theories and practices when the profession is shaped by these twenty-first-century influences? When psychotherapy adopts the language of machine-like processes and thinks of the self as a kind of computer, it will have a hand not only in reflecting but also reproducing that same kind of self – a self that is multiple, flattened, superficial, robotic. In our consumerized economy, this self searches for flashing images, glitzy products, and self-improvement strategies that increase one's aggressive competitive edge. It is hungry for stimulation and entertainment, such as celebrity scandals, violent circuses, catchy slogans, simple questions, and easy answers. It is a self, above all, that requires procedures in order to function properly, and that requires others to follow procedures in order to feel safe from them. This is because a doer–done to landscape is a frightening, dangerous place, and humans within that landscape lose confidence in, or a capacity for engaging in, moral discourse in order to enrich their lives, protect themselves, and improve their society. In such a world, it is thought that only proceduralism – the willingness to follow scientistically produced orders – can save us from one another. When a person aspires to be a robot, programmed rules become the only path to peaceful coexistence.

The technical reflection of a multiple, robotic self is Axis I of DSMs III and IV. Humans are thought of as a collection of specific, concrete behaviors (i.e., signs and symptoms) that have been reduced to their simplest, uncontestable, ahistorical elements – a kind of Lego approach to human psychology. Treatment then becomes understood as the execution of a specific intervention designed for that particular symptom. When the symptom has been properly isolated and broken down to its smallest behavioral denominator, treatment is then thought to be simply a matter of locating and administering the symptom's matching therapeutic intervention: the specific key that turns the particular diagnostic lock for which it has been designed. In this vision, therapy has a predetermined quality: mechanical, unilateral, and surgical in its precision. For every problem, there is thought to be a quick, direct, decontextualized solution, if only the therapist adheres precisely to the script.

It follows from these technical innovations that, in sync with good modern-era thinking, everything psychological can be readily – and clearly – understood. Increasingly, student clinics and community agencies are encouraged to administer a consumer satisfaction survey-like instrument at the end of each session. It is thought the results will indicate whether the patient has been properly understood and empathized with, and the symptoms have disappeared; whether the predesigned therapy plan has been followed, the previous behavioral goals met, the therapeutic alliance properly maintained, and any new goals effectively set. Psychotherapy, then, takes on the cast of a straightforward consumer transaction, like buying a hamster or shopping for a new refrigerator. The relational psychoanalytic value of disagreement and conflict, and the importance of understanding through interpretive processes their causes and meanings

(Stern, 2010), are lost when the patient is thought of as a "consumer" – and the therapist as a "provider" – of therapy.

All this is a relatively new way of conceiving of therapy, although an entirely necessary one, if the profession is to fit smoothly into the scientized world of neoliberal managed care. Once the technological frame has been set, the only problems that come to light are those that can be reduced to the kinds of solutions that procedures and electronic machines can solve. Depression becomes a chemical imbalance or a mistaken way of thinking that can be fixed by the administration of the proper medication or the correct rational thought. Then the patient is quickly returned to the roles of worker and consumer. Depression, anxiety, and dissociation as expressions of moral confusion (Sheehy, 2011), economic insecurity (Bauman, 1999), or political despair (Marin, 1981) rarely come to light in such a world.

The degree to which our psychotherapy theories reduce human beings to this kind of vision is the degree to which our practices support the economic and political forces that created and continue to maintain a world of extreme economic stratification, a militarized police force and racist system of imprisonment, colonial wars of occupation, and spinning electronic circuses. It is these circuses, of course, that make learning and thinking and self-reflection uninteresting, bothersome, and finally unattainable. Increasingly, it seems that we strive to portray ourselves as minor celebrities – we glamorize ourselves online, display our activities, and exaggerate (and invent) our happiest moments: we are our own paparazzi. We are becoming the kind of persons who are uninterested in, and increasingly incapable of, political nuance and creativity, independent interpretive thinking, tolerating difference, or dwelling in a social world of uncertainty.

Scientism brings with it an ever-increasing inability to think philosophically about these important issues and engage with others about the moral understandings these behaviors reflect. Without a better way to engage in discourse, we run the risk of creating the automatic closure of what Gadamer (1989) called dialogue (that is, a meaningful encounter with difference). The absence of dialogue, in turn, will result in the entrenchment of normalizing practices, mainstream values, and the political status quo – all produced through putatively scientific practices. Different cultural beliefs, philosophical questioning, and political critique could soon be in danger of being considered symptoms of what managed care companies call "non-compliance." Whether applied to ever-narrowing APA requirements for graduate-school accreditation or clinical prescriptions in evidence-based, manualized treatments, scientistic procedures are likely to interpret difference, disagreement, or opposition as unprofessional, inappropriate, and perhaps even unethical. This will result in the rejection of an accreditation application or a therapy claim, or perhaps before long the cancellation of a community agency's or private practice's liability insurance.

In other words, governmental agencies and big business develop various rules and practices that suit their financial and political needs, and professional associations like the APA adapt to, justify, and then enforce those rules and practices as their own. These institutions shape a series of interlocking procedures that control the practice of psychology in many ways. The ideology that initiates this vicious cycle and the procedures that police it form a panoptic, self-sealing structure. In managed care, Leyerle wrote in 1994, "providers as well as patients are placed under surveillance by utilization review agencies" (Leyerle, 1994, p. 187). It may be that "the major goal never has been to cut health care costs but to institutionalize the surveillance and control mechanisms themselves" (p. 190). Kaslow et al. (2007), the APA task force on assessing academic competencies in doctoral education, predicted that in the future, through the strict use of academic competencies, a psychology curriculum could "ensure" that graduates would be competent and ethical. In a startling expression of overconfidence, the authors of the eight-page article used the word "ensure" 16 times. The committee was proud to predict that there will be a time when practicing psychologists will be evaluated by a competency system throughout their working lives. Proceduralism will be in complete control; interpretation will be dead.

It is the height of irony that it is this same Nadine Kaslow, President of the APA in 2014, who recently wrote to APA members responding to reports about the APA's collaboration with the Department of Defense's program of torture. In her letter, she seems surprised by the degree and nature of the APA's involvement in the planning of torture practices, its protection and defense of the psychologists who carried them out, and the subsequent cover-up of its own complicity. But any of us who followed the progression of events as they occurred knew what was happening. None of us can claim surprise anymore than could Captain Renault in the movie *Casablanca* who was "shocked, shocked" that there was gambling in Rick's Café Américain.

Sadly, in all likelihood there will be no comprehensive reevaluation of APA ethics nor the way it is taught in APA-accredited graduate programs. There will just be greater vigilance in policing behavior and coercing compliance. At least in its present form, the APA seems unable to question the larger scientistic foundations of its vision. It is unlikely we will see a hermeneutic redesign of and education about the Ethics Code based on the understanding that psychotherapy is a moral discourse. It seems doubtful that mainstream psychology will be able to realize the bankruptcy of its approach and the absolute necessity of a different perspective built on a more solid philosophical framework. No, there will only be the promise of a more procedural scientism. So probably – and sadly – the APA's solution will simply be more of the same. Repetition will compound tragedy.

Conclusion

It seems to me we have a responsibility to resist this convergence of historical forces, to educate ourselves and alert the public. We must tell them that what arrives in the name of consumer protection and the elimination of budgetary waste, in the guise of the march of progressive science and responsible economic policy, is in fact the exercise of power meant to control therapists and researchers in order to increase compliance and conformity in our citizenry. If therapists and graduate students were not controlled by all these panoptic rules, procedures, and protocols, we might be freer to draw from different historical and human science traditions that would enable us to think in more contextual, moral, political, or relational ways. Critical cultural history is a good vehicle for studying and interpreting complex matters like the fit between a cultural/political terrain and the healing technologies that are embedded in that terrain. It can help us realize that to the degree that our practices reproduce the status quo, we are contributing to some of the very suffering we are supposed to be healing.

Being implicated in the ills we are responsible for healing is no way to bring on the Messiah. The way to make the world a better place is to look beyond the triumphalism that neoliberalism guarantees and the safety that militarism and corporate proceduralism putatively "ensure," and to fight against the violence and financial exploitation that Golem-like organizations eventually bring. At times in the life of a people or a nation, it is no doubt helpful to be militarily strong enough to maintain safety, or, in the case of a profession like psychology, influential enough to be respected and financially viable. But too much power, combined with a neoliberal subjectivity, turns strength and the pursuit of status or money into domination and destructiveness. Critique – especially hermeneutic, historical critique framed in an explicit moral stance that leads to alternative social arrangements – is indispensable to a just and good society.

It is not domination and control that save us from fear and despair; in fact, they cause great suffering, create bitter enemies, and bring on the very dangers they set out to avoid. Instead, what saves us from despair and works to help us imagine and actively strive for a more just political world are the moments of care and concern that make meaning in the mutual space between us and can move us to organize in order to fight for larger institutional political change. It is those moments that make life worthwhile, that help us live interpretively, draw on historical and religious traditions in order to resist the urge to comply with fundamentalisms, and instead tolerate absence, become politically active, and thus create a different kind of presence. It is that kind of experience that relational psychoanalysis works to create (Cushman, 2015). In this chapter, I suggest that critical cultural history can have a hand in improving our social world by demonstrating what is missing in our current terrain and what is needed in order to reshape it. It is good that the Golem exists, for a while. But then it must die, for the good of all.

Note

1 Scientism is the belief that only a physical science model of research can determine the truth about all human concerns, including those related to what in the 1830s Tocqueville called "habits of the heart" – that is, moral understandings related to human meaning, relationship, and engagement in public life.

References

Aron, L. (2007). Black fire on white fire, resting on the knee of the holy and blessed one. *Contemporary Psychoanalysis*, *43*, 89–111.

Austad, C.S. & Berman, W. (Eds.). (1991). *Psychotherapy in managed health care: The optimal use of time and resources.* Washington, DC: American Psychological Association.

Bauman, Z. (1999). *In search of politics.* Stanford, CA: Stanford University Press.

Benjamin, J. (1990). An outline of intersubjectivity: The development of recognition. *Psychoanalytic Psychology*, *75*, 33–46.

Buber, M. (1958). *Hasidism and modern man* (Ed. & Trans. M. Friedman). New York: Harper & Row.

Cameron, J. (director). (2009). *Avatar* [motion picture]. Los Angeles, CA: Twentieth Century Fox.

Churchill, S.D. (2012). Humanistic psychology and STEM disciplines: Strange bedfellows? *The Humanistic Psychologist*, *40*, 221–223.

Cushman, P. (1990). Why the self is empty. *American Psychologist*, *45*, 599–611.

Cushman, P. (2005). Between arrogance and a dead-end: Psychoanalysis and the Heidegger–Foucault dilemma. *Contemporary Psychoanalysis*, *41*, 399–417.

Cushman, P. (2007). A burning world, an absent God: Midrash, hermeneutics, and relational psychoanalysis. *Contemporary Psychoanalysis*, *43*, 47–88.

Cushman, P. (2012). Defenseless in the face of the status quo: Psychology without a critical humanities. *The Humanistic Psychologist*, *40*, 262–269.

Cushman, P. (2015). Relational psychoanalysis as political resistance. *Contemporary Psychoanalysis*, *51*, 423–459.

Cushman, P. & Gilford, P. (1999). From emptiness to multiplicity: The self at the year 2000. *Psychohistory Review*, *27*, 15–31.

Cushman, P. & Gilford, P. (2000). Will managed care change our way of being? *American Psychologist*, *55*, 985–996.

Fowers, B.J. (2010). Instrumentalism and psychology: Beyond using and being used. *Theory and Psychology*, *20*, 102–124.

Gadamer, H.-G. (1989). *Truth and method* (Trans. D. Marshal & J. Weinsheimer). New York: Crossroads. (Original work published 1960.)

Heidegger, M. (1962). *Being and time* (Trans. J. Macquarrie & E. Robinson). New York: Harper & Row. (Original work published 1927.)

Heidegger, M. (1977). *The question concerning technology and other essays* (Trans. W. Lovitt). New York: Harper & Row.

Hoffman, I.Z. (2009). Doublethinking our way to "scientific" legitimacy. *Journal of the American Psychoanalytic Association*, *57*, 1043–1069.

Idel, G. (1989). *Golem.* New York: SUNY Press.

Kaslow, N.J., Bebeau, M.J., Leigh, I.W., Lichtenberg, J.W., Nelson, P.D., Portnoy, S.M., Rubin, N.J., & Smith, I.L. (2007). Guiding principles and recommendations for the assessment of competence. *Professional Psychology, Research and Practice*, *38*, 441–451.

Leyerle, B. (1994). *The private regulation of American health care.* Armonk, NY: Sharpe.

Lord, S.P. (2014). *Ways of being in trauma-based society: Discovering the politics and moral culture of the trauma industry through hermeneutic interpretation of evidence-supported PTSD treatment manuals* (Unpublished doctoral dissertation). Antioch University, Seattle, WA.

Magellan Health, Business Wire Press Release (2014). Magellan Health to offer expanded computerized cognitive behavioral therapy services. July 21, 2014, 2:01 p.m. EDT. Retrieved July 27, 2014, 9:32 p.m. WDT.

Marcus, J.R. (1983). *The Jew in the medieval world: A source book, 315–1791.* New York: Atheneum.
Marecek, J. & Gillham, J. (2006). Is three a crowd? Clients, clinicians, and managed care. *American Journal of Orthopsychiatry, 76*, 251–259.
Margolis, M.I. & Marx, A. (1973). *A history of the Jewish people.* New York: Atheneum.
Marin, P. (1981). Living with moral pain. *Psychology Today, 15*, 68–80.
Richardson, F.C., Fowers, B.J., & Guignon, C.B. (1999). *Re-envisioning psychology.* San Francisco, CA: Jossey-Bass.
Sachar, A.L. (1979). *A history of the Jews.* New York: Knopf.
Sandel, M.J. (1984). The procedural republic and the unencumbered self. *Political Theory, 12*, 81–95.
Scholem, G. (1965). *On the Kabballah and its symbolism.* New York: Schoken.
Sheehy, M. (2011). Anonymous: Floaters. In M. Dimen (Ed.), *With culture in mind* (pp. 99–105). New York: Routledge.
Stern, D. (1996). *Midrash and theory.* Evanston, IL: Northwestern University Press.
Stern, D.B. (2010). *Partners in thought.* New York: Routledge.
Stern, D.B. (2013). Psychotherapy is an emergent process. *Psychoanalytic Dialogues, 23*, 102–115.
Sugarman, J. (2015). Neoliberalism and psychological ethics. *Journal of Theoretical and Philosophical Psychology, 35*, 103–116.
Taylor, C. (1989). *Sources of the self.* Cambridge, MA: Harvard University Press.
Wiesel, E. (1966). *The gates of the forest.* New York: Holt, Rinehart & Winston.

Chapter 3

The Golem and the decline of language and magic—or, why our machines disappoint

Joel Rosenberg

Our story begins with the primordial origin of humankind and its fall from divine favor. Here is how it was envisioned by the young Walter Benjamin at the height of what was then known as the "Great War":

> The absolute relation of name to knowledge exists only in God. Only there is naming found, because it is inwardly identical with the creative word … in the human God set language free, set free the medium of creation. … The [later] enslavement of language in prattle [after the fall from Eden] is joined by the enslavement of things in folly almost as its inevitable consequence.
>
> (Benjamin, 1996, pp. 68, 72)

This is a necessary framework for understanding the human creation of the artificial human. If there is a common denominator to much Jewish lore of the android known as the Golem (Clay Man), it is disappointment. This was evident in the prototype of all golem legends, the story of Raba's artificial man in Babylonian Talmud *Sanhedrin* 65b:

> Raba said: If the righteous wished, they could create a world. But, it is said (Isaiah 59:2), "Your iniquities have caused division between you and your Creator."
>
> Raba created a man [*Raba' bara' gabra'*, a multiple pun in Aramaic]. He sent him to Rabbi Zera. [Rabbi Zera] said: You are from my colleagues, the magicians. Return to your dust ...
>
> Rav Hanina and Rav Oshaya used to sit every Friday before the Sabbath and occupy themselves with the *Sefer Yetsirah* [*Book of*

Creation], and created for themselves a calf one-third the natural size, and ate it.

(Epstein, 1994, fol. 65b)

Magical creation, in whatever ways it has been entrusted to human occult wisdom, always, it seems, comes with a catch, a flaw, a shortfall—as if the imitation of divinity it purports to be were but the copy of a copy, and so, doomed to degenerate. Though the magician tries to imitate the divine creation of the cosmos told in Chapter 1 of the Book of Genesis, his artistry seems as if it were passing down in a chain of ever more weakened copies, from one generation to the next (Ben-Shelomoh, 1970, pp. 46–47; Weinstein, 1994, p. 4).[1] Human magical art, like technology, is only as strong as the wielder, and only as the historical era and hour permit. "If the righteous wished," says Raba sadly, "they could create a world." But iniquity and human failing intervene—in such a way that the divinely bestowed creative faculty becomes the image of a kind of hell, like the nightmarish profusion of human arts in pre-Flood times described in a passage from the late pre-Christian-era apocalyptic work *1 Enoch.* This work based itself on an ancient myth of divine beings who descend to earth and corrupt humanity, precisely by teaching humans the refined arts of civilization—imparting, among other things, the art of making weaponry and war, and the arts that presumably (at least for one era of male-dominant culture) help make women the objects of desire (is this why Helen of Troy had become the fount of warmaking?):

> They taught humans medicine, incantation, and the cutting of roots. They taught about plants and the making of swords, knives, shields, and breastplates. About women's bracelets, decorations, and mascara for the eyelids; about precious stones, and coloring tinctures and alchemy. They taught incantation and the cutting of roots; about astrology and knowledge of the heavenly signs and stars, and the course of the moon. They taught the deception of human beings. And the people cried out in pain and their voice reached up to heaven.
>
> (Charlesworth, 1983, pp. 15–16, my translation)[2]

A similar disenchantment prevailed in Jewish legend as late as the twelfth or thirteenth century in a medieval work called *The Book of Letter & Number Lore*. This work by Judah the Pious of Regensburg continues the folk traditions embodied in the Talmudic lore I quoted earlier. It, too, is a golem tale and depicts magical use of the book known as the *Sefer Yetsirah.* Here, it is cast as a tale of Ben Sira, the attributed author of the apocryphal book Sirach, or Ecclesiasticus. Legendarily, though not historically, he was regarded as the son of Jeremiah the prophet. This bit of tradition is remarkable for making its golem (here simply called "a man") not only a speaking being but an ethical being:

> Ben Sira wished to study the [*Sefer*] *Yetsirah* [and make an artificial human being]. Then a heavenly voice went forth: "You cannot make [such a creature] alone." He went to his father, Jeremiah. They busied themselves with it, and at the end of three years a man was created [by them], on whose forehead stood the word *'emet* [א מ ת, truth], as on Adam's forehead. Then the man they had made said to them: "God alone created Adam, and when he wished to let Adam die, he erased the [letter] *'aleph* [א] and he remained *met* [מ ת], dead. That is what you should do with me and not create another man, lest the world succumb to idolatry as in the ancient days of Enosh." The created man said to them: "Reverse the combinations of letters by which I was created and erase the *'aleph* of the word *'emet* from my forehead." They did so and immediately he fell into dust.
>
> (Epstein, 1887; Scholem, 1965, p. 174)[3]

At the core of this preoccupation was the four-letter divine Name YHWH (commonly transcribed as "Yahweh" but traditionally held by observant Jews to be unpronounceable) believed to be the animating power of all life. That name was made synonymous with the word for "Truth" on the precedent of a verse from Jeremiah (Jer. 10:10): "YHWH [your] God is Truth." In Talmudic legend, the name YHWH had already been linked to the potential for catastrophe. There, it was said that when King David was digging the foundations for the Temple he hoped to build, he found a piece of pottery on which the divine Name was inscribed. The shard actually spoke to him and declared that it was forbidden for him to remove it, for it was like a kind of bathtub plug, but in this case holding back the underground waters of the primordial deep from spewing forth. This abeyance of the waters had held true since the time the people Israel had accepted the Torah, the laws of Moses—including, of course, its preface, the Ten Commandments—and will presumably remain in force only as long as they continue to do so.[4]

In rabbinic lore, the divine Name was considered a magical force—its true pronunciation known only to the Jerusalem High Priest and a circle of rabbinic sages privy to magical art. As the grunts and howls of animals were to human language, so, in the rabbinic imagination, was human language to the Name of God. It was, nonetheless, only a small leap to imagine a universe of correspondences within the building blocks of speech itself. This principle was enshrined above all in the remarkable Talmudic-era poem (for a poem it surely was) by a Jewish Pythagorean—a work centrally influential to magical, pietistic, and theosophic Jewish mysticisms of a later era and known by the title *Sefer Yetsirah*.[5]

Whether this work was either identical to or inspired by the mysterious book referred to in the Talmud passage I quoted earlier is not known. But it based its design on the 22-letter Hebrew alphabet and the ten-digit number system, together known as the "32 Pathways of Wonder." It drew boldly imaginative analogies between the fundamental zones of the human speech apparatus (laryngeal, palatal, labial, etc.); the four cardinal elements (fire, water, earth, and air); the six spatial directions (up/down, north/south, east/west); the limbs, organs, and apertures of the human body; the heavenly orbs of our daytime and nighttime sky; the days of the week; and the months of the year. Such efforts to draw connections between domains and dimensions of nature and the components of language tap into the most ancient impulses in Hebrew and Semitic cultures for wordplay, punning, and numerology. The number 32 in Hebrew numerology spells, for example, *Lev* (לֵב), the word for "heart." The whole cosmos is human. It is linguistic. And it is social.

Of particular interest in the *Sefer Yetsirah* were seven letters that had a dual pronunciation, depending on whether or not the letter had a dot in its middle. The Hebrew letter for "b," for example, was pronounced either "b" or "v." The letter for "p" was pronounced either "p" or "f." One possible exception to this pattern was the letter "r," which occurs with a dot (רּ) only once in the whole Hebrew Bible, and may have resulted from a flyspeck on the scroll of the scribe. But it was called into service for the sake of bringing the number of such letters to seven. This allowed the poet of the *Sefer Yetsirah* to rhapsodize on the magical number seven:

> Seven Stars in the universe; Seven Days in the year; Seven Gates in the body [lit. soul or self]. And from them God created Seven Heavens and Seven Earths; and Seven Sabbaths … And these are the Seven

> Stars in the universe: Sun, Venus, Mercury, Moon, Saturn, Jupiter, and Mars. And these are the Seven Days of the year: the Seven Days of Creation. And Seven Gates in the body of male and female ... And therefore, God cherished the seventh of every object under the heavens.
>
> (Anonymous, 1962, 4:2, p. 99; 4:4, p. 51; 4:12, pp. 107–108; my translation)[6]

Such preoccupations were carried forward in later times by Babylonian Jewish sages and late-medieval German-Jewish pietist magic, and, above all, by the kabbalists' virtually Joycean word games.[7] All these influences poured into the later lore of the golem.

The ideas I have culled here from Jewish tradition are difficult—especially, perhaps (though not necessarily), to those who do not consider themselves religious believers. I myself function in an in-between world: between, on the one hand, my own religious conviction as a radical pantheist—that is, as one who believes that divinity is everywhere: in you, in me, in nature, in the totality of the cosmos and beyond, even in alternative universes—and, on the other hand, my outlook as a secular humanist—that is, my allegiance to scientific cosmology, human reason, and Darwinian evolution; to the separation of church and state; and, indeed, to a historical materialist conception of human society, present and past.[8] Nor do I regard these commitments as incompatible with the idea of moral and ethical standards incumbent on humanity at large, whether or not one believes in a higher power or Supreme Being.

I thus believe that the story of Raba's artificial man has an essentially humanistic core: namely, as a reflection on our dual role as creatures and creators. The ancient Jew might have said that we humans are the golems of God. The modern humanist would say that we are creatures of nature and, at the same time, prodigious creators of alternate worlds, of science and technology, of works of the imagination, of modifications of nature, and even of artificial human life: robots, computers, machines, and motion pictures (I am presently a film scholar by trade), and of human social institutions that represent historical, often class-based, decisions.

Many or most of us modern folk are familiar with science-fiction androids, whether through motion pictures or television. It is not hard to understand why the android theme was instantly so successful as a movie plot, and it is fair to suggest that its mythos is a virtual allegory of modernity—or, indeed, of cinema itself, our most elaborated reservoir of artificial human life. The creation of the artificial human was a logical extension of modern humankind's preternatural ability to imagine alternative worlds, and served as a principal means of reflection on the unique and troubled status of *Homo faber*, the fabricating human, the inventor and maker.[9] The nineteenth century, in particular, witnessed radical transformations of human existence through the invention of locomotion and the internal combustion engine, the harnessing of electricity, the establishment of assembly-line production, wire communication, photography, and eventually cinema, radio and TV broadcasting, and sound recordings—all innovations that have further borne fruit, in our own time, in the form of computers, WiFi connections, smartphones, and social media (Facebook, Twitter, etc.), innovations that have more recently become enablers of American fascism. The total trajectory of these steps has collapsed geographical distances, shrunk the barriers between nations, multiplied human productivity to previously unimaginable proportions, and placed the human being into a newly insecure status as a cog or node in machinery itself. This unprecedentedly widespread mechanization of reality inevitably threw into focus the question of the human status of the inventor, and of the power to invent as such.

It is fair to say that most sci-fi traditions of the android are especially indebted to two 1920s German Expressionist silent films. First and foremost was Paul Wegener's cinema classic *The Golem: How He Came into the World* (1920). The second film, perhaps better known today, was Fritz Lang's *Metropolis* (1927), which imagined an underground city where humans worked as slaves and where a workers' rebellion spurred by a charismatic woman rebel named Maria called forth the invention of a female android disguised as Maria, who worked to mislead the workers and to sabotage the rebellion. Wegener's Golem film based itself on the Jewish legend of the sixteenth-century real-life sage, Rabbi Judah Loew of Prague, as the attributed creator of the Golem. The actual Rabbi Loew was indeed a mystic, and also an astronomer, and, according to folklore, was the reputed inventor of the *camera obscura*, ancestor to the motion picture camera. But he was not a magician. Wegener's film, however, made him into not only a magician but also an astrologer, an alchemist, and, indeed, a filmmaker. The Golem was played by Wegener himself. Early in the story, this Clay Man is portrayed as clumsy and awkward, but in the course of the story he begins to discover his human abilities and gradually becomes an independent life.

Wegener follows one strand of the folkloric Golem legends in showing the creature as intended to rescue the Jews from a potentially devastating expulsion from their home city of Prague. Once that mission is accomplished, the Golem is supposed to be returned to lifeless clay. But in the Rabbi's absence, the Golem is reawakened by an assistant named Famulus ("Apprentice"), who, as an archetypal Sorcerer's Apprentice, reactivates the Golem, who then rebels and goes on a rampage, destroying much of Prague's Jewish quarter by setting it aflame. Wegener himself had served in the German Army during World War I, and twice earned the high military honor of the Iron Cross.[10] But because he had known the ravages of war and catastrophe first-hand, he declared himself a pacifist (Wegener, 1954, pp. 13–37). His 1920 Golem film was, whether directly or indirectly, a kind of warning about the catastrophe created by mechanized warfare, which had wrought unprecedented disaster throughout Europe.

Our simultaneously puzzled and titillated reaction to the android stems precisely from uncertainty over where natural boundaries of the self leave off and artificial extensions of it begin. This resembles the boundary between the divine and human but it also expresses the relation of us humans to our own machines. The fact that an automobile has made it possible to cover in minutes a distance that takes an hour or two on foot makes the machine a part of who we are. The computer changes the way we write or calculate, and so changes us. The telephone, by uniting us with far reaches of the globe, extends our person accordingly, but also makes us part of a larger person created by the network of electronic circuitry. We do not have a merely instrumental relation to these conveniences, because our entire conception of time and space, and, in turn, of ourselves, is changed by their use—and shattered by their breakdown once we grow accustomed to them. We are, to this degree, something of a different species from our great-grandparents. And yet, these innovations are no less revolutionary than those extensions of human identity which our distant ancestors created for themselves: the flint, the wheel, the irrigation ditch, the smelting of metals, the instruments of war, the formation of the state, the reading of the stars, the tincture of the eyelids and rouging of the cheeks, the play of costume, fashion, and artifice. A comparable series of inventions comprised the human arts that the ancient Jewish apocalyptic work *1 Enoch* held up as Promethean transgressions, a promiscuous fusion of the elements—symbolically equated with bestiality, sexual license, and what one might call the technology of gender—all of which intoxicated the pre-Flood eras and eventually would lead, according to the apocalyptist, to a divine reckoning and catastrophe.[11]

Jewish mythical and mystical tradition, much like the modern apprehension of the mechanized world, was ambivalent: the creative faculty of humankind was seen as the site both of euphoria, as in the ecstatic strophes of the *Sefer Yetsirah*, and, on the other hand, of horror, as with the grim apocalyptist of *1 Enoch*, and the nausea and ennui of Ben Sira's ethically anguished and suicidal humanoid. The cosmogonic and magical divine Name was both the sum of all truth and, in the wrong hands, a pernicious tool.

Wegener's film thus presents a golem maker who behaves with more or less impeccable propriety, a notion attested in Jewish lore: the Golem was only to be created for a limited time and a set purpose.[12] Once that purpose was fulfilled, it was considered blasphemous to seek to extend its life. The astral and demonic powers that had entrusted the secret for animating clay, while themselves servants of divinity, would begin to assert a claim of their own. As the Rabbi's magical book of instruction puts it (here I quote an intertitle in the film):

> If you have, through word of magic, wakened the dead to life, beware of your own creation! When Uranus comes into the house of planets, the demon Astaroth will demand his creature back. Then dead clay will scorn its master and turn to destroy him, and set itself upon mischief and destruction.
>
> (Ledig, 1989, pp. 122–123; my translation)[13]

The film here casts some ambiguity on the notion, central to the Christian accusation against the Jews, that Rabbi Loew has engaged in black magic. But his magic is in fact a kind of grey magic—undertaken in trepidation; aimed at the salvation of the Jews; striving, though not always successfully, to keep a respectful distance between the practitioner and the powers he has tapped; and mostly remaining mindful of the practice's legal or astrological limits. The magician seems to understand (though later, in leaving the Golem in the care of his apprentice, chooses, at his and Jewry's peril, to ignore) the consequences of unleashing a life that has been borrowed from the cosmos. Danger exists both in the uses others might make of it and in the destruction that the Golem, in turn, is himself capable of wreaking.

Let me conclude this phase of our discussion with some words from one justly regarded as one of the greatest thinkers of the modern era, the

German Jew, Walter Benjamin (1892–1940). His prodigious learning in philosophy, literature, arts, history, and social theory provided, though often in an artful, elliptical, and playful style, a profound critique of modernity and particularly of positivistic and historicist thinking based on false notions of progress and incapable of rendering human experience. Like filmmaker Paul Wegener, he emerged from World War I profoundly shaken by the misuse of the planet that so-called progress-oriented science, allied with imperialism, had brought about—one could call this misaligned use of science the work of a Sorcerer's Apprentice, and thus testament to the decline of magic:

> This much is clear: experience has fallen in value, amid a generation which from 1914 to 1918 had to experience some of the most monstrous events in the history of the world. Perhaps this is less remarkable than it appears. Wasn't it noticed at the time how many people returned from the battlefront in silence? Not richer but poorer in communicable experience? And what poured out from the flood of war books ten years later was anything but the experience that passes from mouth to ear. No, there was nothing remarkable about that. For never has experience been contradicted more thoroughly: strategic experience contravened by positional warfare; economic experience, by the [German] inflation; physical experience, by hunger; moral experience, by the ruling powers. A generation that had gone to school in horse-drawn streetcars now stood in the open air, amid a landscape in which nothing was the same except the clouds and, at its center, in a force field of destructive torrents and explosions, the tiny, fragile human body.
>
> (Benjamin, 1999, pp. 731–732)

Benjamin wrote these words in 1933, the year Hitler came to power in Germany. He would eventually die in 1940 as a suicide after a failed attempt to escape Hitler's occupied Europe. In his lifetime, he saw clearly the role of bourgeois subjectivity even in the rise to power of a madman contemptuous of all human social norms. In my own scholarship, I have tried to portray the political insanity of the 1930s as tied inexorably to the Enlightenment ethos that gave us both science and scientistic reckoning, on the one hand, and a social machinery that could unpredictably come back to bite us in times of crisis, on the other hand. The message is a cautionary one for wielders of scientific reasoning in today's natural and social sciences. We humans have created a Golem intended to serve us in governing and healing, in knowing the world and mastering its forces. But it does not protect us from ourselves. We have the power both to enhance and to destroy human experience and the historical choices we make must be guided by our awareness of both the social whole and ourselves.

My dear friend and colleague Philip Cushman has eloquently comprehended this dichotomy and savored its paradoxes. He cites a rabbinic teaching, found in a midrashic collection of late antiquity, *Song of Songs Rabbah* (literally *Greater Song of Songs*), which declares that only the first two of the Ten Commandments ("I am THE LORD your God" and "You shall have no other gods before Me") were actually spoken at Mount Sinai (*Song of Songs Rabbah*, 1:2; *Pesikta Rabbati,* 2).[14] This commonly known bit of sermonic lore was given a more radical turn by a fourteenth-century kabbalist named Jacob Kohen of Soria, who suggested that only the first letter of the First Commandment was spoken at Sinai.[15] Since the letter *'aleph* (which I customarily represent by the rightward-curved apostrophe: ') is not just the "a" of our own alphabet but a glottal stop that can precede any vowel (e.g., Hebrew *'adam,* human; *'em,* mother; *'im,* if; *'otsar*, treasury; *'ullam*, however), it suggests a deity whose presence inhabits all, but also (as if God were about to say, "Er, . . .") one who is ever trying to get a word in edgewise in human history, even when otherwise regarded as transcendent and supremely authoritative.

The kabbalists used the *aleph* to designate the very first of ten emanations of divinity that constituted the map of Jewish mystical imagination—an array of divine names and epithets taken from the full range of Jewish tradition (biblical, rabbinic, and medieval; narrative, sermonic, liturgical, folkloric, and philosophical). This was a way of making Jewish tradition itself, and even its community of believers, part of the body of divinity—in a way similar to how Christianity wrote the Church into the body of Christ. (This is why, in such contexts, I much prefer the neutral term "divinity" to the historical Hebrew name "God," used both in the Creation story of Genesis 1 and in the Ten Commandments of Exodus 20.) The kabbalists held the first emanation to be the primordially undifferentiated, pre-Creation divine being. It was seen both as a deep, cosmic emptiness and as an infinite, divine fullness, and, equally significant, as predecessor to an infinitesimally concentrated point, called the Supreme Point (itself the second emanation), which was analogous to the tiniest spark of a compressed universe that modern astronomers describe as having preceded the Big Bang in the first microseconds of its existence.[16] To this, the mystics gave the regal name *Keter*, meaning "crown." It is also called *Ehyeh*, "I am becoming" (Exodus 3:14) or, to speak more reassuringly, "I will be with you" (Exodus 3:12).[17]

The scriptural and postbiblical names and epithets associated with *Keter* are, to a large degree, positive and loving: Supreme Sunrise, Supreme Love, Supreme Source, Fount of the Will to Create, Acts of Lovingkindness, Fount of Compassion, the 13 Attributes of Mercy, and Humility (this last in meaningful contrast to the warrior God and stern judge, divine traits that arose in a later emanation). These names thus express the profoundly benign union of divine powers that preceded the biblical act of Creation, and form, as such, a prototype of the creative impulse in human beings and human society. The founders of Hasidism in the early eighteenth century devoted much time and reflection to the serene meditative state they called *Devekut* (Attachment to Divinity), borrowing many of the themes and metaphors associated with *Keter* to craft a spiritual practice that cultivates an inner quietness resembling, one could say, the silence of the letter *aleph*. The earliest generation of Hasidism effected a radical refashioning of the Talmudic orthodoxy of its own era to reckon with the holiness that inhered in all aspects of one's daily life, and to evoke a celebration of divine ubiquity. Eventually, as with many a revolution, Hasidism drifted to the right, but, before doing so, it exerted a profound influence on the Judaism of its time and place, and, I would like to think, on the emergence of the secular Jew, of secular humanism as such, and of the democratic and utopian revolutionary movements of the modern era.[18]

In his contribution to this volume, Cushman evokes with lyrical beauty and an engaging narrative skill the issues underlying the Jewish legend of the Golem, and connects these to the profoundest political and economic crises of our own era—to the misuse of power, the desire to dominate, the distractions and phantasmagoria of consumerism, and the prison we make for ourselves out of our own once well-meaning social practices. At its worst, this evolution has also produced the functionaries of war and torture, whereby, to our enduring shame, psychologists assisted in creating the agony of Baghram, Abu Ghraib, and Guantanamo. But even short of these outrages, the effect on what we misguidedly call ordinary life has wrought a toll of its own—namely, what philosopher Theodor W. Adorno described as an all-pervasive standardization and oppressively "administrative" mentality that marks "the open-air prison which the world is becoming."[19]

Cushman underscores how our social institutions and practices place us in an almost insurmountable dilemma even as we strive to heal the broken self, comfort the grieving, and engender social renewal. As he persuasively argues:

> It is not enough for us only to carry on philosophical and theoretical elaborations and debates as if philosophy and clinical theory are removed from the larger events of the social world around us. It is our responsibility to make a better world by studying the connections between our professional practices and the politics of our world.

Cushman shows us that our social institutions and practices are rooted in our epistemology: how we know, or think we know, has consequences for how the world evolves. Such an awareness can offer "an alternative vision for psychology . . . drawn from hermeneutics, historical study, relational theory, critical thought." These are the worthiest gifts from a Golem born of the Immense *Aleph*. As Cushman puts it most elegantly: "The Immense *Aleph* is without end, pregnant with what is possible, but vulnerable to all the fears and flaws of the human heart."[20] This beautifully double-edged thought expresses both the glory of being human (here we must think of the Clay Man, who falls in love with life the more he occupies it) and the perilous stakes of our making machines whose use makes machines of us.

Conclusion

The aim of this chapter has been to provide the background in traditional Jewish sources for understanding the legend of the Golem, the android prominent in Jewish folkloric imagination, a theme so influential to the later presence of the android in modern popular culture. These lineages go back as far as the second century BCE (i.e., before the Common Era established by the Roman Empire and Christianity from 320 CE onward), and continue across a vast stretch of time into the modern era—though the original mythos of God's creation of humanity "in the image of God" (Genesis 1:27) and the first life-breath of divinity that animated Adam (the first human, formed of clay) in the Garden of Eden (Genesis 2:6–7) had originally formed the nucleus of the myth. The Jewish android described in Talmudic sources had first been an attempt to reflect on the kinship of the human being with divinity, and to explore the paradoxes of humanity's dual identity as both creator and creature. I propose that the purpose of this lore has been a way of explaining our role as *Homo faber* (Human, the inventor), a personification that already haunted post-exilic Jewish mythmaking—especially in Jewish apocalyptic literature of late antiquity, when sectarians rebelled against the established Jerusalem priesthood and social authority, and compared their overreach to the hubris that had given rise to Noah's Flood.

This theme came into special prominence in the modern era, when forces of modernity that gave rise to antisemitic persecution in the Tsarist and Nazi eras, and to genocide in Africa from the 1880s onward, were turning ever more malevolent as a force of fascism and mass ethnic hatred. As Hannah Arendt, herself a refugee from Nazi-occupied France, eventually argued in her well-reasoned and wide-ranging mid-century study, *The Origins of Totalitarianism*, it took a long, complex evolution before European societies were ready for radical antisemitism and the destruction of society that served the interests of fascism and totalitarianism, or what she called "the end of the rights of man" (Arendt, 1964, pp. 267–302). As Arendt argued the case, the radical opponents of democracy and reason were motivated by an aim not just to expunge an imagined enemy—in this case, Jewry—but to destroy civil society itself.

The invention of technology and social dominance described in the first-century BCE Jewish apocalyptic work *1 Enoch* as having provided the premise for Noah's Flood is, for me, a powerful metaphor both for human technological revolution and also, in Cushman's assessment, for the social machinery that psychologists typically imagine as their ally in putting professional therapeutic practice at the beck and call of ideology. Technological and social machinery are interdependent forces, presumably aimed at making things flow more smoothly and efficiently, but which, in the long run, tend to trap us in the paradox of our own intelligence: namely, that our efforts to make things run smoother also predispose us to "dominationist" solutions, and that this has put the therapeutic professions in service to the most abhorrent social practices, such as military conquest and brutality toward the conquered. A solution to this dilemma, if one exists, is to re-imagine the therapeutic professions on a model that recognizes, in Cushman's words, how "[t]he Immense *Aleph* is without end, pregnant with what is possible, but vulnerable to all the fears and flaws of the human heart."[21] Such insight pays respect both to the notion that creativity is a special gift rooted in our species' origins, and to the sad reality that we are most vulnerable, on the same account, to our own failings. We write our machinery into our own history and cultural life, but we often fail to notice how our machinery makes machines of us.

Cushman justly compares this to the conformity of automatons. This paradox of our freedom is perhaps best addressed by a telling adage from Walter Benjamin's final work: "There is never a document of culture that is not, at the same time, one of barbarism" (2003, p. 392). Few have studied the works of modern culture as thoroughly and sympathetically as Benjamin—and fewer still have comprehended as incisively as he their inability to face the threat of fascism and totalitarianism, and the role of the bourgeoisie in engendering and enabling it. The era of the poet Baudelaire was also that of the brutal 1871 suppression of the leftist Paris Commune—another prototype of arguably genocidal massacre, being carried off, in that instance, by the use of automatic machine-gun fire, deployed indiscriminately against men, women, and children. But, equally significant in Benjamin's reckoning was the enervation wrought by the forces of modernity more generally: assembly-line production, the worker as automaton, the consumer as recipient of phantasmagoria and distraction, and, as such, the intermediary of a meaner and more debased culture and politics. We are not as far removed from these ultimate stakes as we might think. May all who behold it cry out.

Notes

1 The degeneration of magic from era to era was a familiar trope of medieval Jewish writers. See, for example, thirteenth-century kabbalist Joseph Gikatilla's introduction to his treatise *Sha'arey 'Orah* ("*Gates of Light*").
2 Author's abridgement and adaptation from the Ge'ez (Old Ethiopic).
3 The work's Hebrew title *Sefer Gematriyot* uses a word derived from the phrase "gamma tria": the letter gamma equals three.
4 See Anonymous (1962, fol. 29a), originally from late antiquity.
5 On this work, see Scholem (1987, pp. 24–35); Idel (1990a, pp. 9–26).
6 Author's abridgment and translation from the Hebrew text.
7 See especially Scholem (1970, 1972). Scholem's immersion in the historical study of Jewish mysticism and its linguistic gnosis was a profound influence on his close friend Walter Benjamin's philosophy of language, expressed most brilliantly in Benjamin's 1916 essay, earlier cited. For the historical Ben Sira, see Skehan and Di Lella (1987).
8 This perspective on history is best expressed, elliptically and provocatively, in Walter Benjamin's final work, written in 1940 (2003, pp. 388–411).
9 See especially Aurich, Jacobsen, and Jatho (2000, pp. 63–69); Biro (1994, pp. 71–110); Biro (2007); Huyssens (1987, pp. 65–81); Kieval (1997), especially pp. 7 and 18, n. 20, and (on the origin of a violent golem), pp. 11–13. On pre-modern

Jewish religious lore of the Golem more generally, see especially Scholem, "The Idea of the Golem," in Scholem (1965, pp. 158–204); Idel (1990a, 1990b). On the golem in Jewish folklore, see Patai (1981, pp. 239, 283, 516–517, 636–642). On the Golem legend in European and, especially, German literature, see Rosenfeld (1934); Mayer (1975); and Schumacher (2008, pp. 85–105).

10 See Wegener (1933).
11 On the theme of sexual and technological promiscuity underlying Noah's Flood, see Patai (1959, 1978).
12 On Jewish practices and beliefs related to magic, see Trachtenberg (1977).
13 Author's translation from the German text.
14 See Kugel (1997, pp. 377–378).
15 See Scholem (1965, p. 30).
16 See Matt (1996, pp. 19–34); Smith (2006, pp. 105–108).
17 On the history and meaning of *Keter*, see Green (1997, 2004). See also Green (2010).
18 See, for example, Buber (1991, 1996); Schachter-Shalomi and Miles-Yepez (2010).
19 See Adorno (1967, pp. 19–34). See also Adorno, Frenkel-Brunswik, Levinson, and Sanford (1950) and Adorno (1973).
20 Cushman (this volume), p. 26.
21 Ibid.

References

Adorno, T. W. (1967). Cultural criticism and society. In T. W. Adorno, *Prisms: Cultural criticism and society, Spengler, Huxley, Kafka, Proust, Schoenberg, Jazz, etc.* (Trans. S. and S. Weber). London: Neville Spearman.

Adorno, T. W. (1973). *Negative dialectics* (Trans. E. B. Ashton). New York and London: Continuum. (The German original of this work was first published in 1966 by Suhrkamp Verlag.)

Adorno, T. W., Frenkel-Brunswik, E., Levinson, D. J., and Sanford, R. N. (1950). *The authoritarian personality*. New York: W. W. Norton & Co./Harper & Row.

Anonymous (1962). *Sefer yetsirah, ha-meyuhas le-'Avraham avinu, z"l* (*The book of creation, ascribed to Abraham our ancestor, of blessed memory*). Jerusalem: Rabbi M. Atyah, publisher; S. Munzon, printer. (My translation from the Hebrew.)

Arendt, H. (1964). *The origins of totalitarianism.* Cleveland, OH and New York: Meridian Books. (Originally written in 1950.)

Aurich, R., Jacobsen, W., and Jatho, G. (Eds.) (2000). *Artificial humans: Manic machines, controlled bodies.* Berlin: Filmmuseum Berlin—Deutsche Kinemathek and jovis verlag.

Benjamin, W. (1996). On language as such and on the languages of man. In M. W. Jennings, B. Dogherty, and T. Y. Levin (Eds.), *Walter Benjamin: Selected writings, vol. 1: 1913–1926* (Trans. E. Jephcott), pp. 62–74. Cambridge, MA and London: The Belknap Press of Harvard University Press. (Originally written in 1916, unpublished in Benjamin's lifetime; my adaptation of the Jephcott translation from the German.)

Benjamin, W. (1999). Experience and poverty. In M. W. Jennings, H. Eiland, and G. Smith (Eds.), *Walter Benjamin: Selected writings, vol. 2: 1927–1934* (Trans. R. Livingstone). Cambridge, MA and London: The Belknap Press of Harvard University Press. (Originally written in 1933, published in *Die Welt im Wort* [Prague], Dec. 1933.)

Benjamin, W. (2003). On the concept of history. In H. Eiland and M. Jennings (Eds.), *Walter Benjamin: Selected writings, vol. 4: 1938–1940* (Trans. E. Jephcott, H. Zohn et al.), pp. 389–411. (Completed in 1940, the year of Benjamin's suicide; unpublished in his lifetime.)

Ben-Shelomoh, Y. (Ed.) (1970). *Sha'arey 'orah* (*Gates of light*), *vol. 1*. Jerusalem: Mosad Bialik. (My translation from the Hebrew of Joseph Gikatilla's thirteenth-century kabbalistic primer.)

Biro, M. (1994). The new man as cyborg: Figures of technology in Weimar visual culture. *New German Critique 62* (Spring–Summer), 71–110.

Biro, M. (2007), *The Dada cyborg: Visions of the new human in Weimar Berlin*. Minneapolis, MN: University of Minnesota Press.

Buber, M. (1991). *Tales of the Hasidim, Book one: The early masters*. New York: Schocken Books.

Buber, M. (1996). *Paths in utopia*. Syracuse, NY: Syracuse University Press.

Charlesworth, J. A. (Ed.) (1983). *The Old Testament pseudepigrapha, vol. 1*. Garden City, NY: Doubleday/Anchor Books.

Epstein, A. (1887). *Beiträge zur Jüdischen Altertumskunde* (*Contributions to the study of Jewish lore in antiquity*). Vienna: n. p. (Manuscript of the medieval Hebrew treatise, *Sefer gematriyot* [*The book of Hebrew letter & number lore*]).

Epstein, I. (Ed.) (1994). *The Soncino Babylonian Talmud: Sanhedrin, chapters vii–xi* (Trans. H. Freedman). London: The Soncino Press. (My translation from the Hebrew and Aramaic.)

Green, A. (1997). *Keter: The Crown of God in early Jewish mysticism*. Princeton, NJ: Princeton University Press.

Green, A. (2004). *Ehyeh: A kabbalah for tomorrow*. Woodstock, VT: Jewish Lights Press.

Green, A. (2010). *Radical Judaism: Rethinking God & tradition*. New Haven, CT and London: Yale University Press.

Huyssens, A. (1987). The vamp and the machine: Fritz Lang's *Metropolis*. In A. Huyssens, *After the great divide: Modernism, mass culture, postmodernism*, pp. 65–81. Bloomington and Indianapolis, IN: Indiana University Press.

Idel, M. (1990a). *Golem: Jewish magical and mystical traditions of the artificial anthropoid*. Albany, NY: SUNY Press.

Idel, M. (1990b). The golem in Jewish magic and mysticism. In E. Bilsky (Ed.), *Golem! Danger, deliverance and art*, pp. 15–35. New York: The Jewish Museum.

Kieval, H. J. (1997). Pursuing the Golem of Prague: Jewish culture and the invention of tradition. *Modern Judaism*, *17*, 1–23.

Kugel, J. (1997). *The Bible as it was*. Cambridge, MA and London: The Belknap Press of Harvard University Press.

Ledig, E. (1989). *Paul Wegeners Golem-Filme im Kontext fantasticher Literatur (Paul Wegener's golem films in the context of fantasy literature)*. Munich: Schaudig, Bauer, Ledig.

Matt, D. C. (1996). *God and the Big Bang: Discovering harmony between science and spirituality.* Woodstock, VT: Jewish Lights Press.

Mayer S. (1975). *Golem: Die literarische Rezeption eines Stoffes (Golem: The literary reception of a motif).* Bern and Frankfurt am Main: Peter Lang.

Patai, R. (1959). *Sex and family in the Bible and Middle East.* Garden City, NY: Doubleday/Anchor Books.

Patai, R. (1978). *The Hebrew goddess.* New York: Avon Books.

Patai, R. (1981). *Gates to the old city: A book of Jewish legends.* Detroit, MI: Wayne State University Press.

Rosenfeld, B. (1934). *Die golemsage und ihre Verwertung in der Deutschen Literatur (The golem legend and its development in German literature).* Breslau: Verlag Dr. Hans Priebatsch.

Schachter-Shalomi, Z. M. and Miles-Yepez, N. (2010). *A heart afire: Stories and teachings of the early Hasidic masters.* Philadelphia, PA: The Jewish Publication Society.

Scholem, G. G. (1965). *On the kabbalah and its symbolism* (Trans. R. Manheim). New York: Schocken Books.

Scholem, G. G. (1970). Der Name Gottes und die Sprachtheorie der Kabbala. In G. G. Scholem, *Judaica III: Studien zur Jüdischen Mystic*, pp. 7–70. Frankfurt am Main: Suhrkamp.

Scholem, G. G. (1972). The name of God and the linguistic theory of the kabbalah. In *Diogenes* 79 (1972), 59–80, and 80 (1972), 164–194.

Scholem, G. G. (1987). *Origins of the kabbalah* (Ed. R. J. Zwi Werblowsky, Trans. A. Arkush). Princeton, NJ: Princeton University Press/The Jewish Publication Society.

Schumacher, F. (2008). *Das Ich und der andere Körper: Eine Kulturgeschichte des Monsters und des küntzlichen Menschen (The ego and other bodies: A cultural history of monsters and artificial persons).* Marburg: Tecten Verlag.

Skehan, P. W. and Di Lella, A. A. (1987). *The Wisdom of Ben Sira: A new translation with notes.* New York: Doubleday.

Smith, H. (2006). *Let there be light: Modern cosmology and kabbalah: A new conversation between science and religion.* Novato, CA: New World Library.

Trachtenberg, J. (1977). *Jewish magic and superstition: A study in folk religion.* New York: Atheneum.

Wegener, P. (1933). *Flandrische Tagebuch, 1914 (Flanders diary, 1914).* Berlin: Rohwolt.

Wegener, P. (1954). Meine werdegang (My career). In K. Möller (Ed.), *Paul Wegener: Sein Leben und seine Rollen (Paul Wegener: His life and his roles)*, pp. 13–37. Hamburg: Rohwolt.

Weinstein, A. (Trans. and Ed.) (1994). *Gates of light: Sha'are 'orah.* San Francisco, CA, London, and Pymble, NSW: HarperCollins.

Chapter 4

Is loyalty really a virtue?

Shame and the monstrous Other

Peter Shabad

Defying the passage of time: the automatism of blind loyalty

Consider the following valedictory maxims: "Till death do us part," "I will always stand by you," or "Honor your mother and father." These declarations of steadfastness imply that just as one has been devoted to one's family, friends, nation, or God yesterday and the day before yesterday, one will continue to honor one's commitments tomorrow and the day after tomorrow. Many of us are proud when we live up to the virtue of such undying loyalty.

But wait … How do we already know today that we will remain committed to a particular cause or person tomorrow or the day after tomorrow? When each American schoolchild pledges allegiance to the flag of the United States of America, does that mean unconditionally "America Right or Wrong?" If so, then we can't be surprised that there was a proliferation of bumper stickers directed at war protesters showing an American flag with the words "Love It or Leave It" during the Vietnam War. The very same steadfastness of honoring a commitment to spouse, family, nation, or religion that we consider to be so admirable and adhere to so diligently is also intrinsic to the robot-like loyalty driving the "Heil Hitler" salute to the Führer.

It is not so much religion or nationalism that lie at the root of every conflict and war, as much as it is group narcissism of loyalty to "one's own kind." As soon as we declare our loyalty to one group instead of another, we create an in-group, "us," and an out-group, "them," on the basis of religion, nation, ethnicity, tribe, race, gender, sexual orientation, or species. When such in-groups and out-groups are constructed, there is a risk that, under certain stressful conditions, individuals who constitute "them" will become demonized as a monstrous Other who must be annihilated. The virtue of honoring unconditional loyalties through "thick and thin" can lead very quickly to acts of evil!

If we consider that life is always in a dynamic process of becoming, then perhaps loyalty becomes encoded as a virtue because we see a kind of elevated heroism in remaining ever constant against the dying of the light. In adhering tenaciously to the meanings we construct through devotion to a person or cause, we seek to create something enduring to fortify us in our defiance of the seeming absurdities of dying and decay.

To the extent that mortality is built into life's flux, however, the unquestioning blindness of automatic loyalty instead may be viewed as a fearful retreat from engaging the finiteness of life on its own terms. This impermanence is our ever-accompanying shadow that is manifest in the birth of incoming moments from future to present, the receding death of those moments as they pass, and then again the rebirth of a new influx of moments from the future. Like each moment, our individual lives also have a finite, never-to-be duplicated quality; as unique persons, we have never lived before and will never live again. How then can human beings best seize the unique opportunities of each passing moment and realize the unique significance of their own lives while they are living it?

It is immensely challenging for human beings to remain open to the onrush of incoming moments without defenses fueled by their shames and anxieties. When we do not open up to the incoming gift of life's fleeting instants and allow them to pass without actualizing our contributions to the human endeavor, the unrealized moments that were not seized while the iron was hot may become sentimentalized after their passing. As if begging the fates for another chance to live out missed opportunities, we shift our openhearted focus from living for and toward the realization of future possibilities, to an enclosed preoccupation with an idealized and reified past as a sanctuary against the steady march of time.

Kierkegaard (1843/2009) refers to this preoccupation with a past that has now been abstracted from the concrete flow of time as "recollection." In contrast, he uses the term "repetition" to describe a passionate movement of freedom to actualize oneself anew in each incoming moment received from the future. He says: "Repetition and recollection are the same movement, just in opposite directions; because what is recollected has already been, and is thus repeated backwards; whereas genuine repetition is recollected forwards" (p. 3).

Carlisle (2005) beautifully summarizes Kierkegaard's thinking on the subject:

> Concrete existence, unlike the necessary being with which logic deals, has reality only insofar as it continues to be actualized at every moment. Existence is always *coming into existence*, arising and passing away and arising again at unfathomable speed. So for an existing thing to endure – to *be itself* – it must be repeatedly renewed, for without the actualizing movement it falls into non-being.
>
> (p. 76, emphasis in original)

As Kierkegaard (1843/1996) famously says: "It is quite true what philosophy says: that life must be understood backwards. But then one forgets the other principle: that it must be lived forwards" (p. 161).

To the extent that the automatic sustainment of commitments depends on an adherence to an abstract recollection of a loyalty oath, it attempts to reduce time's constant flow from one moment into a completely different moment into a static sameness rather than synchronize with its changes through the continually renewable choices of a free human being. Bachelard (1932/2013) states: "Devoted as it is to the contemplation of static being, of spatial being, the intellect must guard against misunderstanding the reality of becoming" (p. 9). When holding to commitments becomes entrenched as a rule of moral virtue that people follow just because it has taken on a life of its own as an abstract norm, then the mechanical aspects of blind loyalty rob our freedom of conscience of its heart and soul.

Inasmuch as love itself is based on the freedom of choice to love or not to love, the unconditional aspects of automatic loyalty preempt the passion of love from entering into our commitments. It is the very possibility of not renewing a commitment to another person that lends ongoing meaning and depth to that commitment.

As Carlisle (2005) states:

> *The constancy of fidelity is grounded not on sameness, but difference.* ... Because existence is temporal and therefore changing, something can "stay the same" only if it becomes new. ... Whether the fidelity in question is truthfulness to another person, to God, or to oneself, this is the kind of truth that needs to be actualized repeatedly, rather than a necessary static truth that merely "is."
>
> (p. 86, emphasis in original)

In this sense, a heartfelt, meaningful loyalty can only be constructed organically on the basis of renewable choice and the freedom to love from one moment to the next. When our attempts to love and be loved fail, and we become preoccupied with defensively covering up our rejected vulnerability, our shame and self-doubts may invert the openness of our passion into a self-enclosed passivity. Encapsulated within ourselves, we hang on to the life raft of our loyalties to provide us with the safety of ongoing sameness, so as not to be buffeted to and fro by the monstrous winds of change and otherness.

Toward the Other: becoming and the passion of renewal

How are we able to renew ourselves with each passing moment? The pre-Socratic philosopher Heraclitus (1974) describes life's constant state of flux when he says famously: "One cannot step twice into the same river, no one can grasp any mortal substance in stable condition; but it scatters and again gathers; it forms and dissolves, and approaches and departs" (p. li).

Like the current in a river, human beings also have a passionate life force that pushes them forward, a life force that Bergson (1911/1998) refers to as *élan vital* or "vital impetus." Our access to the vital impetus of our passion is indispensable to our capacity for self-renewal, and the ability to meet the constant flow of time on its own ever-evolving terms. By helping us remain in synchrony with the ongoing flow of time, our passion enables us to participate and create life rather than merely observe its passage.

While our personal journeys may be fueled by creative passion, that passion alone is not enough to create meaning. Our passionate life force is rooted in a drive for self-realization in which we creatively devote our lives to an Other beyond ourselves, whether that be God, our children, or the essential difference of another person. In this sense, the ethics of living for and toward the Other (Levinas, 1969) is built into the very essence of our passionate life force.

Self-realization ultimately requires that a threshold be crossed from an insulated world of our own making to an Other who lies beyond our creative control, beyond what Winnicott (1960/1965a) refers to as the "sphere of omnipotence." Human agency may be viewed then as the individualized form through which we shape ourselves as creative vessels to be surrendered to someone other than ourselves. A receptive response from an Other mirrors back the special contribution that we are making, providing us at once with both a sense of belonging and significance as individuals who have something of value to offer, thus infusing our labors of passion with meaning. As James Carse (1980) puts it: "Our life is not our own in the sense that it belongs exclusively to us; however, it becomes our own to the degree that we share it, make a gift of it to others" (p. 5).

The shadows of mortality are present in each transition we navigate from the insulated creations of our own minds to an unpredictable world beyond our own making. Maslow (1962) describes this bittersweet aspect of life:

> Growth has not only rewards and pleasures but also many intrinsic pains … Each step forward is a step into the unfamiliar and possibly dangerous. It frequently means a parting and a separation, even a kind of death prior to rebirth, with consequent nostalgia, fear, loneliness, and mourning.
>
> (p. 190)

Miller (1998) delineates in detail the phenomenological journey of suffering that is involved in letting go of one's familiar world to a world beyond one's control.

For Kierkegaard (1843/1983), the process of leaving behind the home comforts of one's mind entails a passionately inspired "leap of faith" in which one's potentiality is repeatedly actualized in each new moment. He uses the metaphor of "leap" precisely to highlight the radical continuity of action, as opposed to mere shifts in thought, and the necessity of exposing ourselves to the risk and opportunity of inspired redemption in order to move through genuine change.

To the extent that the temporal changes required for the unfolding unpredictability of our own growth into the future parallel the shifts in perspective needed to embrace the stranger who is different from us, maintaining access to our passion is centrally implicated in our evolution as ethical individuals. Letting go of oneself in the current moment to engage the future possibilities of who one could become implies also a continuing emergence from the loyalties to oneself and to "one's own kind," whether that be one's own family, nation, religion, species, tribe, race, or gender.

For many years, I have retained an idealized, “Other-oriented” vision that every ethnic group would celebrate the heritage of every other ethnic group with the exception of their own. For example, everyone but Mexican-Americans would march in the parade on behalf of Mexican-American Day and everyone but Italian-Americans would celebrate Italian-American Day and so on. Just as in an election in which one cannot cast a ballot for oneself, each group would celebrate the special day of every other group. It comes too easily to celebrate oneself, but more challenging to go the “extra mile” for someone Other than ourselves.

The tensions mediating the times and spaces between two persons who come face-to-face with each other in their exposed vulnerability are suffused with both the redemptive possibilities of meaningful self-realization and the risks of annihilating shame. When we shield ourselves against the urgent calling of our passion, we desperately hold on to the way things have always been in fear of the unknown person whom we will become. For such individuals, the transitional spaces separating two different persons and the transitional times separating who I am in the present from who I will be in the future—that is, change itself—may take on the antagonistically monstrous appearance of Otherness. When the transitions of one’s life—birth death, and rebirth—are postponed indefinitely, these individuals discover eventually, often to their great regret, that since they were not willing to face their “deaths” from one moment to the next, they were not able to reap the rewards of their accompanying “rebirths.”

Similarly, when we deny the deaths of loved ones and take for granted that they will be with us forever, we also lose a sense of their otherness as mortal subjects in their own right, with the result that our relationships tend to grow stale. Without the capacity to imagine their deaths, we cannot refresh the relationship with their imagined rebirths either. Even though we may remind ourselves that our loved ones could die tomorrow, we nevertheless tend to retreat to the safety of forgetfulness. We may scold our child for trivial matters or hold a grudge against a spouse, all of which would evaporate instantly if we heard that the loved one had 24 hours to live.

When a child then endures the journey of exposed vulnerability in reaching out to the Other, we must ask a question of fundamental developmental and ethical importance: Will the child be helped and inspired on her unique pathway by the welcoming receptivity of the Other? Or will the child be turned away, necessitating that she cover up her helplessness and isolation in her own defensive fashion? A child’s capacity to use her passion and to face the otherness of transition depends greatly on how graciously all of us welcome the most vulnerable into life.

Giving and being received: the inspiration of self-renewal

Although we typically think of development in terms of parents giving love and children receiving it, I would suggest that a human being's passionate life force is first manifested in the reverse: through the child's need to give of himself and to have those gifts accepted by the parent. From the beginning, each created gesture of the newborn is not merely expressed into a void, but is generated as a communicative offering, which is meant to be received and heeded by an Other. Winnicott (1954–1955/1975) thus describes the "spontaneous gesture" of the infant also as a gift gesture of "contributing-in." In this regard, it is interesting to note here that "create" and "generous" derive from the same Latin root *genera*, "to produce, beget." Through the parental reception of the child's expressive offerings as an individual who has never lived before and will never live again, the child is able to gain an indispensable sense of participation within the ongoing human enterprise.

The graciousness with which the mother receives the gift gesture of the child's trust greatly influences the child's initial ethical sense that his passion is constructive, and thus facilitates its usage for further development. When a parent accepts the spontaneous gestures of her baby, her reception conveys to him that his passion will bear fruit, thereby providing him with the initial sense of having something good inside that is worthwhile to someone else. That sense of goodness, in turn, enables children to feel worthy enough to affirm their passion and generate an offering of themselves once again.

A mother's warm "Thank you" after receiving a toddler's drawing as a gift, or her emphatic, excited praise after the child walks across the room for the first time, inspires a gratitude and renewable spirit of generosity in the child to move forward and provide the mother with another such offering of himself again. This generosity to give of himself then facilitates a courage to affirm his passion, move toward the Otherness of the future, and transform the times and spaces separating himself and others into ever-new, creatively fashioned offerings.

Here is a brief illustration of this sort of interchange. A three-year-old child draws a stick figure and says to the mother: "Mommy, look what I did!" and the mother responds by saying: "That's great! Who is that?" The child says, "It's a man!" and the mother responds by saying: "That's the greatest man that I ever saw!" The child, feeling like no one else has ever drawn a picture quite like that before, smiles with great pleasure and then offers the picture to her and says: "This is for you, Mommy!" When she concludes this interchange by saying, "Thank you so much!" the child's passion inspired by her gracious reception moves him to creatively generate another stick figure and present it to her again.

The oscillating developmental rhythms of progression (two steps forward) toward what will be and regression (one step backward) toward what has been are thus intertwined with the evolving interchange of giving and receiving with parents. Each two steps forward through change and growth toward the future is punctuated by a rapprochement (Mahler, 1975) of touching base with the familiar parent, during which there is a crucial exchange of giving, being received, and internalizing the impact of having been received.

The primary means by which parents convey their receptivity is through their recognition of the children. The term "recognition" derives from the French *reconnaissance*, "re-knowing, re-discovering," as in "Oh, I know you. I've seen you before." This definition parallels Freud's (1905/1966) statement that "each finding of an object is in fact a re-finding of it" (p. 222). In this sense, there is an invariable aspect of recognition through which human beings "totalize" the Other (Levinas, 1969) by incorporating his newness into preexisting mental representations. In part, we cannot help but domesticate each encounter with the essential difference of the Other by transforming its strangeness into a re-visiting with a familiar person from the past.

It is true that when we fall in love, for example, we often feel that in some sense we have known the loved one as someone very familiar to us from long ago. It is also true, though, that when we fall in love, we really are becoming acquainted with and discovering someone who had previously been a stranger to us. Recognition may then be viewed as a paradoxical process in which we simultaneously re-find an old object and find an Other *as if for the first time.* The recognition of a birthday is at one and the same time the repeated celebration of the original date of a person's birth and the acknowledgment of the passing of time in the celebration of an age the person has never been before.

Whereas the parent's re-finding of the child helps the child establish a sense of self-continuity through the cycles of the parent's previous "knowing," the parent's finding of the child as if for the first time reflects the acknowledgment of the child's evolving trajectory of self-renewal, of becoming different than he has been previously. These two aspects of recognition are responsive to an implicit question that begins at birth for all of us and is always central to the ongoing quest for self-realization: "Do I exist?" When the answer to this question is a resounding receptivity of recognition, "Yes! We have a special niche in our home awaiting *your* arrival, not just *any* baby," the infant is able to achieve an all-important sense of uniqueness and belonging at the same time.

When a child surrenders his offerings to a parent, he is able to retrieve, through the parent's receptive recognition, a reborn sense of himself that is continuous and that has been transformed by the parent's subjectivity as an Other. Ghent (1990) thus states that the need for self-surrender may express "[t]he centrality, despite its buried secrecy, of a *longing* for the birth, or perhaps re-birth of true self" (p. 120, emphasis in original). The ritualistic process of surrendering one's hold on oneself, receiving back a transformed sense of self through the parent's recognition, and surrendering oneself again is thus inextricably intertwined with the continual transitions of the birth, death, and re-birth of the self.

Mircea Eliade (1954) describes how these repetitive cyclical processes become a way of touching base with a prototype of time and space: "Through the paradox of rite, every consecrated space coincides with the center of the world, just as the time of any ritual coincides with the mythical time of the 'beginning'" (p. 20). If we were to apply Eliade's concept of the prototypical "center" to the ritualistic process of giving and receiving, the transformative mirror of being recognized by the Other may be viewed as a relational center of self-realization that consecrates the child's offerings in a shared time and space. Through this give and take with an Other, children gradually come to realize that they did not merely conjure the world in which they live, thereby reassuring them that they are not all alone. Diane Margolis (1998) says: "When we give gifts, we break down those boundaries and create, instead of me and you or mine and yours, us and ours" (p. 109).

A human life is thus an ethical/relational medium that is both inspired by and generated toward an Other. When the repeated sense of having been received is transposed onto the child's vision of what will be, his passion, now inspired by an imagined welcoming reception from an Other awaiting him in the future, moves him to actualize incoming moments as a new beginning from which to offer himself again. Bachelard (1932/2013) states: "A being that offers itself to life, in its passion for novelty, is itself inclined to welcome the present as a promise of the future" (p. 38).

Repetition is not a means of holding onto a fossilized past in opposition to human mortality and the passing of time, but is in passionately meaningful synchrony with its inevitable unfolding. Even when an individual makes love to the same person repeatedly or performs onstage every night, each occasion is infused with the passion of renewal, which provides the activity with the sense of being engaged *as if for the first time*.

Self-enclosing consciousness: shame and the crisis of exposed vulnerability

What then occurs when children are insulted, injured, and ignored in any assortment of ways without their experiences being validated or consoled? When children suffer alone, they are often not aware of what is triggering their pain, let alone able to convey it to someone else. In taking up the slack for the absence of a compassionate Other who recognizes their experience, children often turn inward and form a self-enclosed relationship with themselves. When children encounter too much suffering, trauma, and cumulative buildup of frustration and disappointment without solace or the recognition of a witness, they reverse the open-faced, hopeful, and giving attitude toward the Other into an inverted self-enclosure.

Elsewhere (Shabad, 1989, 2001), I have described chronic trauma or "traumatic themes" as experiences in which parents repeatedly enact their unmourned character faults onto their children. The psychic loss of a physically present parent, as I have called these traumatic themes, derives specifically from the repeated disappointments of the child's continued hope to change the frustratingly real parent into a wished-for parent. The repeated experiences of being ignored, having promises broken, being harshly criticized, and being intruded upon are just a few examples of such traumatic themes. Eventually, since it is so difficult to bear these chronic experiences of rejected vulnerability for too long, children often dissociate from their wishes that only led to endless disappointment. Inside the defensively self-enclosed counsels of the child's mind, such disappointments, losses, and traumas are no longer just seen for what they are, but quickly become infused with shame because of the overwhelming exposure of the child's rejected vulnerabilities.

If one were to ask a six year old whether he would like his father, who habitually ignores him, to finally hug him, he might nod his head emphatically. If one were to then ask the same question of him at 15, however, he might respond indifferently with "Whatever" or "That will never happen." He no longer is willing to consciously acknowledge shame-ridden desires that are not going to come true anyway.

It is important to understand that children, in particular, do not consider that frustrations, disappointments, and even random misfortunes occur by accident. Instead, they reflexively take on the burden of responsibility for the bad things that happen to them. As Winnicott (1960/1965a) points out, "there is no trauma outside of the individual's omnipotence" (p. 37). When a child embraces his mother and expects her to reciprocate with a smile and a hug, but instead she remains tight-lipped, sad, and oblivious to him, his feeling of being rejected automatically boomerangs as an elusive sense of shame, in which he feels he is in the wrong without knowing exactly how or why.

Through the perceptual filter of their omnipotence, children reflexively transform the helplessness of suffering through their traumas, losses, and disappointments after the fact of their occurrence into a sense of shame. Whereas the omnipotence of positive wish magic is reinforced when our wishes are realized in the external world, we often react to the sufferings of loss and trauma not by admitting the limitations of our powers but as a punitive sign reflecting back to us some wrongness or sinfulness about our most basic passions and desires. The omnipotent burden of responsibility for what occurs in the outside world backfires because now when bad things happen to us, we are at fault for the disappointments and failures that we ourselves suffer. Ricoeur (1967) remarks insightfully: "If you suffer, if you are ill, if you fail, if you die, it is because you have sinned" (p. 31).

In instances of significant relational disruption, children may lose their bearings when their sufferings are not contained by a consoling Other, and attempt reflexively to cover up their exposed vulnerability by forming an enclosed self-conscious relationship with themselves. In self-consciousness, our center of gravity shifts from unselfconsciously looking out at the world from within an integrated mind and body to a disembodied mental state, as if one were on the outside looking at oneself. Sartre (1956/1969) states: "Shame is by nature recognition. I recognize that I am as the other sees me" (p. 222). Morrison (1987) says too that shame is "[t]he eye turned inward" (p. 271). As we train this inward eye on ourselves, however, we seem to shrink in significance, for now we are nothing but an object dwarfed by the overwhelming forces around us. This disturbing consciousness of viewing oneself as an isolated, insignificant object that is incomplete in and of itself is well described in Nietzsche's (1871/2009) statement: "The feeling of shame seems to occur when man is a tool of manifestations of will greater than he is permitted to consider himself in the isolated shape of an individual" (p. 6).

In shame, we no longer are the unselfconsciously lordly creators of our destinies, but mere creatures who are now objectified by our own self-consciousness. Sartre (1956/1969) explains the shameful descent in status from individuals who are extraordinary to humble creatures who are fully dependent on others to confirm our own existence:

> Shame is the feeling of an original fall, not because of the fact that I have committed this or that particular fault, but simply that I have "fallen" into the world in the midst of things and that I need the mediation of others to be what I am.
>
> (p. 384)

For Levinas (1969), this fall from God-like creator of our self-enclosed mind's eye is a necessary disillusionment in our continuing evolution as ethical individuals. Levinas argues that, in forcing us to question the assumptions and expectations created by our own minds, shame allows us to remove the filmy gauze of mental representations through which we view others, and reveal the underlying truth that our human existence is conditioned by each other's subjectivities.

Whereas Levinas (1969) emphasizes that shame, by revealing the fundamental truth of our incompleteness as individuals, opens up "my desire for the Other" (p. 84), I would suggest that the hope and courage required to sustain that openness depends very much on whether our sufferings have been consoled by the receptivity of the Other.

The Other's receptivity as a consoling witness to the expression of suffering is its own return gift to the one who suffers. Ricoeur (2005) emphasizes how the triad of "give, receive, give in return" is central to the development of mutual recognition. He takes particular note of the importance of receiving as a "pivotal category," in that "the way in which the gift is accepted determines the way in which the person who receives the gift will feel obliged to give in return" (p. 243).

Much hinges on whether the sufferer can open himself enough emotionally to receive and be moved to gratitude by the gift of receptive recognition from the Other. Ricoeur (2005) thus states: "Gratitude lightens the weight of obligation to give in return and reorients this toward a generosity equal to the one that led to the first gift" (p. 243). This gratitude inspires a passionate movement of hope and courage through transitional times into the unknown future and through transitional spaces toward the essential difference of the Other.

Without the Other's receptive compassion, the child must rely within his self-enclosure on his own mind to recognize the actuality of his own suffering. Since this attempt by the child to confirm the actual existence of his suffering through his own mind is doomed by the endlessness of obsessive uncertainty, the risk is that the child who suffers alone will be entranced in a fixed gaze of narcissistic self-preoccupation.

Take the example of a three-year-old boy who painstakingly constructs an edifice of building blocks. If the whole structure were to suddenly collapse, he might break into a flood of tears and rage. In identifying himself so closely with his creation, he feels like he has collapsed into a despairing heap as well. At this juncture, if a parent were to immediately jump into the momentary crisis of catastrophic panic, put her arm around him, and soothingly say: "Don't worry, honey. We can build your castle again," his momentary exposure to the abyss is consoled by her compassionate response. On the other hand, if the little boy's desperation concerning his collapsed building blocks were to go on indefinitely without a parent's comforting embrace, he may eventually have to cope with his sense of exposure and inadequacy alone through the protective covering of self-insulating defenses.

In clinical work, we often we see shame-ridden patients who, rather than viewing their limitations as a wake-up call to open up to the Other, instead tyrannize themselves mercilessly within their own self-enclosure. Joan is a 23-year-old woman who lost her mother to cancer at the age of two. Despite being an open, gregarious woman, Joan wonders constantly whether there is something fundamentally wrong and inadequate about her. What was there about her that was not good enough to keep her mother alive? Or was it that she was so bratty that she drove her mother away permanently? Will she always hurt the people she loves? Despite knowing full well the medical reasons why her mother died, these are the doubts that have persistently tormented Joan throughout her young life.

When our helplessness to prevent our sufferings exposes us too transparently to our inherent limitations as flawed creatures, the experience of shame reflects our reflexive denial of those limitations. Instead, shame may be viewed as a hypnotic spell that we cast through the petrifying gaze of self-consciousness, in which we take inordinate responsibility for those all-too-human limitations by transforming them into our fundamental moral deficiency of not being more invulnerably perfect.

There is a heavy cost to pay in taking on one's sufferings as one's burden of shame: the victimizing powers that be, such as God, fate, or one's parents, are not at fault; the enemy now lies within. When a person is raped, sexually abused, or labeled with an ethnic slur, she may blame the victim in herself for being a victim instead of blaming the perpetrator of the aggression. Whether we have big elephant ears, a large protruding nose, uncontrollable zits, parents who never stop bickering, or an abusively alcoholic father, we hound ourselves mercilessly for our all-too-human flaws and weaknesses, as if we had committed the worst of transgressions. The misfortunes we encounter reverberate back reflexively on our passionate life force as shame, sowing doubts in our fundamental sense of worthiness.

Seeking cover: self-doubt and the reversal of passion into passivity

Unsure about the essential goodness of her passion, the child inverts the inherent strength of her passionate life force into a weakened moral state of passive unworthiness. Rather than growth being experienced as a passionately willed process, the passive, self-doubting child comes to experience the uncertainties of separation, transition, and novelty with paralyzing anxiety. As a result, changes are experienced as something that are always happening too quickly, before she is ready. Instead, the child's passion to grow is disowned and projected outward, and then experienced as an overbearing coercive pressure coming from the external world.

In fear and trembling, the child seeks to retreat to the familiarities of his own mind. Kierkegaard (1844/1980) refers to such self-enclosure as "inclosing reserve," and suggests it is animated by the "demonic" element in us. He states: "The demonic does not close itself off with something, but it closes itself up within itself, and in this lies what is profound about existence, precisely that unfreedom makes itself a prisoner" (p. 124). Such freedom can only be found in the renewal of choice that derives from an ongoing, open give-and-take with an Other.

The self-enclosed person searches fruitlessly within the insulated safety of his own being for the wellspring of self-renewal, but it is not to be found there. It is precisely because of the misdirected failure to find the ground of a new beginning within that this individual is caught in the demonic grip of endless compulsion, not unlike a dog chasing its own tail. Significantly, Freud (1919/1966) traces the sense of the uncanny to this compulsion to repeat. He says:

> It is possible to recognize the dominance in the unconscious mind of a "compulsion to repeat" proceeding from the instinctual impulses and probably inherent in the very nature of the instincts—a compulsion powerful enough to overrule the pleasure principle, lending to certain aspects of the mind their daemonic character … .
>
> (p. 238)

However, we are inherently relational beings who have no choice but to communicate. Kierkegaard (1844/1980) thus states that the demonic tendency toward self-enclosure is always haunted by an "anxiety about the good" (p. 123), a needed openness to relationship that is not being lived out. Kierkegaard states:

> The demonic is unfreedom that wants to close itself off. This, however, is and remains an impossibility. It always retains a relation, and even when this has apparently disappeared altogether, it is nevertheless there, and anxiety at once manifests itself in the moment of contact.
>
> (p. 123)

Since the self-enclosed person is so intent on defending against the revelation of vulnerability and limitation of which he is ashamed, he is not able to open up sufficiently to the evolving give-and-take with an Other. In retreating from the "anxiety about the good," he also bypasses the "good" of the mutual vulnerability necessary to a meaningful give-and-take with the Other. Instead, since within the self-enclosed individual's isolation, his need for relationship is not being lived out, it continues to haunt him, until finally emerging with ever-greater intensity in the unswerving guarantees of blind loyalty to an Other.

In order to cover up the shame of exposing oneself to the threat of infinite separateness in relationship to an Other, the self-enclosed individual retreats to a loyalty to his own kind, which he then encodes as a moral virtue. As the child clings to all surrogates of sameness who become associated with a familiarized "us," the passion to change and grow is disowned and projected onto "them," the strangers who embody the threat of indefinite exile and isolation. As Kearney (2003) states: "The figure of the stranger ... frequently operates as a limit experience for humans trying to identify themselves over and against others" (p. 3). The relational ruptures and developmental discontinuities in renewing oneself though an openness to the Other become displaced onto the group discontinuities between "us" and "them." Loyalty to one's own family, ethnicity, religion, nation, or species is set against the different Other, who takes on the monstrous visage of one's own sinful and feared freedom. Bakan (1966) points out that the self-assertive, agentic aspects of ourselves are projected onto the prototypical Other and representative of separateness and exile, the image of Satan.

Usually we think of homesickness as a form of separation anxiety, such as when a child at sleep-away camp feels the ache of longing to return home, or when at the end of the school day, she waits with a single-minded desperation for her mother to pick her up. Such children, feeling lost and alone in a sea of strangers, often cannot be consoled and distracted from the urgency to re-connect with a parent.

While homesickness appears to be a dis-ease of facing the unknown, it also reflects an unstable or disrupted attachment to a parent for which the child has taken on too much responsibility to repair. At the same time that parents warn their children against the dangers of the outside world under the guise of providing a protective shield, they also lay claim to their children as their possessions. This is not coincidental. The parent's caution to beware of strangers, often carrying the weight of a prohibition against the betrayal of venturing too far from home, has a binding effect on children because it stirs up feelings of separation guilt and fear of shame exposure. The homesick child, who suffers through fear and trembling in the anticipation of life transitions, is not crippled so much by an inherent failure of courage, but a self-weakening uncertainty about his right to move forward and sustain his ongoing life.

In loyal solidarity: keeping parents company in their suffering

The self-enclosed individual, who is preoccupied with the cover-up of shame, and doubting his worthiness to move on with life, is left with no choice but to submit loyally to the moral authority of parents, which he infuses with the disowned strength of his passionate life force.

A frequent consequence of the inversion of passion and the emergence of shame morality is that children split off the mask of who they *should* be from the authentic desires that they cover up. This use of a mask or "double face" to preserve something precious about one's essential core is implicit in Winnicott's (1960/1965b) distinction between the True Self and the False Self. Already very early in life, the infant, sensing the threat of exposure to unresponsiveness, instinctively makes do by instead developing a mentalized False Self to adapt and "care" for the mother's needs.

When a depressed parent, for example, does not recognize or enjoy the offerings of her child, the child may feel excluded from the inner sanctum of the parent's life, and fall back on fantasies of omnipotence to compensate for his actual inability to have a lasting effect on the depressed parent. Tormented by a perfectionistic sense of omnipotence that knows no bounds, a child may drive himself mercilessly to do more, always more, to alleviate a parent's misery. Failure simply is evidence of his own inadequacy and shame.

As many attempts to give of himself come to a dead end in a parent who cannot or will not receive the child's offerings of help, the child is confronted with the predicament of knowing about the parent's unhappiness without being able to do anything about it. The frustrated wish to give and take care of the parent, now "backed up," infiltrates the child's mental spheres of imagining, knowing, and thinking. Since the parent is not accessible to the child's offerings, the child's gifts of *doing* are necessarily restricted to the mental gifts of *worrying*. Each wish to give that is frustrated in actuality, stillborn at its conception, is recycled in the incessant false starts of worrying or obsessive ruminating.

In the meantime, the child's burden of mental responsibility for the parent's unhappiness continues to weigh heavily as from the unremitting pressure of a debt that never gets repaid. For children who have been rebuffed in their attempts to contribute to their parents' lives, those experiences may surface in their solitude in the form of negative introjects.

A sense of unacceptability may conspire with self-castigating voices to declare incessantly that they are not worthy or good enough to fit into the lives of others, such that the experience of aloneness comes to signify the loneliness of isolation and exile. Freedom of choice, and thinking itself, is not very enlightening when each thought and each decision occurs under the watchful, critical eye of a perfectionistic consciousness. Forever knocking on the door of inclusion and acceptability without being able to get in, and intent on escaping their individual selves, such children bind themselves loyally to parental authority.

When no other offerings are deemed sufficiently acceptable, the child's primary means of assuaging his sense of indebtedness and placating the envy of previous generations is by offering himself as an imitative replica to parents. In circumstances in which a parent does not appear to appreciate or benefit from her child's offerings of love in any lasting way, the child may feel an increasing paradoxical pressure to give up more of himself in order to separate from the parent's unhappy state with good conscience.

One of the symptomatic actions that often baffle many individuals could be described as "becoming the parent one hates." A number of years ago, I saw a nine-year-old boy named John in therapy whose parents had recently been divorced. John was referred to me because he was getting into fights at school and then put into detention every day after school. His father had beaten his mother and finally committed a robbery for which he was serving time in prison. In the meantime, John had been willingly inculcated by his mother into a "correct" way of viewing his father as a "no-good asshole." After all, he himself was a witness to his father beating his mother and, of course, he consciously took his mother's side in those parental battles. In our sessions, he was quite sincere about having "no use for his father" and did not care if he never heard from him again. At what cost to himself did John disown any relationship he may have had at one time, or ever wanted to have had, with a father of whom he was ashamed?

When I inquired at the time of John, whether he missed his father or wished his father would contact him, John shrugged his shoulders with marked indifference. Yet, John too, just like his imprisoned father, was constrained against his will in school detention as punishment for his behavior. Against all common sense and any "correct" moral ideology, John was identifying with his father's crimes and punishment of imprisonment.

One way to understand John's behavior is that the exiled desires to love and be loved by his father had been idealized precisely because John turned away from the disillusionment of his shamed wishes. As a result, they had never found an actualized voice in the outside world, although they, too, belonged to John. What better way for John to compensate for a love that never existed and bridge the gulf between himself and his father than to embrace his father in loyal solidarity by joining him in his suffering of imprisoned solitude, as if to say: "Don't worry, Dad. I did not really abandon you in your unhappy misery. I will keep you company in your experience of exile."

In a broader sense, the loyal maintenance of ritual in adherence to parental values and traditions becomes a means of paying sacrificial dues to previous generations. In the mortifying aftermath of shame, by taking cover under the cloak of parental traditions and appropriation of parental values, children are able to cover their sense of individual inadequacy and give themselves a reborn sense of moral right to move forward with life again. By infusing himself with a pride gained from incorporating the power of one's traditions, the individual can re-present himself to the world again with a new "persona," or the masked face of a reborn personhood. As Wurmser (1994) says:

> In shame one wants to change into another being or hide, not to be seen anymore. The mask changes the shamefully exposed into the shameless exhibitionist, one who fears to be seen as weak into one who is now feared as strong.
>
> (p. 306)

Hiding in the crowd: conformity and the concept of "cool"

For most individuals, the masks of adhering loyally to parental traditions evolve eventually into the masks of conforming loyally to group norms of peer relationships. Through the mutual jeopardy of exposure and shame, the masks of conformity bind each group member's self-esteem to every other group member's self-esteem on the paradoxical basis of covering up and inhibiting one's individual difference.

If a hypnotic trance is an unconscious collusion between the hypnotist and the willing suggestibility of the hypnotized person, then the loyal adherence to the moral authority of social norms may be viewed as a "slow-motion hypnosis," in which individuals can surrender the wearying hypervigilance of watching over their individual shames to the group. Powerful loyalty pressures, with the coercive aim of enforcing uniformity, are brought to bear on each individual to uphold a group pride in which all participants invest their hopes to transcend their own limitations.

Focusing on the moral judgments of group norms diverts each individual from his own freedom of conscience and the genuine remorse he may feel for hurting somebody he loves. It is for that reason that Nietzsche (1887/1989) suggests that punishment may *impede* the development of the very feelings of guilt it is supposed to awaken. He says: "Punishment makes men hard and cold; it concentrates; it sharpens the feeling of alienation; it *strengthens the power of resistance*" (p. 81, emphasis added). To brace for potential accusations from his peers for deviating from group norms, each group member summons his energies to preempt the risk of excommunication, thus leaving very little mental space for the self-reflectiveness of a free conscience.

Very early in childhood, we learn to collude with each other's defenses by constructing group standards of "cool" that are often based on nothing more substantive than image and appearance. We all want to be accepted for who we are as unique individuals, but we often defeat our own purposes when we don masks of cool to fit into a group.

Take the sixth grader who combs his hair a certain way and wears baggy pants and uses a particular jargon to gain entrée into his peer group. In buying the approval and respect of his peers with the imitative mask of acting and talking in a certain way, he hinders his own aims to be accepted for who he is. He is still left in some doubt as to whether he would be acceptable in and of himself if he were to reveal himself in greater depth. On the contrary, he may observe how his fellow group members project their disowned shames and doubts about their own individual acceptability onto the nerdy, parent-oriented kids who have not mastered the images of cool, and who are teased mercilessly for their "geekiness" and "babyness."

Teenagers learn quickly enough, if they have not done so already, that it is not "cool" to wear their hearts on their sleeve or to get too hot and bothered about anything that deviates from group norms. "Chill" is the watchword for "Relax, don't show you care too much about anything. Be cool." The pecking orders of high-school culture, based in large part on the ability to master the values and language of cool, still haunt many individuals long after adolescence and inform the norms of adult conformity.

In capitalistic societies, such as the United States, making and having money becomes a culture-wide norm of cool that provides status, power, and influence. In this light, it is interesting to note that the word "materialism" derives from the Latin *mater*, "mother." Perhaps one must emphasize the proud appearance of surrounding oneself with much "mother" to cover over the deficiency of not having internalized one's mother at a deeper level.

Kierkegaard (1846/1962) strips the emperor of his clothes to reveal the illusory quality of these group and cultural constructions of "cool." He says: "In order that everything should be reduced to the same level, it is first of all necessary to procure a phantom, its spirit, a monstrous abstraction, an all-embracing something which is nothing, a mirage—and that phantom is *the public*" (p. 59, emphasis in original). Eugene Ionesco's (1960) play *Rhinoceros*, in which every person mysteriously turns into a rhinoceros, also depicts the absurd lengths to which human beings will go to conform blindly to meaningless social norms—all to cover up their exposed isolation as separate individuals.

Far from being fair-weather friends, the relations between rivalrous siblings of a given culture become governed, at least in part, by the "Misery loves company" motto of rainy-day friendships. Bound together by the dangers of exposing one's individual passions to the envious "evil eye" of others (Shabad, 2001), culture ties the interests of its disparate members together through the loyalty of shared commiseration. Kierkegaard (1846/1962) notes that: "In an age which is very reflective and passionless *envy* is the negative unifying principle" (p. 47, emphasis in original).

The problem here is that just as Narcissus's enchantment with his own appearance constricts his ability to actually live, the cultivation of image is an extension of narcissistic defenses in which we attempt to avoid the mortification of exposed vulnerability by not getting too deep, by lowering the stakes of our expressive life. As in a large enmeshed family, the mutual possessiveness of one for all and all for one becomes a cultural mandate that narrows each individual's vision of what is possible.

Group standards of cool can be viewed as a kind of narcissistic reflecting pool by which we become enamored with an image of ourselves at the expense of the actuality of our being. In order to attain a sense of security and significance, we adapt to and immerse ourselves in what Becker (1973) calls the "borrowed meanings of others" at heavy cost to our own truths.

Furthermore, we must do so without fully knowing what we are doing and how much we need others to prop up our self-esteem, for any shame consciousness of our profound limitations as self-sustaining individuals would expose the anxieties and sense of weakness that underlie unconscious conformity.

This unconscious use of borrowed meanings prompted Becker (1973) to describe the narcissism of human character as a "vital lie." Narcissism is vital because the self-forgetful deception and ignorance as to the energies we really draw on enables us to go on living securely and serenely; narcissism is a lie because we do not want to admit how much our sense of individual significance depends on the meanings of others. In describing the problem of living according to these masks of group norms, Becker (1973) concludes: "It is fateful and ironic how the life we need in order to live dooms us to a life that is never really ours" (p. 56).

Us and them: hierarchy and scapegoating the monstrous Other

Perhaps it is because differences connote exclusion and separateness, and arouse hidden anxieties of isolation as insignificant individuals, that we often feel compelled to distinguish hierarchically between "us and them." Adam Phillips (2002) poses a basic question: "Why is hierarchy a reflex response to difference?"

In retreating from the anxieties and self-doubts of shame exposure by taking shelter under the cover of loyalty to our own kind, we attempt to obliterate the limitations of our individuality by resurrecting ourselves behind the guise of group pride. In our attempts to master the experience of our own shame, we externalize the dynamic of self-contempt and worthlessness by constructing hierarchies between people according to that same dynamic of oppressor and oppressed from which we suffer so much. Such hierarchical distinctions allow *us* to distinguish ourselves from *them*—other lesser mortals—and, at least on this earthly stage, to strut around proudly for a brief period of time.

Whereas in shame we objectify ourselves, within the externalized "us and them" hierarchies endemic to group narcissism we objectify others as alien and Other. In this sense, Goffman (1963) describes how shame is related to the stigma of social pollution and has historical roots in the notion of defilement. Girard (1977) also suggests that the threat of being infected with such defiling impurities through its contagious spread has played an influential role in social relations. This mortal fear of being flooded over with impurities emanating from a monstrous Other helps us to understand the desperate need to demarcate rigid boundaries between us and them, and between the pure and the impure. Ricoeur (1967) thus states: "Dread of the impure and rites of purification are in the background of all of our feelings and all our behavior relating to fault" (p. 25).

The in-group of "us" may attempt to undo this traumatized sense of defilement and shame through purification rituals of sacrifice. We project our own disowned vulnerabilities onto others and attempt magically to kill off the existential insult of death, which is now inscribed in those frailties. The omnipotent defense of denying one's mortal limitations may become coupled with its projection onto a monstrous Other, such that a life-or-death struggle of "kill or be killed" must ensue between "them" and "us." Becker (1975) asserted that in the zero-sum logic of scapegoating, one becomes stronger through the death of the scapegoated victim by incorporating his life force. The scapegoat, embodying our disowned death, is sent off into the never-to-be-heard-from wilderness, so that we can continue to live deathlessly. Rank (1936) says: "The death fear of the ego is lessened by the killing, the sacrifice, of the other through the death of the other; one buys oneself free from the penalty of dying, of being killed" (p. 180).

Klaus Theleweit (1989) examines the fantasies of right-wing German stormtroopers immediately following World War I. He notes that the overflowing, soft, fluid liquid of the female body was viewed as a dangerously contagious Other that the stormtroopers feared would overwhelm their male identities with its impurities. Theleweit suggests that these men, to whom he insightfully refers as the "*not fully born*," were hell-bent on armoring their bodies with a physical "hardness" in order to ward off their symbiotic anxieties. Elsewhere, I have suggested that this fascistic idealization of hardness is an attempt to defend against the shame of being born of a woman from whom one never separated and who therefore is forever feared as a lurking presence within (Shabad, 2007). In subsequent years, Hitler played on this fear of the underlying symbiotic mother and feminized man to spur a re-invented, self-created Aryan superman whose firm musculature and emotional hardness delineated rigid boundaries to armor him in a genocidal war against the impure threat of the parasitical, feminized Jew.

The sociologist Hugh Duncan (1968) says: "We cannot become humane until we understand this need to visit suffering and death on others" (p. 39).

It is not only Nazis and other perpetrators of genocide who divide "us" from "them." Many of the self-styled virtuous among us attempt to cleanse themselves of their shame by conveniently projecting their sense of "sin" onto perpetrators who already have committed crimes or wrongdoing. We thus extend the dichotomy between loyalty to our own kind and the externalization of shame onto the monstrous Other to correspondingly inconsistent ways in which we either seek to understand or cast blame on others. We may exert efforts to understand the motives of our family and friends when they do something wrong, while not extending the same benefit of the doubt to the strangers in our midst. We seek to understand those we love and we blame our enemies.

Many people view criminals or sexual abusers or Nazis or serial killers as nonhuman "monsters" who must be held accountable for their misdeeds, but who are not worth understanding in depth. The punitive tone with which the word "accountability" often is uttered belies the displaced resentments and moralistic judgments of "innocent" bystanders, who are simultaneously exempting their loved ones from such harsh judgments. Perhaps if a parent of one of those bystanders were to say something sadistically hurtful, one might hear something like, "Mom didn't really know what she was saying. Besides, she can be difficult sometimes because she had a really bad relationship with her own mother." By means of defensive splitting, our inconsistent attributions of a punitive accountability often depend on the extent to which, on the one hand, we have "no use for" certain people and, on the other hand, the extent to which we use rationalizations as a means to erase wrongdoing by persons we either idealize or need.

I have occasionally conducted a thought experiment when teaching trainees. I ask the class to imagine a picture of Adolf Hitler as a young kindergartner raising his hand to ask if he can go pee-pee. The teacher then escorts him by the hand to the bathroom. A number of trainees have said that they are quite discomforted by the juxtaposition of incongruent images of good and evil. Mixing Hitler's evil with the image of goodness normally attributed to a child's innocence can be challenging to the normal tendency to split good and evil. Some people may find it more difficult to hold the adult evil Hitler responsible for his actions if they actually picture that he was an innocent child at one time. This difficulty may be compounded if they were to conjure up an image of innocent little Adolf being beaten by his father.

For many who forego understanding in favor of condemnation, knowing why someone does something may be tantamount to excusing or condoning that person's actions. After all, sometimes explanations sound all too much like rationalizations, even justifications, for wrongdoing. Perhaps there is a fear that to understand the reasons behind a person's wrongdoing is to risk dissipating a sense of righteous indignation. As clinicians, many of us are well aware of patients who, not wishing to have their resentments softened, do not want to know the reasons why parents did or did not do the things they did. Or when patients attempt to quickly bypass their resentments by attempting to understand their parents' motives, many clinicians may suspect that they are protecting an idealized image of those parents.

When perpetrators are understood, they are often transformed from monstrous targets of scapegoating and blame into three-dimensional persons. The further we probe into the depths of the human soul, the more we discover that we are all more human than otherwise. We cannot isolate understanding from its ethical underpinnings of empathy and compassion. In ways that words cannot describe, human beings have a deeply rooted sense of kinship with each other's suffering. For those of us who study the workings of the human psyche, it is incumbent to ask ourselves how the "might makes right" morality of shame colludes with the group narcissism of loyalty to one's own kind to obscure these compassionate echoes of an individual's conscience.

References

Bachelard, G. (2013). *Intuition of the instant.* Evanston, IL: Northwestern University Press. (Original work published in 1932.)

Bakan, D. (1966). *The duality of human existence: An essay on psychology and religion.* Chicago, IL: Rand McNally.

Becker, E. (1973). *The denial of death.* Glencoe, IL: Free Press.

Becker, E. (1975). *Escape from evil.* New York: Free Press.

Bergson, H. (1998). *Creative evolution.* New York: Dover. (Original work published in 1911.)

Carlisle, C. (2005). *Kierkegaard's philosophy of becoming.* Albany, NY: SUNY Press.

Carse, J. (1980). *Death and existence.* New York: Wiley.

Duncan, H. (1968). *Symbols in society.* London: Oxford University Press.

Eliade, M. (1954). *The myth of the eternal return.* Princeton, NJ: Princeton University Press.

Freud, S. (1966). *Three essays on the theory of sexuality. The standard edition of the complete psychological works of Sigmund Freud, Volume VII.* Ed. and trans. J. Strachey: 125–245. London: Hogarth Press. (Original work published in 1905.)
Freud, S. (1966). *The Uncanny. The standard edition of the complete psychological works of Sigmund Freud, Volume XVII.* Ed. and trans. J. Strachey: 217–252. London: Hogarth Press. (Original work published in 1919.)
Ghent, E. (1990). Masochism, submission, surrender: Masochism as a perversion of surrender. *Contemporary Psychoanalysis*, 26, 108–136.
Girard, R. (1977). *Violence and the sacred.* Baltimore, MD: Johns Hopkins University Press.
Goffman, E. (1963). *Stigma: Notes on the management of spoiled identity.* New York: Touchstone.
Heraclitus (1974). *The cosmic fragments.* Ed. G.S. Kirk. Cambridge: Cambridge University Press.
Ionesco, E. (1960). *Rhinoceros.* New York: Vintage.
Kearney, R. (2003). *Strangers, gods, and monsters.* New York: Routledge.
Kierkegaard, S. (1962). *The present age.* Trans. A. Dru. New York: Harper & Row. (Original work published in 1846.)
Kierkegaard, S. (1980). *The concept of anxiety.* Trans. R. Thomte. Princeton, NJ: Princeton University Press. (Original work published in 1844.)
Kierkegaard, S. (1983). *Fear and trembling.* Trans. H. Hong and E. Hong. Princeton, NJ: Princeton University Press. (Original work published in 1843.)
Kierkegaard, S. (1996) *Papers and journals: A selection.* Trans. A. Hannay. London: Penguin Classics. (Original work published in 1843.)
Kierkegaard, S. (2009). *Repetition.* Trans. M.G. Piety. London: Oxford University Press. (Original work published in 1843.)
Levinas, E. (1969). *Totality and infinity.* Pittsburgh, PA: Duquesne University Press.
Mahler, M. (1975). *The psychological birth of the human infant.* New York: Basic Books.
Margolis, D. (1998). *The fabric of self.* New Haven, CT: Yale University Press.
Maslow, A. (1962). *Toward a psychology of being.* Princeton, NJ: Princeton University Press.
Miller, J. (1988). *The way of suffering.* Washington, DC: Georgetown University Press.
Morrison, A. (1987). The eye turned inward: Shame and the self. In *The many faces of shame* (pp. 271–291). Ed. D. Nathanson. New York: Guilford Press.
Nietzsche, F. (1989). *On the genealogy of morals and Ecce homo.* New York: Vintage. (Original work published in 1887.)
Nietzsche, F. (2009). Early Greek philosophy and other essays. In *The complete works of Friedrich Nietzsche, Vol. 2* (p. 6). Trans. M. Mugge. Ithaca, NY: Cornell University Press. (Original work published in 1871.)
Phillips, A. (2002). *Equals.* New York: Basic Books.
Rank, O. (1936). *Truth and reality and will therapy.* New York: Knopf.

Ricoeur, P. (1967). *The symbolism of evil.* Boston, MA: Beacon Press.
Ricoeur, P. (2005). *The course of recognition.* Trans. D. Pellauer. Cambridge, MA: Harvard University Press.
Sartre, J.P. (1969). *Being and nothingness.* Trans. H. Barnes. London: Routledge. (Original work published in 1956.)
Shabad, P. (1989). Vicissitudes of psychic loss of a physically present parent. In *The problem of loss and mourning: Psychoanalytic perspectives* (pp. 101–126). Eds. D. Dietrich and P. Shabad. Madison, CT: International Universities Press.
Shabad, P. (2001). *Despair and the return of hope: Echoes of mourning in psychotherapy.* Northvale, NJ: Aronson/Rowman & Littlefield.
Shabad, P. (2007). Of woman born: Womb envy and the male project of self-creation. In *Jealousy and envy* (pp. 75–90). Eds. L. Wurmser and H. Jarass. Hillsdale, NJ: The Analytic Press.
Theleweit, K. (1989). *Male fantasies*, Vol. 2. Minneapolis, MN: University of Minnesota Press.
Winnicott, D.W. (1965a). The theory of the parent–infant relationship. In *The maturational processes and the facilitating environment* (pp. 37–55). New York: International Universities Press. (Original work published in 1960.)
Winnicott, D.W. (1965b). Ego distortion in terms of true and false self. In *The maturational processes and the facilitating environment* (pp. 140–152). New York: International Universities Press. (Original work published in 1960.)
Winnicott, D.W. (1975). The depressive position in normal emotional development. In *Through paediatrics to psychoanalysis* (pp. 262–277). New York: Basic Books. (Original work published in 1954–1955.)
Wurmser, L. (1994). *The mask of shame.* Northvale, NJ: Aronson.

Chapter 5

Toward a psychoanalysis of passion

Jerome A. Miller

In our current vernacular, as well as in the current discourse of philosophers, psychologists, and psychoanalysts, "passion" and "desire" are usually treated as synonyms. On occasions when calibrating desire is important, we may reserve "passion" for an especially intense, especially energetic modality of it. Used in this way, "passion" brings to mind "addiction," with the result that these words also come to be used interchangeably. The one word whose meaning all these others seem to somehow share is, of course, "love." Usually, we don't give a second thought to our practice of using these terms without discriminating among them. But there seems to be something profoundly incongruous about this practice. For these terms serve as the vocabulary of human motivation—and our motivations are complicated and conflicted in ways that cast suspicion on a linguistic habit that implies that a chain of synonyms can do justice to them. Perhaps synonymy is camouflage we use to cover up motivational tensions and antinomies we're loath to acknowledge. This is, of course, just the kind of suspicion that both philosophical and psychoanalytic self-examination tends to awaken. But if those of us accustomed to operating in the world of interiority are relying on linguistic camouflage ourselves, it may be because it's reinforced by assumptions that are especially deep-seated.

The assumption that underlies our dependence on synonyms when talking about our motivations is, I believe, easily identified, and its historical provenance easily described. From Plato to Freud, almost without exception, desire has been considered primal in us, and other kinds of motivation, if acknowledged, have been discussed and understood in terms of it. The Christian tradition, for example, distinguished *agape* from desire/eros—but viewed desire as naturally primal and attributed *agape* to supernatural influence. By assuming the primacy of desire, we're able to suppose that even our most primordial conflicts are due not to different motivations but simply to conflicting objects of desire. There are now emerging, however, compelling reasons to question this view, some of which come from the theorizing and practice of psychoanalysts. In this chapter, I will be trying to explore and articulate the alternative conception of motivation and, indeed, of the human person that their work adumbrates.[1]

Passion

I'll begin by briefly describing and then reflecting on an experience I had with my granddaughter Camille when she was 18 months old. Taking a seat in the sunroom where she was playing, I was intent on reconnecting with her after a fairly lengthy absence. She, on the other hand, was intent on Minnie Mouse, her constant and favorite companion. But as I was watching her, she gave Minnie one last look of gladness, walked over to where I sat, smiled, and gave her to me. Returning her smile, I thanked her heartily. Camille returned to her toys, picked up a stuffed animal, and brought *that* to me. Before long, I was cradling a pile of her things.

Camille repeated these actions time after time, day after day, during her stay with us. Someone employing the classical psychoanalytic heuristic would find nothing surprising in them: unlike little Ernst, she was motivated to hand over her things so as to win my affection in return. But contemporary psychoanalysts such as Peter Shabad who are less inclined to employ a hermeneutic of suspicion would not hesitate to say that Camille was giving me gifts that had previously been given to her. Seen in this way, she was already beginning to operate in, and demonstrating a rudimentary understanding of, the kind of gift-economy Lewis Hyde (1983) describes. Shabad, from whom I've learned much about these matters, suggests that the gracious reception of a child's "offerings" is "essential … to the development of [her] healthy self-confidence and the creative unfolding of [her] identity" (2001, p. 32). Implicit in this claim is the suggestion that what's crucial to the child's positive sense of her self is her belief that her gifts to the world are singularly important and worthwhile.

Although this may strike us as a plausible but relatively innocuous insight, it has the potential to revolutionize our very conception of selfhood. It suggests that the human self is primordially oriented toward self-donation. Shabad himself (2001) doesn't hesitate to affirm that this is the case:

> The notion of a meaningful life that transcends the self is not merely an existential appendage that becomes relevant only after our most basic needs are met and biological survival is secured. To attempt to disentangle the urge for transcendent meaning from the entirety of a human life is misguided. Living for something or someone other than oneself is fundamental to being human.
>
> (p. 38)

"Transcendent meaning," as Shabad construes it here, is no abstraction. It's immanent in, incarnate in, the other toward which or toward whom one's generosity is directed. The belief that the "urge" to self-donation is primal in us isn't just pivotal to Shabad's psychoanalytic theorizing. It informs his clinical practice and underlies his diagnostic conviction that psychic knots can often be traced back to the devastating rejection of one's gifts in early childhood. This is not a kind of trauma that traditional psychoanalytic practitioners were inclined to suspect. And given our normalized understanding of evolution,[2] according to which all the operations of human intentionality derive from and are finally explainable in terms of primal biological imperatives, we may find the claim that an "urge" to self-transcendence is "fundamental" in us highly implausible. But it's not only the occasional generosities of very young children that encourage us to consider it. In the Nazi and Soviet camps, where we would have expected the ordeal of meeting primal needs to preclude even the thought of the other, there were acts of self-donation that defy Maslow's hierarchy of needs as well as the usual assumptions of our evolutionary theorists (Todorov, 1996). In our theorizing about the human self, we're obligated to try to learn the truths such acts have to teach us, even if doing so requires us to question assumptions long considered unassailable.

The psychologists whose theorizing centered on "self-realization" may have been trying to appreciate the kind of self-donative action that I'm discussing here. But it is crucial for us to recognize that, far from being synonymous, "self-realization" and "self-donation" differ fundamentally because radically different ways of understanding possibility are implicit in these two concepts.

According to Aristotle (1940), from whom the concept of self-realization derives, the actions we're capable of performing are limited by the invariances of human nature. But there are, in his view, potentialities immanent in our nature that we're able to develop, and in developing these potentials, we're actualizing/realizing ourselves—becoming more fully the selves we originally were. The existential conception of self-realization (Sartre, 1970) on which humanistic psychologists drew emphasized in a way Aristotle didn't that our possibilities open the unprecedented historical future to us. In actualizing these possibilities, we're not more fully actualizing our original nature; we're creating our own identity. Heidegger (1962) called our attention to the fact that there's one unprecedented possibility toward which we're moving but which we can't actualize: the possibility of nothingness. Instead of our being able to actualize it, *it* will utterly undo *us*. Nevertheless, Heidegger insists that this possibility belongs to us. Indeed, he calls it our "*ownmost*" possibility (1962, p. 294, emphasis in original). This view helps us to recognize that, in spite of their very significant differences, the Aristotelian and existential conceptions of possibility employ the same heuristic and share a crucial assumption: they view possibility from the point of view of the agent about to act, and assume that this possibility is his and his alone to actualize or not. When he does actualize it, he's actualizing himself (irrespective of whether nature or historicity is constitutive of this self).

But if I suppose that the possibilities that are open to me are *my* possibilities, I'm overlooking the fact that every possibility, including the primal possibility of breathing, places me in relationship to alterities that transcend me. I'm not just always already exposed to and inescapably borne toward the dreadful heterogeneity of the *not* about which Heidegger (1993) speaks. I'm also exposed to, inescapably borne toward, and inextricably caught in the throe of the *not* of heterogeneity—the whole universe of others that is irreducible to me. Because the throe of alterity is constitutive of possibility, possibility doesn't belong to me and hence isn't mine to actualize. Irrespective of how I respond to any of the possibilities open to me, none of them is part of my autobiography because autobiography is an oxymoron. The graph of human *bios* is heterological.

According to our sciences, and especially our ecologies, what I've just said of the human self is true of every being: every one of the possibilities that are usually thought of as belonging to it actually place it in relationship to heterogeneities that are irreducible to it. Living beings aren't just related to alterities; their development as living beings is dependent on alterities. Conscious living beings to some degree experience this dependence, this needfulness. But it's in the human self that awareness is broken open to alterity *as such.* Even in her infancy, the human self doesn't just consciously experience her dependence on alterities. She's traumatized by anxiety when they're absent. That the infant suffers such anxiety was one of the late Freud's most important insights. "The earliest anxiety of all," he said, "is brought about on the occasion of a separation from the Mother," (Freud, 1959, p. 66) and the condition of helplessness that results from this separation. A phenomenology of felt need confirms this. Its immediacy and urgency makes the absence of the needed all too real. It's not just that Mother is not present, not available, to the infant; it's that this *not* induces excruciating distress in her. Her being as a whole is experiencing its dependence on a future that doesn't belong to her. Her cry expresses not just primal needfulness but primal impotence. Conscious human life is exposed, from the beginning, to traumatizing absence that already portends—already in some sense signifies to it—the possibility of death. Like all living beings, we're ontologically vulnerable to the *not.* But, for us, vulnerability is affect-ability—our capacity to be affectively pierced by the *not.*

Were we affect-able only by excruciating absence, affect-ability would be a curse. But thankfully this isn't the case. Not even an infant is entirely bound by need, or related to alterity by need alone. Need is an invariant condition of life but felt need is intermittent. When it passes, the child can remain alert. She can be attentive to now this, then that, then something else—to whatever happens to be right-here-now-in-front-of-her.[3] Usually, it's something seen; sometimes, it's something heard; it's best, perhaps, when it's something tasted. Once a certain point is reached, that which she's attending to doesn't have to be right-here-now-in-front-of-her; it can also be over-there-beyond-reach. Not long thereafter, what's over there turns out to be reachable; the child can pick it up and carefully examine it. As the process of examination evolves, something profoundly transformative happens in awareness to awareness, though it's a transformation that psychoanalytic theorizing has generally and inexplicably ignored: the child's sensory awareness is broken open to, and broken open by, a possibility that she can't assimilate into herself—the possibility that there's more to that-which-is-right-here-now-in-her-hands than is right-here-now-in-her-hands.[4] Call it primal astonishment or original amazement or the first absolute surprise. The infant evolves into the child—becomes childlike—not by crawling or walking or speaking a rudimentary language but by beginning to live in relation to the wondrous. The very transcendence of the wondrous throws her out of and beyond herself by calling her toward it.[5] Here I think once again of Camille, and my other grandchildren, and the way the wondrous moves them. Unwilling to withhold themselves from it, they're wont to run into whatever mystery is summoning them. When they do so, they're usually jubilant. Let their joyous surrender of themselves to the wondrous serve as a paradigmatic example of passion.

It's not the only one. When I say the very young child is "moved," I'm speaking of the same thing that happened to us when we were nine and the Saturday morning sun drew us out of a backyard tent, or when at 20 a mountain summoned us to ascend it, or when at 40 we were carried inside Bruch's Concerto by Nadia Salerno Sonnenberg's violin. What moves us may be wondrous or awe-full. In either case, the subject is caught by and in the throe of an alterity that surpasses her. By virtue of this throe, she's carried beyond herself without ceasing to be herself; she becomes a participant in alterity without becoming fused with, hence indistinguishable from, it.[6] We can call this self-transcendence, provided we recognize that the self who experiences it (a) continues to be herself, and (b) doesn't achieve self-transcendence on her own but only by being drawn into the throe of the other by the other, and entrusting herself to this throe.

Now insofar as the throe breaks the self open to the possibility that there's more to what's right-here-now-in-her-hands than is right-here-now-in-her-hands and accessible to her senses, the self can enter into it only if her intentional consciousness is vulnerable to—able to be affected by—what can't be sensed. Her intentionality has to be capable of being amazed. It's appropriate to call this ability "human intelligence," but important to keep in mind that intelligence can't cause itself to be astonished—it can't make itself wonder or shudder in awe. It has to be moved to astonishment by the wondrous or the awe-full. But the crucial point is that intelligence is able to be so moved; it's affect-able by the astonishing. I call this, borrowing from Keats (1952, p. 71), its negative capability. It makes all the difference. It enables intelligence to be caught in the throe of alterity.[7]

Once it's brought intelligent consciousness under its sway, the astonishing can pass into the recesses of interiority and, from there, into one's being as a whole. Here, I'm thinking of Camille dancing. Even for an 18-month-old infant, there's more to music than just sound that's sensible to the ear. A simple melody and rhythm can be "catching" and draw a child into its throe. When this happens, she isn't taking the music—assimilating the music—into herself; she's becoming assimilated into—beginning to live inside—what transcends her. And because the child's vulnerability is unguarded, her being in its entirety is available to, hence affect-able by, what her intelligence accesses. We typically think of emotion as one "part" or dimension of the psyche. But affect isn't localizable. We place it metaphorically in the heart only because the heart signifies the very core of the person and the negative capability of her being as a whole—her capacity to be utterly overcome. When the poignancy at our core is touched, there's no part of us that's unaffected.

The affect that's thereby engendered is passion—from the Latin *passio*, meaning "to undergo." It's here that the full import of what I've called our negative capability becomes clear. We don't create our enthusiasms or cause ourselves to become impassioned. It's the radiance of the wondrous, the sublimity of the awe-full, that quickens or bowls over, that springs on the child, and perhaps still on us, an enlivening grace or an empowering summons. Passion is born in our primordial vulnerability. Our grandchildren are moved to run out into the unprecedented future by the gladness this mysterious future awakens in them. Could the child express what she's experiencing, she would answer the sort of question that Socrates poses to Euthyphro without hesitation: she doesn't find the wondrous wondrous because it gladdens her; it gladdens her because it's wondrous. Unlike pleasure, which is wrapped up in itself, joy can't contain itself. It radiates as if to reciprocate the effulgence that engenders it. Passion is donative *elan.* It's a mistake to think of it as, or compare it to, energy that's to be discharged. For that conception of it overlooks the fact that, while it's engendered in the subject by alterities that transcend her, it's the subject *as* subject—the subject as intentional agent—who voluntarily expends it. And she does this precisely by giving her impassioned self to the alterities that engender it in her. The child's gladness is a kind of freshet from which primal gratitude and praise-singing spring. The child runs to give her exorbitant assent to life as an unfolding mystery. Running is the primordial, pre-lingual "yea." This is love in action. It provides us a paradigmatic image of the entire process of human evolution, as Shabad (2001) conceives of it. We can think of it, he says, as an "impassioned [movement] toward an other who we imagine is awaiting us in the future. Our life derives its continuing meaning to the extent that it can be fashioned as a creative gift to be surrendered to this imaginary other" (p. 34).

This is, it would seem, the way we ought to live—the way that, from the beginning, we're being called to live by the wondrous, awe-full alterities we're moved to love. These alterities are real, not imaginary. To the child, they signify—and perhaps still signify to us—normative order itself, the Good as such that calls us to and incites us to give ourselves to it.

But hidden within this wondrous, awe-inspiring gift-economy lies a horrifying possibility. What if one's gift of oneself is rejected? How is one then to live with oneself? The answer to this question is unequivocal—and devastating. One can't.

Expulsion

I've turned to rejection rather abruptly because that's how it occurs. Rejection happens out of the blue as a world-shattering rupture.

When Camille's antics prompt me to laugh in delight, she is, I'm happy to say, moved to join in. But there are different kinds of laughter, and not all are encouraging. I found it hard not to guffaw when, instead of crawling, our youngest daughter hopped across a room on her bottom. The same intelligent affect-ability that enables the young child to find more in music than audible sound enables her to hear in loud, boisterous laughter a portent of ridicule. How is such discernment possible? How is it that a child still lacking even the rudiments of language can tell one kind of laughter from another? Intelligent affectivity is, it seems, morally sensitive from very near the beginning. Even a hint of mockery can pierce. The cry that issues from this wound is also a response to a *not*. But it's not a *not* that signifies absence; it's a *not* that signifies expulsion from the bonds of human affection.

Rejection is a judgment that, in one way or another, disesteems and devalues (even when, as in a prospective employer's letter, it's carefully qualified and tempered by an expression of regret). Only the human other can make such a judgment because only she is able to imagine the Good, think the Good, speak of the Good, and so seem to *be* the Good itself (when one tells a lie, one is trying to take advantage of the fact that the power to speak with moral authority is inherent in the human voice). As a judgment, rejection involves an exercise of intelligence; but it's the affect discernible in the other's tone of voice, rather than the content of what she says, that enables the child to experience the full brunt of rejection. For it is feeling that speaks through intelligence to feeling and says not through words but through a tone of embittered impatience, "I'd rather you didn't exist."

One of the piercing, inescapable facts of human life is that we're entirely subject to and affect-able by the other's judgment long before we're capable of forming our own. Kant's (1993, p. 38) conception of us as morally autonomous doesn't take this into account because, unlike depth psychology, he didn't attend to our earliest experiences and the formative impact they have first on the depths of interiority and later on all our self-consciously intentional operations. Our earliest decisions are voluntary but not deliberate because deliberation, and hence moral response-ability, are not yet possible. Negative capability is the young child's only moral capacity: she can respond to moral order because she's affect-able by the voice the other gives it. This affect-ability is needful—but also impassioned. It's traumatized by absence—but never more so than by rejection and the shame that rejection engenders (Shabad, 2001, p. 73). To appreciate the profound reverberations of shame in the child, we have to remember that, unlike an adult, she can't consult her conscience to assess whether the condemnation she receives from others is deserved. For she doesn't yet have a conscience but only the original inklings of it that come from the voice of the other. For her, this is the voice of God.

Nothing in life is more traumatizing than hearing that voice expel me from community. Rejection doesn't mean only that Mother is leaving me. It means that Mother is turning away from me, as if from someone she can't abide. It's not just that she abandons me. She abandons me to my being my unlovable self. This is what I can't bear—to be expelled from her throe. She who gives the world to me, and me to the world, wants nothing to do with me. Without her gravity, I start drifting out into empty space. There's no air. I'm gulping to catch my breath and can't find it. I'm choking on myself and beginning to suffocate. In the yawning abysses of space, there's nowhere that's habitable. When Mother can't abide me, abiding is no longer possible.

Being rejected by an other who speaks for the world makes it impossible to live. I don't mean simply that the rejected child feels it's impossible to live. I mean that being rejected by the Mother really does make living impossible. For relationship with alterity is, for reasons argued above, constitutive of possibility as such. Here we can begin to appreciate why our normalized conception of recovery from trauma is so deeply problematic. We now customarily suppose that the labor of grief, however prolonged, will at some point bring one to accept loss and so enable one to "move past it." But one can't ever live with being unlovable. One can't get past it to a future that lies beyond it because it's precisely the future—the entire order of the possible—that is rejecting one. Insofar as it ends one's future, the experience of being identified with that-which-others-cannot-abide is analogous to the dreadful anticipation of the terminal *not*—the possibility that is the undoing of all possibilities. But we can and sometimes do live with the possibility of nothingness. In fact, doing so is, according to Heidegger (1962, p. 341), the condition for living our lives authentically. But contrary to what he claims (p. 294), death isn't the trauma that can't be surpassed; it isn't the trauma than which none greater can be conceived. The dreadful pales when compared to the horrifying because the horrifying jeopardizes sanity itself, as Heidegger had occasion to realize. Bearing the dreadful authenticates and dignifies one's humanity. Being identified with what-cannot-be-borne dissociates one from humanity.

We would, of course, prefer not to be exposed to the possibility of being judged unlovable. We'd prefer it if adults were incapable of so judging a child. But because we humans are not only conscious of the Good but drawn toward it by its impassioning effulgence, we can't not recoil in horror from what we judge to be violations of it—and from those who, because they've committed such violations, we judge to be responsible for the horrific. No small child can ever bear such responsibility because moral responsibility presupposes the capacity to make deliberate choices. But this fact doesn't protect them from our guffaws and embittered impatience, or from what are to them, and often to us, the inexplicable eruptions of anger that analysis might be able to trace back to our own experience of expulsion. As Freud helped us recognize, children are always already caught in the throe of our moral histories, are always already being traumatized by them, are always already evolving into participants in them. The question they'll have to face, as we've had to face it, is whether there's an alternative to repeating them.

Desire

The trauma of absence and the trauma of rejection can dovetail to form a single catastrophe for the child when the Mother upon whose presence she is totally dependent can't bear the sight of her. We can hope that such a catastrophe is rare. But whether it happens rarely or frequently, it is the universal terror that roils the psyche of the human child simply by virtue of the fact that the Mother on whom she relies to meet her needs is the one to whose judgment she's habitually exposed. From the moment that she's born, the child is vulnerable to and affect-able by an alterity from whom affirming sustenance and sustaining affirmation may—or may not—come. The child experiences in the very alterity of the Mother the traumatizing possibility of being abandoned and rejected. And because trauma is possible, every possibility has the potential to be traumatizing. This means that, for the child—and therefore for all of us, since we're always carrying our childhoods with us—time itself is inherently terrible, inherently charged with the power to devastate us. The future is always already rupturing the present, always already exposing us to the dreadful and the horrifying, always already introducing the *not* into our experience. Does there not arise in every child, hence in every one of us, a desire not to suffer this *not*?

From the viewpoint of classical psychoanalytic theory, the fact that I'm only now raising the topic of desire is an indication that I've failed to recognize its primordiality and hence am not in a position to appreciate what the psychoanalytic hermeneutic of suspicion has taught us about its protean character and the crucial, if subterranean, influence it has on the evolution of conscious intentionality. The pivotal psychoanalytic concepts, such as repression and sublimation, were developed to explain how the psyche succeeds or fails in working out a compromise between desire, with its pleasure principle, and the real world that inevitably fails to satisfy it. When Freud (1961) postulated a "life-instinct" and a "death-instinct," he went "beyond the pleasure principle" as the *urgrund* of the psyche. But he wasn't questioning the primordiality of desire; he was hypothesizing that it moves in opposite directions in an effort to achieve conflicting goals: in the one case, the evolutionary goal of unifying with the desired object; in the other, the devolutionary goal of regressing to inorganic existence. Freud speaks, of course, about our experience of felt need and about emotion (what I've called passion). But he understands both need and passion as modalities of desire. And desire isn't just the most primal and primordial of our motives. Equipped with the hermeneutic of suspicion, classical psychoanalysis aspired to show that all other motives are disguised, sublimated versions of it.

But if psychoanalytic theorizing is to be consistent, it can't simply assume the primacy of desire, or infer it from the reductionisms of normalized evolutionary theory. It has to submit desire itself to the hermeneutic of suspicion by tracking its genealogy and examining the purposes it serves. The arguments that I've laid out in the preceding pages lead me to believe that there are compelling reasons for undertaking such an examination. For they encourage us to hypothesize that desire arises as a response to the traumatizing *not*, and hence presupposes an experience that's more primordial than it—namely, the agon of an affect-ability traumatized by the possibility of abandonment and rejection. Whether this hypothesis can be a fruitful diagnostic and clinical heuristic can be determined only by practitioners. But we'll have a better sense of its plausibility if we examine phenomenologically just what it is that desire aims to do, and how it goes about trying to do it.

Let's begin by considering the kind of desire that's at play in what Freud called the "life-instinct." Such desire seeks union with the "object" desired, whatever this object might be. This desire for union with the desired is one common definition of "love," and desire/love supposedly gets charged with "eros" when it starts to become the focus of my affect-ability—when my being as a whole begins to center on it. Plato and many of his Christian heirs distinguished "carnal" eros from "heavenly" eros, and made conversion from one to the other the overarching purpose of human life. But it's important to recognize that the difference between these two kinds of desire is due only to the difference in the object desired, not to any difference in the character of the desire itself. In each case, desire seeks union, whether with God or something earthly.

Now as Plato recognized (1999, line 200a), we wouldn't seek union with the loved/desired object if we were already united with it. We seek only what we lack. It follows from this that desire presupposes a prior experience of the distance between, hence the difference between, the one desiring and the object desired. The *not* is constitutive of this distance, this difference: the desired object is not present, not here-with-me-now; it belongs to the future. It's not united with me but separate from and hence heterogeneous from me. If I am to achieve union with that which I desire, I have to bring it so close to myself that the distance between it and me—indeed, the between itself—is entirely effaced. If union is to be complete, the absent has to be made present; the other has to be absorbed into, assimilated into, the same. This means that desire aims at eliminating both the heterogeneity of the *not* and the *not* of heterogeneity.

This is, to use the existentialists' word, desire's "project." What makes this term relevant here is the fact that desire is self-assertive. It doesn't want to wait—and if it gets its way, it won't have to wait for the desired to come to it. It doesn't want to have to practice patience because doing so would make it the patient of alterity and the patient of the future. It doesn't want to suffer absence; it doesn't want to be subject to the *not*. When we gather all these preferences together, we're able to recognize that they're fingers of a hand that is clenched: desire doesn't want to practice negative capability. It wants to make the desired subject to it, and is liable to become enraged if the desired resists. Here, I confess, I can't help but think of my grandchildren's "tantrums." I'd be inclined to say they're paradigmatic examples of the temperament of desire, if they did not provide the mirror image of what I do on the golf course when the ball disobeys my instructions. Even when it's 70 years old, desire is still childish. It's not just that it always wants to get its way. It's always determined to get its way. It's active in a way that aims at eliminating the suffering inherent in negative capability.

But if our desire refuses to suffer negative capability, it presupposes that we've experienced it. And we don't have far to look to find this experience. Beginning in infancy, the child's dependence on the alterity of the Mother makes her affectivity vulnerable to a *not* that isn't just troubling but dreadful, *angst*-producing, traumatizing. And this same affectivity makes her vulnerable to what's more traumatizing than the dreadfulness of need: the horrifying possibility that Mother will prefer that she not exist. Every Mother is liable to be absent from her child and liable to impatiently, angrily, lash out at her. No Mother is good enough to make dreadful and horrifying possibilities impossible. But it's precisely the impossible that desire desires. It doesn't just want Mother to always be present; it wants to eliminate the possibility that she might be absent. It doesn't just want to avert rejection; it wants to eliminate the possibility of rejection. Put positively, it wants to entirely absorb the Mother into itself and the unprecedented future into the present. To recognize in this the Oedipal project, as Freud understood it, all we have to do is recognize in the *not* the stereotypical Father, the signifier of the reality principle that traumatizes the child's affect-ability. Desire desires to eliminate the father—the heterogeneity of the *not* and the *not* of heterogeneity—so that it can make Mother its own.

As Freud recognized, this is not only the primal desire. It's the prototype of all desire. Desire is protean insofar as it can pursue different objects; it can graduate from a popular toy to popularity itself, from car replicas to actual automobiles, even from things in this world to God. One can argue, as classical psychoanalysis did, that as desire is taught to sublimate, it pursues substitutes for the Mother who had to be renounced. But the pivotal insight is that, irrespective of how it is sublimated, or the substitutes on which it fixates, desire itself remains unaltered. Whatever I may happen to desire, my goal is to get it, gain possession of it, make it mine. Prior to achieving this objective, the desired object is not present and not mine. It's separated from me by the alterity of the *not* and the *not* of alterity. If I do achieve my objective, I've succeeded in eliminating both of these *nots*. The other is no longer absent because I've made it present; the other is no longer other because I've made it mine. However, getting what I want doesn't suffice. For time doesn't stop. The present is always already being ruptured by an unprecedented future that's irreducible to it. This prompts me to desire to keep what I've made mine—to avert the possibility of traumatizing loss that's inherent in possibility itself. Irrespective of what I desire, the kind of union with it that I seek can be achieved only by gaining control not only over it but over the future itself.

Once we recognize that the desire for union is an exercise in gaining control, we're in a position to appreciate the amphiboly inherent in it. Because desire fixates on an object, and can become addicted to it, we're inclined to suppose that this object is its principal or, as in addiction, its exclusive concern. But in the very act of seeking its object—its perceived good—it's subjecting this good to its project of gaining possession of and control over it. This has profound moral implications. For the good that centers normative order is categorical. One can't subordinate it to something other than it without violating it. But this is just what desire does, and does automatically, simply by virtue of the fact that it prioritizes possession of the good over the good itself.

It's precisely in this respect that desire differs most profoundly from both passion and need. The impassioned violinist enters the throe of the music and means to give herself entirely to it. Her relationship to it consists in her offering to it the donative response it evokes from her. Desire, on the other hand, is an exercise in domination. It reaches out toward the other not for the purpose of giving itself to the other but in order to seize hold of it. Need, for its part, is self-regarding in a way that passion isn't: the one in need views the other as that which she needs. But immanent in the intentional experience of meeting a need is the possibility of gratitude to alterity. The smile that the infant who has supped gives her Mother is a portent of this gratitude. Desire, on the other hand, wants to control alterity, and eliminate the possibility of losing what it has. It's therefore intent on overcoming the vulnerability and dependence on alterity that's constitutive of need.[8] Its desire to "unite" with alterity is, in fact, an aspiration to repress alterity.

But if Freud's insights in *Beyond the Pleasure Principle* were correct, this account of desire is not exhaustive. For there he hypothesized a kind of desire that differs fundamentally from the kind I've been describing—a "death-instinct" that's regressive rather than progressive, a desire that doesn't seek union with an object but wants to devolve back to an inorganic state. When we take into account the fact that desire is not primal but presupposes, and is a response to, a traumatizing experience that precedes it, this Freudian hypothesis becomes not only plausible but compelling. For whether it's the result of excruciating need or unbearable rejection, trauma makes the present unlivable. And because trauma is a lived experience of temporality, desire's response to it is temporally conditioned, and so can move in opposite directions. The modality of desire described above aims to eliminate the alterity of the *not* and the *not* of alterity; it's focused on the future because it aims to control it, reduce it to presence, and so make trauma impossible. But another alternative is available to desire. Instead of trying to fight the *not*, it can flee from it. Instead of trying to control the future, it can recoil from it. When it does so, it runs back toward the womb from which it was originally expelled—back to a place it imagines to be perfectly secure, perfectly insulated, perfectly protected, utterly invulnerable and impregnable. This too is an Oedipal desire. Desire can get the security, the protection, the impregnability that it seeks when it's recoiling from the trauma of birth only by enclosing itself in a womb so perfectly sealed that no alterity can possibly penetrate it.

Desire, then, can move in two diametrically opposed directions—toward union with, and control over, an object belonging to the future, or back into the past it imagines it has left behind. But the fact that both of these desires are Oedipal suggests that they are, finally, indistinguishable from each other. It's true that the "life-instinct" desires union with its object. But it can't achieve this union until it makes its possession of this object secure. And it can't make its possession secure unless it can find some place that's perfectly protected from the *not*, some place that makes the possibility of trauma and the trauma of possibility impossible. There is and can be no such place in the world, though we tirelessly try to find or make it. It exists only in our imaginations, as the imaginary womb of an imaginary Mother who saves us from trauma by not giving birth to us. The real womb is open. But we desire to return to it only in the hope of shutting it behind us. Freud was mistaken in attributing this desire to a "death-instinct" because it's the dreadful *not*, as well as the horrifying *not*, that we're trying to flee. But he wasn't mistaken in supposing that, if this desire were to succeed, we'd regress to an inorganic state. For inside the womb imagined by desire, we'd be entirely cut off from the future, entirely cut off from the play of possibility. There, the affect-ability constitutive of us would be unaffectable. This is the supreme object of desire. But one can achieve it only by becoming a corpse. The womb desire imagines doesn't belong to any Mother because the real Mother is, for each of us, the primal other. In giving birth to us, she placed us in the throe of possibility, the throe of the unprecedented, unpredictable future. The imaginary womb to which we desire to return isn't a womb at all but a coffin.

Ego

When my spouse and I leave our granddaughters and grandsons, we do so in a Camry. Unlike the 2017 Buick Enclave, it doesn't have heated and cooled power-adjustable front seats, a Bose 10 speaker system with navigation, power-folding outside rearview mirrors, ultrasonic rear parking assist and rearview camera, or tri-zone automatic climate control. But it does have cruise control, and that's enough to give me a sense of what driving in the Enclave would be like. Even the Enclave isn't as "cool" as James Bond's amphibious vehicle. But driving it would still be comparable to traveling inside the womb of the imagination. It seems we don't ever cease to be childish.

Shabad (2001, p. 236) suggests that the "traditional psychoanalytic ideal of mature adulthood" was "enclosed self-sufficiency"—what's commonly called "autonomy." Driving an Enclave provides us with an image of what "enclosed self-sufficiency" would be like but it is, of course, an illusion to suppose that any vehicle will provide it. The driver herself must be cool, unflappable, self-possessed—able to deal with, handle, manage any situation that may arise without losing her composure. We might be inclined to say that such composure and self-possession require that she have a strong, adaptable, resilient ego. But in putting it this way, we distinguish the person herself from the ego she has. What we mean to say is that if a person is to be self-possessed, the ego must be firmly established as the control center of the psyche—the operator of the vehicle. It's only by operating egologically, in the Levinasian sense, that she can negotiate the twists and turns of swerving temporality without careening off the road. The psyche as a whole has to be organized around the ego and ready to put its egological, apparently rational project of control into practice. Freud recognized in a way Levinas didn't that this configuration isn't immanent in intentionality. It has to be constructed by intentionality. And in the Freudian view, it has to be constructed from and by what is immanent in and constitutive of the psyche—namely, desire. Desire has to evolve; it has to learn to shift its cathexis from objects that reality refuses to let it have to those that reality permits it to get. Most importantly, it has to learn to be patient. But this patience has nothing to do with being a patient and practicing negative capability. On the contrary, it requires desire to renounce immediate gratification and work for gratification as a goal that lies in the future.

Desire balks at and stubbornly resists this requirement. It goes through "stages of grief," from denial to anger to bartering and even a kind of depression before it finally accepts that it has to abandon its preference for presence. But working for a goal is something that its self-assertive character makes it eminently qualified to do. All it needs is driver education. There will, of course, be potholes and flat tires. This is why desire has to learn how to deal with/cope with/manage interruptions so that they don't discombobulate, don't upset, don't render it impotent—so that they don't become ruptures. One must learn to master the *not* immanent in time and alterity so that one won't have to suffer it. It's true that, in undertaking the project of mastering the *not*, one is not only recognizing its reality but accepting the fact that it makes work unavoidable. But what's crucial is that one refuse to let it negate one's capabilities—refuse to let it reduce one to negative capability.

Now if it were true, as Freud thought, that desire is what's primal in the psyche, the ego, once constructed, would have no problem re-energizing itself since it would be able to continuously tap into primal desire. The psyche with the ego as its control center would be autonomous and "self-sufficient." But as the ego's project of control, which both sublimates and operationalizes it, makes clear, desire is repressive. This means that desire cannot be primal because repression presupposes what it represses. And what it represses is the traumatizing experiences of our primordial affect-ability. Freud would be quick to object that, if this were true, there'd be nothing to empower desire to practice the repression I'm attributing to it. But Freud himself has shown us the way to answer this objection. Repression, in his view, draws upon the energy it represses. Employing this Freudian insight, we can say that desire draws upon, hence depends on, the passion engendered in our primordial affect-ability. But if we put it this way, we're still implying that desire exists separately from passion, without explaining this separation. This defect can be remedied if we hypothesize that desire is the inversion of passion—that it's the recoil of passion from its very vulnerability. Camille's passion is donative. It's extroverted, self-exposing, self-expending; it carries her beyond herself toward the wondrous and awe-full alterities that draw her. Passion *as desire* does the opposite: it shrinks back from its very vulnerability. It's self-assertive, self-aggrandizing, for the purpose of self-protection and self-possession. If this hypothesis is correct, the primal tension in the psyche isn't between id and ego, pleasure principle and reality principle, life-instinct and death-instinct. For all of these, as Freud explains them, are variations on desire. The primal tension isn't between two separate powers of the psyche. It's the tension inherent in affect-ability itself by virtue of the fact that it can either entrust itself to its negative capabilities or try to master them. Because our affect-ability isn't localizable but impacts our being as a whole, our being as a whole can respond to our time in the world and the alterities in it in either of these ways. Intentionality can give itself to the throe of the future and the throe of the other through the exercise of its negative capabilities; *or* it can aspire to control the throe so as to avoid being the patient of it; *or* its intentions can be characterized by a profoundly ambivalent, profoundly conflicted conflation of these incompatible purposes. Who among us doesn't experience such ambivalence?

But if intentionality does aspire to master, if it operates as the control center of the psyche and carries out its operations in an egological manner for an egological purpose, we can predict that, if the hypothesis proposed here is correct, it will inevitably run dry. For we are, as I said at the beginning, incapable of producing any of our enthusiasms. We're incapable of causing ourselves to be impassioned. This incapacity is the fundamental impotence of the human heart. But it doesn't doom us to be care-less. For the heart that can't produce its enthusiasms is blessed with a negative capability: the capacity to be moved, affected, overwhelmed, devastated, by alterities that transcend it. I remember lying in my sick-bed as a child, riding a toy horse up the mountainous folds of a brown army blanket. I remember my father ushering me to an upper-deck seat at Forbes Field, where I experienced for the first time in the flesh the do-or-die drama of Pirates baseball. I remember staying up all night in a Milwaukee boarding room reading my first Dostoevsky novel. No one can know ahead of time what will draw her, summon her, because the summons comes from the dreadful, exhilarating—and potentially horrifying—play of possibility. The passion we spend on alterity is generated in us by alterity.

That is the rub, and it rubs all the way down. Once we're bent on control, we can't succeed unless we organize our psyche around the project of mastery. We can't organize our psyche around the project of mastery unless we repress the vulnerable affect-ability that is constitutive of our very being. If we do this well enough, we can staunch the flow of blood from our primal wounds—those inflicted by the absence of the one most needed and the word of excommunication coming from the mouth we took to be the mouth of God. Who among us doesn't desire to repress these wounds and the memory of them? But to repress them, we have to place a tourniquet on our affections; to make the repression succeed, we have to tighten the tourniquet until it renders our affect-ability inoperable. With such a tourniquet in place, we have no difficulty handling whatever happens to us. Nothing can upset or unsettle us, move us or affect us. For the core of us has been made into an enclave of impregnability and invulnerability. But this turns out not to be the utopia we imagined. The fundamental condition of a heart impervious to all affect is depression.

Psychoanalysis

Science, as Freud conceived of it, involves a "dispassionate," "disinterested" exercise of intelligence. And because the practitioner of psychoanalysis has to be acutely attentive to the various strands of transference and counter-transference if she is to employ them to the benefit of the patient and avoid becoming entangled in their affective complexities, it's long been considered essential that she maintain a certain kind of "detachment" and "professional distance" from the analysand. Here is another set of terms not unlike and not unrelated to those I've been discussing throughout this chapter. The assumption that "passion" and "interest" are synonymous is another revealing instance of the failure to distinguish passion as passion from passion as desire. Passion as passion is disinterested because, unlike passion as desire, it's not self-serving or self-assertive, but self-donative. Taking this difference into account enables us to recognize that *The Interpretation of Dreams*, far from being the product of a scientific mind dissociated from affect-ability, or an egological noesis intent on mastering its noema, is a paradigmatic example of impassioned intelligence giving itself to the throe of unprecedented truths. As understood and practiced by contemporary analysts such as Shabad, the clinical process involves an analogous kind of thoughtful generosity: it requires the analyst to offer the other an impassioned receptivity that welcomes the terrible, unbearable truths that she's borne unknowingly ever since being traumatized by them.

If desire were primal in the analysand, her deepest truth would be that she is and has always been, just like the rest of us, the enemy of civilization (Freud, 1964). For desire, as both Freud and Plato recognized, is tirelessly inventive and polymorphous in its perversity. Today, it's usually the psychoanalyst who gets closer to its monstrosity than anyone except the victims and perpetrators of the violence inherent in it. But every one of us has, at some time, in some way, been close enough to monstrosity to be both of these. We'd prefer not to know this—not to learn the truths hidden under the camouflage. But it's these very truths that the psychoanalyst invites us to give her. Because monstrosity is unbearable, her receptivity seems a human impossibility—and so it would be if each of us were, as the polymorphous perversity of desire leads us to suppose, monstrous at the core. In the heart of all our hearts, there'd be only darkness.

But, on occasion, what we think unimaginable, inconceivable, impossible happens. It doesn't happen because the analyst is able to make herself an impassioned listener to the darkest truth. It happens because there's more to the patient's resistances and compulsions than resistance and compulsion, more to her neuroses and monstrosities than neurosis and monstrosity, more to her desires than desire. Entangled with all these, suffering under all these, there's the inexhaustible patience of an unprecedented heart, an unprecedented affect-ability, an unprecedented self. This affect-able self, in her unfathomable singularity, isn't an enemy of civilization. She's a gift. It's this gift that engenders in the analyst her impassioned willingness to receive and unwrap it, session after session, month after month, year after year, until the patient realizes, in a way and at a time that can't possibly be planned, that all along she has been giving it.

The "of" in the title of this chapter is meant to be both an objective and subjective genitive. In it, I've tried to offer some philosophical reflections on passion and how psychoanalytic theorizing might be affected if its primordiality and difference from desire were recognized. I've been moved to do this by what I've tried to describe here at the end: the impassioned generosity of psychoanalysis itself. I've said desire acts as a tourniquet.

The passion of psychoanalysis is to remove it. It's tempting to finish by saying that it succeeds. But is that not exactly the wrong word? Success, as our culture understands it, is a product of work: what's achieved through the self-assertions of desire. What happens in psychoanalysis involves something very different from this: the play of a terrible, excruciating grace. But this grace is efficacious only because the analyst and the patient allow it to draw them out of the enclave they would otherwise inhabit and willingly entrust their vulnerabilities to its throe. The psychoanalytic process is a prototype of donativity. It models how we're meant to live.

Notes

1 I've previously addressed the issues I'll be discussing here in Miller (2014).
2 See, for example, Dennett (1995).
3 I'm adapting a phrase used by Lonergan (1992).
4 I explore this experience more fully than I'm able to do here in Miller (1992).
5 In arguing that this is the case, I'm disagreeing with Levinas's (1998) account of intentionality, according to which it is always trying to assimilate alterity. This would be true of wonder if, as is normally the case, it's identified with "the desire to know." Desire, I will be arguing, does aspire to assimilate the desired. But this is one very important reason why it's crucial to distinguish desire from passion. I'm suggesting that, primordially, wonder is impassioned. And inquiry, when impassioned, doesn't aspire to assimilate noema into noesis; it aspires to be true to—faithful to—the other as other.
6 Levinas opposes what he calls the ethical relationship with the other to both the assimilation of alterity and the fusion with alterity. I am arguing that there's an alternative to both of these: namely, impassioned, self-donative participation in alterity. Such participation is ethical in character but differs in crucial respects from the Levinasian concept of ethical relationship.
7 If one overlooks the negative capability of intelligence and its far-reaching implications, it becomes difficult, if not impossible, to disagree with the Levinasian claim that intelligence always aspires to assimilate alterity. See Levinas (1998, *passim*).
8 In *Totality and Infinity*, Levinas develops an egological interpretation of need which makes it indistinguishable from desire. This prevents him from recognizing that desire aspires to autonomy and hence seeks to eliminate need. See Levinas (1969, pp. 143–51).

References

Aristotle. (1940). Ethica nicomachea. In R. McKeon (Ed.), *The basic works of Aristotle* (pp. 935–1126). New York: Random House.
Dennett, D. (1995). *Darwin's dangerous idea: Evolution and the meanings of life.* New York: Simon & Schuster.

Freud, S. (1959). *Inhibitions, symptoms and anxiety.* (J. Strachey, Trans. & Ed.). New York: W.W. Norton & Company.

Freud, S. (1961). *Beyond the pleasure principle.* (J. Strachey, Trans. & Ed.). New York: W.W. Norton & Company.

Freud, S. (1964). *The future of an illusion.* (W. D. Robson-Scott, Trans., J. Strachey, Ed.). Garden City, NY: Anchor Books.

Heidegger, M. (1962). *Being and time.* (J. Macquarrie & E. Robinson, Trans.). New York: Harper & Row.

Heidegger, M. (1993). What is metaphysics? In D. F. Krell (Ed.), *Basic writings* (pp. 41–58). San Francisco, CA: HarperSanFrancisco.

Hyde, L. (1983). *The gift: Imagination and the erotic life of property.* New York: Vintage Books.

Kant, I. (1993). *Grounding for the metaphysics of morals.* (J. W. Ellington, Trans.). Indianapolis, IN: Hackett Publishing Company.

Keats, J. (1952). *The letters of John Keats.* (M. B. Forman, Ed.). New York: Oxford University Press.

Levinas, E. (1969). *Totality and infinity: An essay on exteriority.* (A. Lingis, Trans.). Pittsburgh, PA: Duquesne University Press.

Levinas, E. (1998). *Otherwise than being or beyond essence.* (A. Lingis, Trans.). Pittsburgh, PA: Duquesne University Press.

Lonergan, B. (1992). *Insight: A study of human understanding.* Toronto: University of Toronto Press.

Miller, J. (1992). *In the throe of wonder: Intimations of the sacred in a post-modern world.* Albany, NY: SUNY Press.

Miller, J. (2014). Desire, passion and the politics of culture. *The Montreal Review*, May Retrieved from www.themontrealreview.com/2009/Desire-Passion-and-the-Politics-of-Culture.php.

Plato. (1999). *The symposium.* (C. Gill, Trans.). New York: Penguin Books.

Sartre, J-P. (1970). The humanism of existentialism. In W. Baskin (Ed.), *Essays in existentialism* (pp. 31–62). New York: The Citadel Press.

Shabad, P. (2001). *Despair and the return of hope: Echoes of mourning in psychotherapy.* Northvale, NJ: Jason Aronson Inc.

Todorov, T. (1996). *Facing the extreme: Moral life in the concentration camps.* (A. Denner, Trans.). New York: Henry Holt & Company.

Chapter 6

Living in the shadows of the past

German memory, trauma, and legacies of perpetration[1]

Roger Frie

The bombing raids were always at night. The blackouts created a suffocating darkness that was broken only by tracers and spotlights that searched for the bombers flying high overhead. It was on one of these inky black nights, in late September 1943, that a bomb fell on my mother's house. The explosion left a huge crater in the ground. The destruction was massive. But because it was not an incendiary bomb, there was no fire. That was fortunate as my grandfather was in a so-called strong room in the cellar, on the opposite side of the house from where the bomb hit. Somehow he survived; the house did not.

My mother had spent the night in the local bomb shelter with her younger brother and my grandmother. When the three walked home early the next morning, they made their way carefully around a host of deep craters where bombs had fallen. When my mother reached the house, it looked normal, at least from the front. My grandfather met them on the street and took them around the back of the house, which was no longer there. Their relief at seeing my grandfather alive was tempered by the loss of all they knew and owned.

Growing up in Canada, I would sit comfortably in the safety of my family's house, listening to the stories my mother shared of her past. Each story seemed to culminate in a nightly sprint to the bomb shelter, my mother's small fingers trying to keep hold of my grandmother's sweaty hand. Her childhood took place in Hanover, Germany, in a time and place so different from my own as to be nearly incomprehensible. While I would never know these events directly, my mother's memories came to possess me. The anxiety I felt at a young age generated a host of images and sensations: the drone of the air raid sirens; the rumble of squadrons of bombers; the sound of bombs whirring down; the impact of multiple, successive explosions that made the dash to safety so difficult—all culminating in the bombing and destruction of my mother's home.

Bombs and bomb shelters play a prominent role in Germans' memory of World War II. My mother began to use the local bomb shelter soon after it was constructed in February 1942, the year the bombing raids on Hanover intensified. She was six years old at the time. The bomb shelter was designed as a so-called high-rise bunker and was built to house several hundred people. Three stories tall, with windowless concrete walls and a red tiled roof, it survives to this day, empty and locked up, a haunting reminder of the Nazi era.

Following the destruction of their house, my mother and her family spent the remainder of the war living in small rooms in nearby buildings that had remained intact. Visits to the bomb shelter increased with time. As the war progressed, my mother increasingly stayed in the shelter from one night to the next. My aunt was born in the spring of 1944 and lived in the bomb shelter for most of the first year of her life, separated from the chaos outside by concrete walls that were over a meter thick.

As a child, I created a mental image of the bomb shelter, a dark and frightening place, but also one of safety, with the potential to survive mortal threats. I was always relieved to know there was a place that had offered my mother protection. The bomb shelter held my attention. I even recreated a version of the shelter in the form of what I called my "fort" under the stairs. There were, of course, no bombs falling in the Canada of my childhood. The shelter I built was an echo of another time and a place to keep peril at bay. World War II casts a long shadow. It would be many years before I grasped the connection between my fort under the stairs and my inherited memories—inchoate sensations of the past that were handed down to me. From a young age, I had become an unwitting participant in a world of pain and sorrow, perpetration and slaughter that preceded me.

The topic of German wartime experience is controversial and difficult. German civilians endured many years of unrelenting bombings that led to widespread death and destruction. The fact that such experiences could result in trauma is hard to question. But how does one address the notion of suffering in a nation that perpetrated the Holocaust, orchestrating monstrous crimes against humanity? After the Holocaust, is it really possible to talk about "German trauma?" More importantly, when Germans focus on their own suffering, do they avoid talking about moral responsibility and the indescribable suffering their nation caused others?

The questions I am posing are not rhetorical. Talk of German wartime trauma quickly loses sight of the historical contexts in which it occurred. When this happens, intergenerational memory discourse in German families is transformed into a narrative of victimization. The kind of moral slippage I am describing creates narratives of the past that are shared in isolation of the horrors committed, keeping the Nazi past and the role of family members as perpetrators at bay. As a result, German suffering is remembered as a form of victimization on a par with the suffering that Germans inflicted on their victims.

The shadows of the past shape how memory is transferred from one generation to the next. The intergenerational transmission of memory in German families often includes unspoken experiences of the Nazi past, intergenerational secrets that make their presence known in silences that are transmitted between generations. The unspoken experiences of first-generation Germans who were participants in the Nazi past were passed down to their children and their grandchildren who covered them over with feelings of guilt and shame and maintained a community of silence. My grandparents selectively shared with my mother and her siblings the events of the Nazi era. My mother, in turn, told me about some aspects of the past, and I heard what my emotional understanding allowed me to. I dissociated those aspects of my family history that I found too painful or threatening to my identification with my grandparents. The intergenerational process I am describing suggests that we are burdened by traumatic histories. Using examples from my own family and my work with a former psychotherapy patient, I will suggest that for descendants of perpetrator groups, the emotional consequences of the transmission of memory should not be underestimated. As psychoanalytic scholar Stephen Frosh (2013, p. 44) points out: "What is left unresolved in history works its way into the present as a traumatic haunting that is profoundly social yet is lived out in the deepest recesses of individuals' lives."

Discourse of German suffering

I inherited memories of German wartime trauma and postwar hardship and suffering from both my parents. Whereas my mother lost her home in the war, my father lost his own father and many relatives. Both of my grandfathers were drafted into the German Army and fought in the service of Hitler's war machine. One survived the war, the other died in combat. My parents were both nine years old when the war ended. In the late 1950s, they chose to leave their difficult childhood and adolescent years in Germany behind and emigrated to Canada in search of a new beginning. As a result, I was born and grew up in a country that was at war with Germany and became a destination of hope for many Holocaust survivors. When I was 17 years old, my parents returned to Europe, first to Switzerland, where I lived for a time, and then to Germany. I was raised bilingually; crossing the historical and cultural divide between English and German became second nature to me, though it was not always easy. From a young age, I was confronted with the knowledge that my German family and its history were connected, however directly or indirectly, with the perpetration of the Holocaust. I learned about Germany's guilt and shame for the Holocaust from my parents when I was a young child. But what was not talked about was the fate of the Jewish neighbors who lived in the city in which my parents grew up. Nor did I know definitively whether my grandparents supported Hitler's heinous regime. The experience I am describing is typical of many postwar German families, in which the Nazi past is often shrouded in silence, creating a situation in which it is both known and unknown, spoken and unspoken (Schwab, 2010).

Saul Friedlaender (1993), a historian of the Holocaust and a child survivor, has noted that Germany's struggle with the Nazi era may actually stem from an inability to remember. What do Germans remember and what do they forget? At the level of collective public memory, Germany has done much to atone for its terrible crimes. There are few nations that live so closely with the painful reminders of their history in order to help them remember and act more humanely in the future. In contrast to many of its European neighbors, contemporary Germany provides a haven for refugees and its policies embody the democratic and tolerant outlook that has developed since the end of the war. German students tend to know more about the Holocaust than these of any other nation outside of Israel. But at the level of private family memory, knowledge of the Nazi past often remains gray and murky.

A study undertaken in the early 2000s by social psychologists Harald Welzer, Sabine Moller, and Caroline Tschuggnall (2002) showed that the vast majority of third-generation Germans like myself, the grandchildren of the first generation, actively decried the massive horrors of the Holocaust.

But at the same time, most of those questioned did not believe that their own grandparents had actively participated in or supported the Nazi regime. Clearly, the Holocaust remains a fulcrum on which the question of German memory turns. As Friedlaender (1993, p. 17) states,

> The extermination of the Jews is at the very core of the German struggles with memory: it was the ultimate in Nazi criminality and remains its fundamental expression . . . This theme, even when unmentioned, is never far from the surface.

What does it mean to live with the Nazi past? In many German families, the powerful but elusive wish for a history free from any Nazi association creates significant challenges to the process of remembering. How does a nation of former perpetrators acknowledge the enormity of its crimes? How does the collective responsibility to acknowledge the past exist side-by-side with the personal desire to be free from the past?

Since the turn of the millennium, a host of books have been published on the topic of German wartime experience, spurred on by a widespread belief that there has been a taboo on open discussion of German suffering since the war. The central focus of these works is the Allied bombing of German cities. The most provocative is undoubtedly Jörg Friedrich's *The Fire* (2006), which discusses the aerial war from the perspective of the citizens of towns and cities that were bombed. Friedrich's descriptions of death by incineration, asphyxiation, or melting asphalt that resulted from the widespread use of incendiary bombs are horrific to contemplate. The firestorms that followed the bombing of cities like Hamburg caused tremendous loss of life and a lifetime of traumatic memories for those who survived. Over 40,000 people died in the port city of Hamburg during "Operation Gomorrah," the code name given to several nights of bombing raids in July 1943. The utter destruction of Dresden in the fire bombings that occurred on February 13, 1945 has long been a rallying cry for those Germans who feel their victimhood has been overlooked.

During the course of the war, some 380,000 Germans were killed in the bombings, a high percentage of whom were elderly, women, and children (Overy 1980, 2014). While there can be no question of the human toll or the sheer destruction caused by the bombings, my concern is with how the bombings are remembered. In Friedrich's description of the air war, it is German civilians who are terrorized. He thereby creates, whether purposefully or not, a direct comparison with the Holocaust. In the process, Friedrich gives voice to a longstanding belief on the part of many Germans that the aerial bombardment constitutes an unacknowledged "Holocaust" in its own right, unleashed against them by the Allies.

Friedrich's book supports the view that nation states behave much like individuals: they identify their own pain and suffering before they recognize the suffering they have inflicted on others. It is surely easier to focus on the deaths of German civilians than to think about the six million murdered European Jews, of whom over one million were children; it is easier to see the bombing as a catastrophe that has befallen the innocent than it is to explain the path that led to the destruction of German cities. The popularity of Friedrich's book can be explained by the fact that German memories of suffering are usually associated with strong affect—what is commonly known as felt memories (Welzer, 2005). Conversely, knowledge of the Holocaust is commonly based on a learned, cognitive awareness. This divide makes it easier for many postwar Germans to connect with the suffering of family members than to see these same relatives as perpetrators and bystanders; it also reinforces the separation of German suffering from moral questions of guilt and responsibility.

The recent shift in Germany's public memory discourse to the question of suffering gives voice to private narratives that have existed since the end of the war. Indeed, at the local level, Germans have always talked about their own suffering. In her 1950 essay, "The Aftermath of Nazi Rule: Report from Germany," the German-Jewish philosopher, Hannah Arendt, provides a glimpse into the thinking of everyday Germans in the immediate postwar years. It was first time Arendt had been back to Germany since escaping in 1933 and she describes the paradoxical interaction of German indifference and suffering that she encounters there:

> Indifference, and the irritation that comes when indifference is challenged, can be tested on many levels. The most obvious experiment is to state what the other fellow has noticed from the beginning of the conversation, namely, that you are a Jew. This is usually followed by a little embarrassed pause; and then comes – not a personal question, such as "Where did you go after you left Germany?"; no sign of sympathy, such as "What happened to your family?" – but a deluge of stories about how Germans have suffered (true enough, of course, but beside the point); and if the object of this little experiment

> happens to be educated and intelligent, he will proceed to draw up a balance between German suffering and the suffering of others, the implication being that one side cancels the other and we may well proceed to a more promising topic of conversation.
>
> (Arendt, 1950, pp. 342–343)

Despite the passage of time, the dynamic Arendt describes in relation to German suffering is familiar to me. My knowledge of German history was first and foremost a felt awareness that I received from my parents. They were both born in Germany in 1935 and lived out their childhoods during the period of National Socialism and World War II. Both experienced significant loss and trauma as children. Whereas my mother has always talked about her history, my father has largely been silent about this time in his life. I visited Germany often as a child to see my grandparents and I came to assume the war was a natural topic of conversation among family members. There was a tacking to and fro between the past and the present. Stories were shared about the past week and then conversation morphed into stories from long ago, of suffering and struggle. In the context of these family gatherings, my grandparents would engage in telling familiar stories of hardship. The continual retelling became a kind of ritual that would shape how events were portrayed and understood, structuring what was said and what remained unsaid. My parents, aunts and uncles, all the members of the second generation, would generally listen in silence or share versions of these same stories. The third generation, of which I am a member, thus became the bearers of inherited memories and family narratives.

The focus on German suffering meant that the suffering of the victims was pushed aside, if not altogether excluded. Only very seldom and then quite suddenly would the horrors of the time break through. There was little talk of guilt and responsibility. No mention of my grandparents' support for a regime whose intent on genocide was surely clear for anyone who wished to see it. There were no questions asked about the disappearance of Jewish neighbors or of the historical forces that led to the bombings. There was only talk of hardship. It was generally accepted that everyone had suffered, regardless of background. Terrible things had happened and suffering was the result. Mine was not the only family to experience bombings and talk about its own suffering to the exclusion of guilt and responsibility. It was commonplace; perpetrators and victims had, in effect, become equal in their suffering. While the official discourse of postwar Germany may have frowned on such talk, it took place in private conversations, spurred on by a deep-seated feeling of victimization.

The city of Hanover

As a child, I remember standing in Hanover's "new city hall" staring transfixed at a set of giant models of the city. I was a curious young boy, a visitor from afar, yet strangely linked to what I beheld in front of me. The two models showed, in great detail, different versions of Hanover: one as the city appeared in 1939 before the start of the war, and the second in 1945 at the end of the war. The models of the city were large-scale replicas, remarkable in their level of architectural detail. The first model showed a city with its medieval center intact and the grand avenues and plazas that surrounded it; the other showed a city in utter ruin. The damage was severe. In the center, over 90 percent of the structures had been destroyed. It was very much like looking at a before and after photograph, the architectural rendering adding a further dimension that made a strong impression on its viewers. The designers of the models dared viewers to imagine what it was like to live through bombings that had reduced an entire city to rubble.

My fascination with the models of Hanover was inherently connected to my family history. The models provided me with a visual sense of the overwhelming destruction my parents lived through. Looking at the models was akin to seeing a photograph of an event that one has heard of but never before seen. A photograph can provide a new and more tangible perspective. The physical destruction of the city was shown in forbidding detail. But like any photograph, the model of the ruined city was also inherently limited. Despite its lifelike features and accuracy, the model of Hanover in 1939 showed no Nazi flags, no Nazi insignias on major buildings, no adults or children in Nazi uniforms. Nor was there any indication of the once thriving and very old Jewish area of the city. The model did not tell its viewers of the terror that persecuted Jewish neighbors endured as they hid in fear for their lives, or that Hanover's industries relied on forced labor from seven sub-concentration camps and hundreds of forced labor camps located in and around the city center. In fact, the destruction of Hanover's Jewish community did not result from the Allied bombing campaign but from the National Socialist policies carried out willingly by the citizens of Hanover before and during the war. These were the same citizens of

Hanover who lived through the terrible destruction portrayed in the model of their ruined city. No amount of falling bombs, physical damage, or emotional trauma in the midst of war would change the legislated policy of extermination. While my mother and family sought shelter from the falling bombs, Hanover's Jewish citizens had nowhere to flee. In the midst of the Allied bombing raids, the Nazis intent on annihilating the city's Jewish population continued unabated. As the German-Jewish journalist Ralph Giordano, who survived the Holocaust in hiding in Germany, has observed: "The end of the Third Reich was at hand, everything was falling down about them, yet Eichmann's deportation machinery was still running" (2003, p. 166).

When the Nazis came to power, Hanover had one of the ten largest Jewish communities in Germany. It was a vibrant community that dated back to the thirteenth century.[2] The Nazi regime's anti-Semitic policies were evident soon after its election in March 1933. The first deportations occurred directly after the *Kristallnacht* pogrom of November 9, 1938, when the central synagogue was destroyed and German-Jewish businesses and homes were ransacked. Those who could, fled the country. By 1941, any chance of leaving had been shut down and the first major deportation of approximately half the remaining Jewish population took place. They were sent to the ghetto in Riga and of this number very few would survive. Seven more deportations to Theresienstadt, the Warsaw ghetto, and Auschwitz would take place before the end of the war. In early 1945, the only remaining Jewish citizens, those who were married to non-Jewish Germans, were deported and by war's end all who had not already emigrated or escaped had been murdered.

Hanover's Jewish community has grown significantly since the end of the war. Yet, few of its original members survived, and each death involves a tragic family history. One such history belongs to the Israeli psychoanalyst Yecheskiel Cohen, who left Germany for Palestine in 1938. He lived with his family in the town of Bernburg, where his parents ran a department store. When Cohen was six years old, his father was imprisoned for a period of eight weeks after refusing to sell the business to the Nazi authorities for a fraction of what it was worth. During his father's imprisonment, his mother gave up the business and the family managed to buy their way out of Germany. Cohen's parents had visited Palestine in 1933 with the knowledge that they might one day have to emigrate, though they hoped to remain in Germany. Looking back, Cohen has only a single memory of the day his family were forced to leave Germany: it is of his father, breaking down in tears at the Bernburg train station. It remains a singularly painful recollection to this day.

I met Cohen through my work on German memory and the Holocaust. When Cohen learned of my family's history in Hanover, he revealed that his own mother was a member of Hanover's Jewish community. In his first letter to me, he wrote:

> Dear Roger, I want you to know that we share something very crucial: my mother was born and raised in Hanover! And here a sad story: my mother had 4 siblings. One emigrated to the U.S. in the thirties after Hitler came to power. One came to Israel (which was then still Palestine) and their mother (my grandmother) went after him. But, she felt that the circumstances here are so different and so difficult that she returned [to Hanover]. She claimed that nothing will happen to her as she lost one son (my mother's other brother) in World War I and received a special medal for his sacrifice ... but you may imagine what the reality was – she was sent to Theresienstadt and died there.
>
> (personal communication, 2013)

The deportation of Cohen's grandmother and, indeed, the murder of Hanover's entire Jewish community occurred in the same cultural context and in the same geographical location as the childhood experiences of my parents.

After Cohen's parents moved to Palestine, they were able to maintain a small measure of contact with family members who had remained in Germany. These included his grandmother on his mother's side and his grandfather on his father's side. They corresponded through the Red Cross and Cohen remembers that each letter was limited to 25 words. He has shared three of these letters. In the first, his grandfather responded to a letter from Cohen's parents in Palestine: "Very happy about news. Am healthy. The longing for you, big. Warmest congratulations on your birthday." He then adds, referring to other family members: "Willi, Eugen, Julchin, no news." In the second letter, his grandfather states: "Willi, Eugen, Julchin gone away." And in the final letter, he states only: "I am going away." Cohen's grandfather was leaving for Theresienstadt where, like Cohen's grandmother, and like Willi, Eugen and Julchin, all were murdered.

Felt memories

When I was a child, my felt sense of the suffering of my family loomed large. Looking back, it was perhaps easier for me to imagine what my family went through than to imagine the indescribable pain and suffering endured by Nazi Germany's victims. This was obviously a form of emotional dissociation, generated by the social context in which I grew up and my fear of relinquishing the idealized image I had of the grandparents I loved; I could not bear to accept and acknowledge that the entire generation to which my grandparents belonged was responsible for the horrors of the Holocaust (Kohut, 2012). My parents' own shame and struggle to share and discuss what unfolded when they were children meant that the silence with which they had grown up also became a part of my own childhood. How do you make sense of the fact that your parents, or indeed your grandparents, are capable of morally intolerable beliefs and indefensible actions?

In order to fill the gaps in my family history and move beyond my family's own felt sense of the past, I read widely about the experience of Germany's victims and the civilian use of German bomb shelters during World War II. The racist ideology of the Nazi regime was entrenched in every aspect of Germany's civilian life. Entry into the local bomb shelter and indeed into all shelters throughout Germany was forbidden to Jews. I eventually found some local history books that shed light on the experience of the individuals who used the same bomb shelter as my mother. In one of these books, I encountered an account of a family that seemed vaguely familiar. I had to read it numerous times before I realized that the names on the page belonged to my own family members. It was the story of my grandmother and aunt who was born late in the war. The words themselves are unambiguous:

> The Andresen family is living in the city hall and is awaiting the birth of a new child. The house of the Andresen family was the first in Vinnhorst to be bombed . . . On the night of April 10, 1944 a girl is brought into the world with the help of a midwife. The birth takes place in a room in the city hall . . . The air raid siren sounds and everything must be packed up in order to reach the bomb shelter. The newly born infant is put in a carrier as the first bombs fall. Halfway to the bomb shelter cover is sought in a ditch beside the road. The mother

> and infant reach the bomb shelter unscathed, where they remain for the next nine days, resulting in a widespread rumor that the child was born in the bomb shelter. . . . The Americans enter into the northern part of Hanover on April 10, 1945, the child's first birthday. The father carries the little girl on his arm as the Americans march into Vinnhorst. She doesn't need to go into the bomb shelter any longer.
>
> (Meyer & Klingebiel, 1996, p. 15, my translation)

I assume this account was recorded by a local historian, but exactly where and when is a mystery. I asked my mother and aunt but it is as much a surprise to them as it is to me. The image of my grandmother in a ditch with my newly born aunt, only a few hours old, as bombers fly overhead dropping their payload, is now seared in my mind. As I reflect on the words on the page, I realize I have heard some version of the story before. My mother once described to me how she entered the bomb shelter on the night of April 9, 1945. It was the eve of my aunt's first birthday and the day before the Americans arrived. Bombs were already falling and the earth was shaking from the many explosions as she ran with my grandfather to the shelter. The next day, when the entire family emerged from the shelter, they saw the dead bodies of Hitler Youth who had made a suicidal attempt to stop the American advance. These are the kind of haunting images that refuse to be stilled. Despite my attempt to keep stories like this at bay, the fears and anxieties I feel are little diminished by time.

The wartime traumas experienced by Germans are neither fictitious nor inconsequential. But, as I have suggested, the focus on suffering in the absence of sustained reflection on moral guilt and responsibility for the Holocaust constitutes a grievous injustice against the victims and their families. As a child, it was clearly easier for me to imagine a bomb shelter than a concentration camp (Frie, 2014). Whereas one structure was meant to save lives, the other was designed to carry out a policy of genocide. Both were the creations of the Nazi regime. The bomb shelter did not belong to my everyday life, yet it was, in a way, just as real as the world in which I lived, thousands of miles away. By contrast, when I first visited the concentration camp of Bergen-Belsen outside of Hanover, I experienced a palpable sense of "unreality" as I sought to grasp what I saw and the horror I felt in the face of the atrocities that had taken place. The powerful emotional reactions that followed—my sense of deep sadness, anger, and revulsion at what had been done—pushed aside my inherited family memories.

After this knowledge, how do I understand the experiences of my family? How can they exist side-by-side with the responsibility I have to remember and acknowledge the crimes committed by my grandparents' generation? The meaning I accord my inherited memories of the bomb shelter will vary according to the perspective I take about the past. From the perspective of German wartime experience, the bomb shelter becomes the site of suffering endured in the aerial bombing raids. From the perspective of the horrors unleashed by the Nazi regime, the bomb shelter stands as an unmarked symbol of the complicity of an entire people in genocide and war. It is all too easy to conflate these two views. This leads to the misleading if not spurious account of history that the German-Jewish philosopher Theodor Adorno (1986) had in mind when he criticized German attempts "to come to terms with the past," a kind of facile remembering that is really an act of forgetting.

The reality of the bomb shelter and my received memories of it exist within an irreducible historical and moral context that must inform how I respond to the past and live in the present. Over time, the potential safety I first associated with the bomb shelter as a child has been transformed into a sense of foreboding. Its physical presence, in contrast to my childhood image of it, represents a historical reality full of terrors that can no longer be explained away or dissociated. The bomb shelter makes the past—the childhood of my parents and the crimes of the generation of my grandparents—a lived reality for me. It is a reminder of what transpired. I am unable to see or imagine the bomb shelter today without asking the question of "How could this possibly have happened?" Yet, as with so much German history, people walk by the structure on a daily basis without reflecting on its multiple meanings. Indeed, how does one live with a surfeit of memories that are so fraught with meaning? Our powers of dissociation are strong, motivated by the need to distance ourselves from shameful histories of perpetration.

Shadows of perpetration

The histories of perpetrator nations often remain unassimilated, casting long shadows into the present. Postwar Germany has sought to openly account for its genocidal actions, which surely rank amongst the worst atrocities ever committed. Whatever the problems confronting Germany's memory culture, it stands in contrast to those countries that refuse to acknowledge the catastrophes they imposed on their own or on other people. My aim has not been to enter into a critical discussion of Germany's official policy of remembrance but to point to the tensions at work between public and private memory. I have suggested that German family histories often remain unspoken and unknown (Frie, 2017; Welzer, Moeller, & Tschuggnall, 2002). As a result, inherited guilt and shame about what took place in Nazi Germany is juxtaposed with a silence that shrouds the actual beliefs and actions of family members in the Third Reich. The dynamic I am describing is not unique to Germany. It can be observed in many nations that perpetrated acts of mass violence.

What remains unsaid in the gaps and silences of the past that are handed down from one generation to another? I once worked with a psychotherapy patient who had grown up in one of the U.S. states that belonged to the Confederacy. She was a married, white professional from an established upper-middle-class family with a long history in that state. She grew up in an urban setting, but throughout her childhood she often visited her grandparents and extended family members who lived in a bucolic, rural setting and resided in a large house on what had once been a tobacco farm. My patient described exploring the former farm and its many buildings, most of which had fallen into ruin as a result of disuse. She was especially fascinated with small, dilapidated shacks that dotted the property, remnants of another time and place. No one seemed to know what the shacks had been used for.

My patient entered into psychotherapy because she was struggling with the emotional distance that had emerged between herself and her parents. The strain was evident in almost every aspect of their relationship, and was made especially poignant by my patient's choice of career as a youth worker with inner-city, predominantly African-American children. Her parents had expected my patient to follow in the family's footsteps and carry the mantle of privilege with which she has been raised. My patient, in turn, seemed to disappoint them every step of the way. Eventually, she stopped visiting her parents altogether, unable to withstand their deep disapproval. Yet, throughout our work together, she continued to visit her relatives on the old family farm where she always received a warm welcome. In contrast to her parents' home, it was a place full of tender memories and a respite from her demanding work.

As the psychotherapeutic relationship developed, I came to realize that at least in one key respect my patient and I shared life experiences.

Although we grew up in vastly different places, each with distinct cultures, we were connected by inherited histories of perpetration that remained unspoken, if not unknown. It was not until my patient engaged the youth in a civil rights project that she connected the dots. She realized that the shacks that no one spoke about, and which had been a source of childhood fascination, were once the homes of slaves, and then of indentured share-croppers. My patient was confronted with the recognition that this criminal past was irrefutably connected to her family. The privilege and wealth that her family took for granted was built on a foundation of slave labor, a history that had been silenced through the passage of time. The fields that had fallen into disuse were once full of slaves. It was a dark history that no one acknowledged or thought to question. But, as my patient learned, it was there for all who wished to see.

How do we make sense of this kind of "not-knowing" in the face of obvious historical evidence? My patient was a socially motivated and politically aware individual, concerned about the welfare of her fellow citizens. However, when it came to her own family history, there was a powerful dissociation at work. This emotional distancing was buttressed by the lack of any oral history beyond the experiences of her immediate family members. There were no spoken references to the culture of slavery and racist ideology that enabled a group of immensely wealthy white individuals, including her forefathers, to wield absolute and terrible power over the lives of others.

My patient was no longer able to deny a history she had long questioned but been afraid to articulate. Looking back, she recognized that she had inherited a longstanding sense of guilt and shame but never fully understood its source. Her physical discomforts and bouts of anxiety, perhaps even her choice of career, now took on added meaning. The shadow of slavery in the history she was bequeathed could no longer be avoided. The work of remembrance that followed was difficult and painful, marked by anger, grief, and an overwhelming sadness. Lingering in the background was the question of whether my patient might have known about this dark history all along. Did she fear what "knowing" about the past might mean for her relationships with family members who seemed unwilling to talk about it? Was the shame my patient felt so overwhelming as to remain silent? The struggles of my patient were familiar to me, given my own quest to understand my German family history (Frie, 2012, 2017).

The legacy of unassimilated perpetrator histories has been described by Erna Paris (2000) in her powerful study *Long Shadows: Truth, Lies, and*

History. Paris explores the theme of collective memory and how nation states respond to their shameful mistreatment of others and murderous actions. In the course of writing her book, Paris travelled to Germany, France, Japan, the United States, South Africa, and the nation states that emerged out of the former Yugoslavia. When she was researching the collective memory of slavery in the United States, Paris visited an opulent plantation home in South Carolina. What she encountered there illustrates the extent to which the effects of slavery and racism continue to be denied. As Paris describes it:

> The tour guide is circumspect about slaves. When obliged to mention their existence as the obvious backbone of this lavish world, he carefully describes them as "servants" and calls the shacks where they lived at the back of the big house as "dependencies." We pass by the old slave market without hearing a word about its origin except to learn that there are bargains to be found in the shops there. It's the same old story: There's an elephant in the salon, but we're too polite to notice.
>
> (Paris, 2000, pp. 195–196)

While so much has changed since the time of the Antebellum, racism continues to be a central aspect of contemporary American society. What does it mean to live in a society in which racial prejudice is not only widespread but also tolerated? And how might the views and actions of our own family histories come into play? While my patient and I were both confronted with the reality of the perpetrator histories we inherited, it can be hard for members of the normative, white majority to recognize the need for change, particularly if they are not directly affected by institutional racism. Indeed, the very notion of apologizing for past wrongs is anathema to many. Individuals may be willing to apologize for their own actions, but the idea that the society to which they belong should apologize for its history is often treated as nonsensical. Thus, whereas some nations actively seek to atone for their past crimes, others remain steadfast in their belief that no wrong was committed or that any wrongs were the work of a previous generation, implying that current generations have no responsibility to remember.

Remembering is an integrative process that requires us to recognize the longstanding effects of historical trauma into the present and to feel our way into the experience of the victims. Acknowledging the reality of past crimes—be they individual or collective—is not easy to do, especially if our own families are implicated. But understanding the role that these traumas continue to play—be it emotionally, socially, or politically—is an initial step toward recognizing the historical effects of racism and prejudice. I have suggested that there are ambivalences at work in the process of remembering that are not easily resolved. I may associate with my family's pain and suffering in the Allied bombing raids in World War II, but this does not excuse me from seeking to understand the feelings of another person or the meaning and implications of the crimes that were committed against that person and his or her community. As the German psychotherapist Barbara Heimannsberg (1993, p. 169) suggests, "a part of successful work of remembering is also repeating and the experience of overcoming ambivalent conflicts over and over again." In order to remember the past and fashion our lives in the present, we need to appreciate our emotional relationship to history. Only then, I believe, can we truly engage in the social and political realities in which we participate.

Notes

1 This chapter draws on material from the author's new book (Frie, 2017).
2 For information on German-Jewish history in Hanover, including the period of the Third Reich and the Holocaust, see: www.jewishvirtuallibrary.org/jsource/judaica/ejud_0002_0008_0_08378.html.

References

Adorno, T. (1986). What does coming to terms with the past mean? In G. Hartman (Ed.), *Bitburg in moral and political perspective* (pp. 114–129). T. Bahti and G. Hartman (Trans.). Bloomington, IN: Indiana University Press. (Originally published in 1959.)

Arendt, H. (1950). The aftermath of Nazi rule: Report from Germany. *Commentary*, *10*, 342–353.

Frie, R. (2012). Memory and responsibility: Navigating identity and shame in the German-Jewish experience. *Psychoanalytic Psychology*, *29*, 206–225.

Frie, R. (2014). From memorials to bomb shelters: Navigating the emotional landscape of German memory. *Psychoanalytic Inquiry*, *34*, 649–662.

Frie, R. (2017). *Not in my family: German memory and responsibility after the Holocaust*. New York: Oxford University Press.

Friedlaender, S. (1993). *Memory, history, and the extermination of the Jews of Europe*. Bloomington, IN: Indiana University Press.

Friedrich, J. (2006). The fire: The bombing of Germany, 1940–1945. A. Brown (Trans.). New York: Columbia University Press. (Originally published in 2002 as *Der Brand: Deutschland im Bombenkrieg, 1940–1945*, Munich: Propyläen Verlag.)

Frosh, S. (2013). *Hauntings: Psychoanalysis and ghostly transmissions*. London: Palgrave Macmillan.

Giordano, R. (2003). Ein Volk von Opfern? [A nation of victims?]. In L. Kattenacker (Ed.), *Ein Volk von Opfern? Die neue Debatte um den Bombenkrieg 1940–45* [*A nation of victims? The new debate about the air war, 1940–45*] (pp. 166–168). Berlin: Rowohlt.

Heimannsberg, B. (1993). The work of remembering: A psychodynamic view of the Nazi past as it exists in German today (C. O. Harris & G. Wheeler, Trans.). In B. Heimannsberg & C. J. Schmidt (Eds.), *The collective silence: German identity and the legacy of shame* (pp. 163–170). San Francisco, CA: Jossey-Bass.

Kohut, T. A. (2012). *A German generation: An experiential history of the twentieth century*. New Haven, CT: Yale University Press.

Meyer, H. & Klingebiel, J. (1996). Bunker in Vinnhorst. [Bombshelter in Vinnhorst]. In C. Grund (Ed.), *Vinnhorst: Ein Stadtteil verändert sein Gesicht* [*Vinnhorst: A city municipality changes its face*] (pp. 13–17). Hannover: Arbeitskreis Stadtteilgeschichte Vinnhorst.

Overy, R. (1980). *The air war, 1939–1945.* Washington, DC: Potomac Books.

Overy, R. (2014). *The bombers and the bombed: Allied air war over Europe, 1940–1945*. New York: Viking Press.

Paris, E. (2000). *Long shadows: Truth, lies and history*. Toronto: Vintage.

Schwab, G. (2010). *Haunting legacies: Violent histories and transgenerational trauma*. New York: Columbia University Press.

Welzer, H. (2005). *Grandpa wasn't a Nazi: The Holocaust in Germany family remembrance*. New York: American Jewish Committee.

Welzer, H., Moller, S., & Tschuggnall, K. (2002). *"Opa war kein Nazi": Nationalsozialismus und Holocaust im Familiengedaechtnis* [*"Grandpa wasn't a Nazi": National Socialism and the Holocaust in the collective memory of the family*]. Frankfurt am Main: Fischer.

Chapter 7

Haunting and historicity

Jerome Veith

Introduction

When Lauret Savoy, in her recent book *Trace* (2015), describes her travels across the U.S. in search of her ancestors and their stories, she is piecing together hidden facets not only of her own biography, but of a broader collective narrative. Yet, while the end result certainly reads like a significant uncovering, it is not immediately clear wherein the disclosure lies. Savoy's project does not amount to groundbreaking historiographical research; nor does her treatment of literal sedimentation—she is a geologist by training—deliver the moral impact. In most instances, as she herself underscores, what she discovers or recounts is already well documented and archived (such as the number and role of slaves on an antebellum South Carolina plantation). If that is the case, then why does her account seem to touch a nerve? Why does it seem as if one is bearing witness to some significant discovery?

It is because, despite those facts being available somewhere, the failure until now to give them appropriate recognition represents, as Sue Campbell (2014) might put it, a "moral, epistemological, and emotional distortion" (p. 26). The lives that these facts trace when connected have remained outside of our country's overt and nostalgic narrative of self-reliance and liberty. In this instance, the culturally enforced silence around the intricate legacy of slavery has kept many Americans' experience from being formulated, shared, understood, and integrated into a collective identity. Layers of internalized oppression have kept it from even being sought. When it is finally formulated, it can thus be doubly chilling: first, in light of the very texture of the atrocities that are recounted; second, for the recognition of this experience having remained silent for so long. Both of these together reverberate as reminders of how intensively the past can haunt us. It is haunting in both its retrieved presence and in its often irretrievable absence. After one such disclosure, the possible hauntings of history seem inexhaustible.

Articulations like Savoy's do not fit neatly into any existing disciplinary practice or genre of writing. *Trace* is neither a memoir nor a social study. Despite their overt intention and ability to disrupt a nostalgic narrative, Savoy's "traces" do not seem likely to induce institutional change or broad cultural reflection. Nevertheless, this contribution is deeply necessary. Yet, because this necessity is so difficult to articulate, since silences and their traces are so liminal, so difficult to grapple with on any level (be it individual, dialogical, communal, or cross-cultural), and because we often simply do not know how pervasive they really are, it is worth wondering what we can do with, or how we can relate to, this sort of historical haunting. How should communities, institutions, or families deal with their unclaimed experiences? By what means should we bring to light and commemorate silent aspects of the past? From a psychological standpoint, how can one conceptualize haunting in the therapeutic encounter?

To address these questions obliquely, one of the essential preliminary steps is to articulate conceptually what is captured in the experience of history's haunting—which, put less artfully, names the way that experiences of extremity reverberate throughout human memory and identity, whether they are overtly recollected or not. I argue that a proper grasp of haunting demands a reconceptualization of human memory and temporality, that the concepts for this revision are available to us in philosophical hermeneutics, and that the current cross-disciplinary "memory crisis" demands a turn to precisely these concepts. To help substantiate this conceptual direction, I will subsequently draw on two works of literature that exemplify, in my view, both the experience of haunting and our possible responses to it: W. G. Sebald's *Austerlitz* (2001) and Toni Morrison's *Beloved* (1987). These works will return us to the question of how we engage with haunting, where I think a parallel between collective history and personal trauma is instructive. Just as there is a drive to be witnessed and an "impossibility of telling" for one who has suffered personal catastrophe (Laub, 1992, p. 79), so one may find that, on a collective level, historical haunting demands to be recognized, but also necessitates coming to terms with its irretrievability or inexhaustible ambivalence.

Haunting and the memory crisis

What is captured in the experience of haunting is, at least in part, an overflowing of the typical memory-categories of linear temporal ordering and spatial (especially mental) localization. The haunting past is perceived to be present in a way that does not adhere to the usual static pastness-register of established facts, archived material, or settled narratives. Nor does it seem confined to (or by) coherent internal structures of self-identity. In this exceeding of containment, haunting disrupts what we have typically taken memory to mean and be capable of. It is no exaggeration, then, to say that haunting constitutes the rupture of a certain conception of time and memory.

In this way, the experience of historical haunting mirrors a burgeoning recognition, across many fields of inquiry, of the elusiveness of memory as a concept. This parallel is no coincidence. The memory crisis had its beginnings, in fact, in attempts "to explore forms and manifestations of Holocaust memory, consequences of trauma, and the distorted remembrance (and forgetting) of historical events that in some fundamental ways contradicted the traditional notion of memory" (Brockmeier, 2010, pp. 9–10). Thus, one might say that the experience of haunting, once recognized and reflected upon, uncovers a philosophical impasse at the heart of any discipline or activity dealing with memory. In what follows, I will not elaborate in detail how the experience of historical haunting contributed causally to the present *aporia* concerning the nature of memory (for this, see e.g. Terdiman, 1993 and Brockmeier, 2015). What will hopefully become clear, however, is that the memory crisis demands precisely the sort of clarification, and leads in the same conceptual direction, as attempts to make sense of historical haunting.

The memory crisis is, in brief terms, an increasing dissolution not only of "the idea of memory as storage, an archive of the past", but also of memory as a delineable system, a localized mental process, a "more or less unitary individual capacity" (Brockmeier, 2010, p. 7, p. 8). Considered as a paradigm shift, the new model emphasizes memory's trans-individual distribution across social fabrics, its co-constructed rather than representational nature, and its embeddedness within practices, spaces, and artifacts. Some of the main fields experiencing and contributing to this conceptual shift are the social and human sciences, media and technology studies, neurobiology and neurocognition, and the arts (especially literature).

Brockmeier (2010) has already given a detailed account of each of these fields, so I will merely provide an overview here, indicating how these various directions of inquiry both discover and engage with the perplexity of memory. In the final section below, I will address the ways in which the field of psychoanalysis takes up some repercussions of the memory crisis.

In the fields of social and human sciences, there is now a widespread recognition that engagement with the past does not constitute a relationship with a static and given object, but is instead an ongoing process of constructive re-presentation (Erll, 2008, p. 7). This insight leads directly to questions about the shape that this process is to take at any present moment. It reveals that memory is a task not just of accumulated and diversified documentation, but of carrying the past forward according to constantly re-negotiated standards and needs. The sheer dimension of atrocities in the twentieth century, for instance, has demanded not only that attention be directed back to initially overlooked details and narratives, but also that memory take the form of witnessing, of remembering the memory of others (this process is often also called "postmemory"; Hirsch, 1997). Shifting from memory as a static entity to remembering as a process thereby also leads to the recognition of the role that power and privilege play in remembrance and forgetting. Who remembers, and by what means, become equally decisive concerns as the question of what is remembered. The social and human sciences are thus deeply interested in scrutinizing the various ways that memory is delimited and performed, and advocating on behalf of silenced, ignored, or repressed pasts.

Media and technologies have long been implicated in discussions of how and what people remember. From the wax tablet to the hard drive, the technologies of capture and storage have tended to generate the very material basis of memory, and to become stand-in metaphors and conceptual frameworks for the larger process of memory itself. In the twentieth century, the camera and the solitary digital processor predominantly held this role. Now, the multimedial digital network is quickly becoming the guiding framework not just of how people interact socially in the present, but also of how they remember. The fact of a network's distributedness, exemplified in the notion of the "cloud," challenges the distinctions between personal and collective, public and private. It "changes traditional conventions for autobiographical remembering, undermining, among others, any idea of memory as a predominantly cerebral property of a human being" (Brockmeier, 2010, p. 15). Further, since the distributed network is not ordered according to any predefined categories or standards, it disrupts the traditional delineations of archival memory: it blends facts, impressions, narratives, and imaginative constructions. It thereby mirrors and exemplifies the concept of human memory as an ongoing and non-linear process. Finally, the engagement with memory through a global digital network may paradoxically draw attention to the very spatial and social configuration of artifacts, sites, and contexts that an archive model of memory, through its reliance on representation and (mental) storage, failed to notice. In this way, the multimedial network may be especially attuned to tracing the history of sites and artifacts, giving voice to previously silenced groups, and finding gaps and exclusions in narratives.

Literature stands out among the arts as a practice that, over the course of human history, has both generated the narrative works by which we remember cultures, events, and identities, and that has also thematized and scrutinized the very intricacies of remembering as an intrinsically human activity. In this reflexive capacity, it has contributed directly to the memory crisis by revealing the mutual interdependence of remembering and narrative identity-construction, thereby pointing to the inherent fluidity of the subject and toppling the notion of an archival consciousness that is fully present to itself. This also gives literature its exceptional capacity to reveal historical haunting, which I will return to in the treatment of *Austerlitz* and *Beloved* below.

Of the fields mentioned here, the broad conglomerate field of neuroscience has been the most resistant to the paradigm shift in memory, still clinging in much of its conceptual framework to archival notions of encoding, storage, and retrieval. Nevertheless, there are developments even in this field that point to deep reassessments of the traditional memory model. One basic yet crucial finding is that there is "no biological correlate that allows us to distinguish between what we traditionally call acts of remembering the past from acts of perceiving the present" (Brockmeier, 2010, p. 20). From this, it is only a short step to realize that a person's accumulated experience cannot be stored neurologically, and might not be said to accumulate at all. Instead, one might need to speak of neural events being cognitively organized in various temporal registers, but this in turn points to narrative meaning-construction and socially distributed models of memory, as the registers in question would not appear to have any strictly biological existence. From a neuroscientific perspective, then, the most that can be said is that "memory is structurally like perception, a generative event occurring in the present" (Brockmeier, 2010, p. 25). This connects powerfully with the findings from other fields, and seems to entail that, if we are to locate haunting as an aspect of memory, we must treat it as happening now, not as a completed occurrence in the past.

If we take these developments seriously, we encounter a need across a broad range of human inquiry to reconceptualize what we mean by memory. But we should also note that this revision of concepts, however drastic, does not just entail a changing of theoretical models. It also demands a shift in how we concretely engage with or live out the past, and a reflection on what we value in our memory practices. Thus, it is as much a matter of social, cultural, and ethical considerations as it is one of theoretical investigation.

As Campbell (2014) has pointed out, thinking merely in terms of competing theoretical frameworks can have confusing consequences, as the very terminology of a paradigm shift can lead to undesired commitments (p. 19). Like Brockmeier, she points to many of the recent attempts in psychology and neuroscience to replace the archival, representational model of memory with a reconstructive one. However, since so much of the current research on the reconstructive model underscores memory's subjective character and its distortive possibilities (Campbell mainly targets Elizabeth Loftus and Daniel Schacter in her text), it seems to lead many adherents of the new paradigm to treat all instances of biographical subjectivity ("story truth," in Loftus' words) with deep suspicion (cited in Campbell, 2014, p. 22). Yet, to account for this suspicion, those proponents of reconstructive memory who stress its subjectively distortive tendency have to rely on standards (such as reproductive accuracy) that are derived from the very storage model of memory that they purportedly reject.

Campbell (2014) thus notes that much of recent science, while offering valuable insights, does not actually articulate a complete new paradigm of memory, and she advocates that we "give up proposing the archival and the reconstructive as competing models of memory processes" (pp. 22–23). In her view, there are more subtle ways of undertaking the revision of memory concepts that recognize the significance of our subjective situatedness without sacrificing the dimensions of truth and faithfulness—what Campbell (2014) refers to as "good remembering" (p. 20). Those latter aspects, after all, are crucial to what we value about remembering, and that valuation plays an important balancing role over against the seeming relativizing entailments of the new paradigm. Just because memory is reconstructive, in other words, does not mean we give up our desire to remember well—whatever that might mean.

To explore this meaning, and to grasp the subtler approach that Campbell advocates, it bears considering that a sheer factual memory "does not prevent recollection from being distorted or inaccurate in a sense having precisely to do with its selectivity or appropriate significance," as in the case of nostalgia (Campbell, 2014, p. 26). The standard of objective or intersubjective accuracy is thus not enough to assure good remembering. One could think of the situations that Savoy encounters over and over, in which someone may technically be remembering correctly, but omitting much that is uncomfortable, unformulated, or unclaimed.

Whether someone explicitly relies on storage models of memory is therefore not the point. The idea or metaphor of an archive is, as such, not the culprit. It is in the motivated abuse of representational objectivity as a "moral, epistemological, and emotional distortion" of memory that one can recognize a threat to good remembering, and a major source of haunting. In these very distortions, one also sees how haunting demands an ethical response (Campbell, 2014, p. 26). By calling our attention to such occlusions and silences, haunting insists that we *can* remember more (or differently), that we *ought* to remember more (or differently), and that we ought to do so for the sake of an *other* (alive or dead). Without directly naming haunting as such, Campbell (2014) vaguely describes what such an ethical response might entail: "To remember the past faithfully is to properly capture its significance to the present and future" (p. 25).

From truth and reconciliation commissions to interactive memorials, recent decades have been rife with attempts to describe and undertake precisely such faithful recollections. Following Campbell's skepticism of the paradigm-shift terminology, I would argue that it is more than just the sedimentation of a theoretical framework that hinders those efforts. While it is indeed important to grasp the bare conceptual underpinnings of the experience of haunting (which I will attempt to describe in the next section), the broader ethical hurdle might be something like a failure of imagination. If one cannot imagine how silent aspects of the past can continue to have an effect, then one will not be receptive to them. If one cannot envision remembering differently, if one is motivated to sustain a sedimented narrative against all possible revisions, then a commission report or new museum will probably not have an effect. Put differently, if one cannot hear haunting as making an ethical demand, then a mere change in memory models is not likely to develop one's ability to listen. It will be worth wondering, when we engage with the two novels below, whether literature is capable of prodding or cultivating the sort of imagination necessary to hear haunting.

Just as there is no simple, model-based solution to the memory crisis, there is no outright method that would guarantee an adequate response to historical haunting. At the very least, however, it is clear that both the crisis and the experience of haunting demand a reconceptualization of human temporality. Put less theoretically, there is an ethical demand to look at and listen to the past differently. This would constitute a change in practice rooted in changes in concepts and imagination. Luckily, we do not have to undertake these changes from scratch. Heidegger recognized aspects of the memory crisis almost a century ago, articulating aspects of temporality that Gadamer took up and extended. One might even say that these thinkers (among many others) induced and abetted the present extremity of conceptual rupture. In turning mainly to Gadamer's hermeneutics in the next section, I will elucidate features of human historicity that guide us through the crisis to a comprehension of historical haunting. Turning to *Austerlitz* and *Beloved* in the subsequent section will reveal ways that literary imaginings can exemplify what it means to hear the haunting of the past, and thereby hone our ethical responsivity.

Haunting and hermeneutics

As we have seen, historical haunting challenges notions not just of archival memory, but of time, subjectivity, meaning, and narrative. It also reorients the very practice of remembering, challenging standards of representational accuracy and factuality. In some of their most fundamental gestures, the fields of phenomenology and hermeneutics recognize and address these very challenges. One of phenomenology's most powerful insights concerns the enacted nature of consciousness—even to the point that the term "consciousness" may be considered too reifying. Rather than treating our minds as static containers for representations of the world, we are to grasp ourselves as making meaning with and through our contexts. Early in his career, Heidegger posed himself the task of making sedimented phenomena and ideas "fluid" through a radical re-conception not only of what phenomena as such might be, but of our very being as meaning-makers

(Veith, 2015, pp. 46–53). Articulating our inextricable "hermeneutic situation" throughout the 1920s (Heidegger, 2009, pp. 38–61), Heidegger attempted in various ways to name and describe this enacted character of our own being, always insisting on its event-like nature. The fundamental insight of *Being and Time* is thus that being (in particular our being as humans) should be considered temporalizing. If we can be said to exist, then it is as lived, "worlding" processes rather than as objects alongside the other things of the world.

Gadamer's hermeneutics inherits and extends this basic point of Heidegger's phenomenology, taking the latter's notion of Dasein's "thrown projection" as a universal lens for human understanding (Heidegger, 1962, p. 265). If we are processes of inextricable involvement with the world, then, according to Gadamer, in order to grasp (and perhaps improve) our meaning-making, there are two equiprimordial features of our being that deserve special attention and clarification: our linguisticality and our historicity. The former stresses our entwinement in discourse and dialogue, emphasizing that truth is provisional, intersubjective, and always an occurrence rather than a product. The latter involves recognizing our situatedness in history. This means not only that we are constant heirs to past meanings that are not our own, but that we continually enact and reinterpret those pasts as well.

Gadamer insists that both of these dimensions of our being have the character of a response. In the case of our linguisticality, this may be more straightforwardly comprehensible. To say that "language is reply" (Gadamer, 1995, p. 123) means, foremost, that our communication never occurs *ex nihilo*: it is always drawing from, contributing to, or in some relation with the utterance of an other. It is inexhaustible, in the sense that there is always something more to reply to. Yet, response, if it is a character of our being, is also not something that could ever be finalized or complete. There is thus no final word, no ultimate conclusive articulation, and no definitive account. There is always more to say. We are inextricably, incompletely, and inexhaustibly linguistic; hence Gadamer's penchant for citing Hölderlin's line "we are a conversation" (Gadamer, 2001, p. 39).

If one tries to translate this to the historical, however, the characterization becomes far less obvious. What would inextricable, incomplete, and inexhaustible responsivity mean with regard to our historicity? Where is the "always more" in our relation to time? With regard to the future, this makes some immediate sense, but what about with regard to the past?

Answering these questions will, perhaps, get us closer to grasping how we are susceptible to haunting and how we might respond to it.

If historicity means that we are inextricably situated in history, we should make sure that this does not evoke the wrong image. Gadamer does not mean that we are contained within a stable narrative arc or fixed entity that could be totalized as "history." Nor, conversely, does he think that history is an endless, unintelligible medium in which we are—by some unhappy coincidence—submerged. Instead, our historical situatedness entails an involvement or intertwining. To have historicity means to be historical—to be of the same stuff as history. This entails some sort of equation of ourselves as fluid with a history that is fluid—or at the very least at an "interplay" between the two (Gadamer, 2000, p. xxv). That the two are not truly separate—that historicity is a unitary phenomenon or structure—is captured in Gadamer's reference to "one great horizon" that encompasses all individual horizons (Gadamer, 2000, p. 304). To elaborate on this unity, it is necessary to grasp two features of horizons that run in seemingly opposite temporal directions. One might also, like Gadamer, employ the metaphor of "inner" and "outer" for these aspects.

Common to both of these aspects is the general notion of horizon, which—whether linguistically or historically—involves our peculiar perspectives, prejudices, and experiences that make up our respective subjective standpoints. There are certainly tendencies and textures to these unique horizons, but as limits they are continually shifting as we move about in the world, revise our conceptions, or find ourselves surprised by new experiences. The outer direction of horizons is the easiest to grasp, and is often equated with horizons as such (it is often, in fact, the only direction that readers of Gadamer notice). From this angle, our temporal limits are incomplete: they are continually revisable in a future-directed openness, always leaving the possibility of learning more, phrasing things differently, or arriving at a new understanding with an other. When Gadamer speaks of the "infinity of the dialogue" (Gadamer, 2000, p. xxxiv), he may mean precisely this incompleteness and ongoing revisability of horizons: there is always more to say in response. Translated firmly into historicity, this would correspond to a recognition that narratives are always incomplete, that we will always need to tell them from the standpoint of the present, and that we will thus never be finished encountering the world and applying ourselves to every new situation.

If this were the only direction to horizonal limits, we could be taken to have a firm starting point from which we engage, and a possibility of using that point of departure to arrive at increasing clarity about the world and others. Our horizons would be incomplete, but not inexhaustible; deferred, but not haunted. However, just as this one-sidedness does not capture the character of our linguisticality (there is always more to hear as well as to say), it is ultimately an untenable interpretation of historicity. There is also an inward trajectory to horizons, having an inexhaustibility that Gadamer calls "inner infinity" (Gadamer, 1976, p. 68). This latter is far more difficult to grasp, and is often overlooked in treatments of Gadamer's hermeneutics, perhaps because it is initially so puzzling (cf. Risser, 2002 for an excellent clarification; cf. also Veith, 2015, pp. 109–115). If the outer direction of horizons indicates an incompleteness with a futural inflection, then the inner direction insinuates that there is always more to what has been.

This direction would include all that is overtly accessible to historical consciousness, but also that which we take over from the past unawares, both in the silent dimensions of our own biographies and in the furthest hidden reaches of our cultural contexts. It would not be limited to what is, even just hypothetically, accessible. Inexhaustibility of the inner horizon would also—or even especially—involve the present silences of the past that cannot be given a voice (Caputo, 2004). If the outer horizonal direction is a limit that is open to encounter with the new or unexpected, and therefore not surveyable in its ultimate reach, then the inner direction, equally unfathomable, appears to possess an alterity that would always impede full transparency and self-possession in the present. It may well be that this alterity is what haunts.

With this opacity at the core of historicity—which amounts to an ungrounding of subjectivity—Gadamer is giving a crucial inflection to what might otherwise risk becoming a project of Hegelian consumption. If it were merely a matter of moving forward into an infinite dialogue, one could conceive of this as an independent subject's process of inevitable growth that begins with their own projects and claims (this is the charge leveled by Caputo, 1987, pp. 108–115 and Caputo, 2000, p. 55). By insisting on the inner infinity of historicity, Gadamer underscores that the hermeneutic subject does not begin with its own delimited identity or resolved narrative. We do not begin from a known situation only to eventually encounter what is strange or perplexing. Instead, through the opacity of our situation, we are forced to acknowledge that the subject has no point of inception, no circumscribable past, but exists rather from the outset in a position of receptivity and response. Our thrownness, just as our projection, is horizonal or perspectival.

Further, since the range of the inner horizon is just as far-reaching as the outer one—their infinity expresses precisely their inexhaustibility—it would be delusional to expect an eventual grounding of one's starting-point through an exhaustive inventory of one's (personal or cultural) inheritance. Always being in response means never fully comprehending the strange background to the familiar into which one is thrown; it thus entails never arriving at full self-understanding. While we nevertheless pursue such understanding, it never amounts to a pure or total retrieval. It is always a historically situated retrieval, inflected with the meanings and expectations of the present enactment. Just as one's outer horizon is mobile and flexible, so too with the inner horizon: one can always understand one's having-been differently. Though one might be tempted to reify the past as the totality of that which has been, it will always exceed that delimitation. That excess is another name for the haunting that pervades our experience of the past. It exists within and contributes to one's present horizon.

These hermeneutic contributions resemble or help to pave many of the inroads to the memory crisis, and help us to grasp just what makes the experience of haunting possible. As underscoring the opacity and responsivity that is already at the core of our being, Gadamer's concepts also help to convey the mode in which haunting afflicts us and seems to demand a reply. I have shown elsewhere (Veith, 2015) that Gadamer considers this reply an "ethical task" (p. 11) of engaging the past in the present, and that the historical human sciences are central to that endeavor (pp. 145–161). In the remaining sections, I wish to explore some concrete literary practices and psychotherapeutic stances that exemplify this ethical task, and make the engagement with historical haunting explicit. A common theme that arises here is that of witnessing.

Literary witnessing

W. G. Sebald's *Austerlitz* and Toni Morrison's *Beloved* are novels that exemplify historical haunting. As works of literature, they can certainly take metaphorical liberty with the experience, and include literal hauntings through seemingly supernatural devices: both texts prominently feature ghosts as well as unlikely coincidences and transformations. Yet, more significantly, the books also feature figurative or stylistic disturbances—what Wolfgang Iser (1978) refers to as textual "negations" (pp. 221–222)—that not only portray haunting within the narrative, but directly evoke an experience of it on the part of the reader. In doing so, both texts urge their readers to consider what it would mean to respond to the respective historical hauntings being thematized: in the case of *Austerlitz*, the Holocaust; in *Beloved*, slavery in the United States.

Of the concepts considered in this chapter thus far, *Austerlitz* most directly captures the opacity that Gadamer points to in our historicity. The book's overt story is a recounting of the eponymous protagonist's gradual yet incomplete uncovering of a hidden identity he has carried with him since childhood: growing up in Wales, he had been unaware of being a Czech refugee rescued from the Continent in 1939. It is only through several devastating memory breakthroughs in the 1990s that he recalls his childhood in Prague and his flight by rail across Europe. As helpful as archives and museums are to his subsequent search, he is never able to definitively trace his parents' ultimate fates or the mechanism by which he had sealed off his past.

Despite having plumbed obscure psychological depths and retrieved parts of himself, then, Austerlitz is brought to mournfully recognize "the vanished past of his family and his people which, as he knows, can never be brought up from those depths again" (Sebald, 2001, p. 297). This irretrievability complicates the mourning, for it doubles the sense of loss, leaving forever unclear what exactly is being mourned. Yet, the abyssal vanished past makes up an essential part of who Austerlitz is; he, too, will therefore always be incomplete.

Having seen the way in which Austerlitz's past afflicts him—along with his breakthroughs, he suffers several breakdowns—we as readers can sense the force with which this abyss of irretrievability must haunt him. What is more, since we have accompanied him sporadically through his process of discovery, hearing of new developments through his encounters with the anonymous narrator, we have undergone an analogous development from ignorance and puzzlement to pursuit, (re)collection, and frustration. The closure that is missing for Austerlitz remains absent for us as well. The reader becomes a recognizing witness to Austerlitz's affliction.

However, we are also at least twice removed from Austerlitz's personal journey, and this adds another form of negation and opacity. After all, we hear of the entire story through the narrator's layers of reported speech, making the actual events of the book seem hazily distant and even more irretrievable. We are, at best, witnesses to a witness, occupying a space of postmemory in which any notion of intervention, direct response, or repair is out of the question. Sebald solidifies this distance with a slow and lapidary prose style that is distinctly "not of this time" (Silverblatt, 2007, p. 78).

Sebald admits that all of these opacities and obstructions in the text serve to circle around an "invisible referent," the "silent presence" of the Holocaust (Silverblatt, 2007, p. 79). One major reason for this indirect mode of thematization is Sebald's recognition that direct confrontations with the horror of the Holocaust rarely result in "discursive thinking" or the honing of our "moral capacity" (Silverblatt, 2007, p. 80). He thus wants to challenge the notion that the sheer and blunt documentation of atrocities is the means by which one best responds to the past and approaches its silences. Memorialization and archival memory are useful, but their form of mourning rarely addresses the abyss of the irretrievable or the haunting that remains even when all available facts are gathered. Yet, the gauzy texture of the novel also echoes a more personal experience of Sebald's, namely the "conspiracy of silence" (Wachtel, 2007, p. 44) that pervaded Germany for decades after World War II, and which has remained pervasive until very recently (Frie, 2014; Bilger, 2016).

Sebald imaginatively draws our attention to hauntings in our cultural history, but "seems to say in and through his work that we must take haunting personally" (Diedrich, 2007, p. 274). This entails considering the place of opacity not just in the life of a fictional character, but in the lives of other victims and in our own as well. In having us bear witness, even if only indirectly, to Austerlitz's painful but necessary process of incomplete recollection and self-discovery, Sebald underscores the importance of carrying memory onward even if it is just an ongoing reminder of irretrievability. Since, as we have seen with Gadamer, memory is an incomplete process even when such drastic abyssal opacities are not an issue, we can see that the witnessing Sebald has in mind is an endless task. He may thus be highlighting, in Kelly Oliver's words, the notion that "witnessing is at the heart of subjectivity" (cited in Diedrich, 2007, p. 260): to fully be ourselves, to stand in the best possible relation to the past, is to recognize and continually respond to historical haunting—to the silent voices of others who could not even demand to be heard.

If *Austerlitz* exemplifies the witnessing of a haunting irretrievability, then Toni Morrison's *Beloved* invokes the possible recovery from historical haunting—or at least a healing engagement with it. Here, the eponymous character is herself a ghost who haunts her mother. Sethe, an escaped slave, had murdered her infant daughter in desperation, rather than allow her to be stolen into slavery. Instead of defending her infanticide through any outward explanation—an impossible rationalization that would have merely confirmed Sethe's enslavement within a logic of human economy—she maintains her humanity by repressing the overwhelming trauma of her act and living an isolated but relatively stable existence. Yet, the catastrophic murder, through Beloved's spectral return and increasingly concrete presence, nevertheless demands a response. Sethe is gradually brought to face her pain and shame and eventually finds the ability to live with her past through a ritual of "clearing."

Sethe's past can be read as symbolizing the traumatic collective past of the African-American community, so her individual engagement with the past parallels the processing that might occur on a broader cultural level. Since memory is lived spatially and intersubjectively (Morrison, 1987, p. 43), Sethe's experiences of unendurable suffering are not just hers in isolation, nor are they annulled with the abolition of slavery; they form a collective inheritance "that lives right here where we live" (Krumholz, 1992, p. 395) and that, like Sethe, we must somehow learn to face (or else allow to haunt us in unconscious ways).

Morrison's novel underscores that this learning does not proceed in a demonstrative fashion; it is not about factual memorialization or methodology, but about continually and personally revisiting something that is barely articulable. Yet, even if one cannot speak objectively or definitively about the pain of the past, one can still engage with it. The book outlines this engagement as being akin to ritual healing, in which indefinite voices form a communal backdrop to personal pain and assure that suffering, however indescribable, is heard and held (Krumholz, 1992, p. 403). Our possible response to, and recovery from, historical haunting might also demand such an oblique approach of witnessing. At a minimal level, this would be a reframing of response away from the passive dissociation of trauma—through standardized narratives of the dominant white culture, for example—to an active opening up of memory to further recovery.

Beloved ends by noting the impossibility of simply handing down a narrative (Morrison, 1987, p. 324). On the one hand, it thus contests precisely the sort of textbook narrative of slavery that insists on closure and diminishes its victims to the level of passive object-lessons. On the other hand, it serves to remind us that the story itself is incomplete; it cannot be passed on because there is no possibility of closure regarding historical atrocities like slavery. Just as the haunting Beloved, who represents the "spiteful, beautiful, painful past," merely recedes from overt presence at the end of the novel, so she "will live on to haunt us" (Krumholz, 1992, p. 401). We will therefore continue to be haunted by slavery; it is solely up to us how we respond to that haunting.

The narrative arts seem uniquely poised to portray historical haunting and imaginatively cultivate the capacity to face it. They can circumscribe it, invoke it, and suggest ways of engaging with it, all without having to explain it or even name it as such. In fact, it may be that, by approaching it so obliquely, by bringing the reader to encounter the opaque, the irretrievable, and the inexpressible, literature can first get us to acknowledge the presence of historical haunting in the first place. We are so accustomed to the ideal of objective and exhaustive archival memory that it may not occur to us to consider incompleteness, opacity, or silence as intrinsic aspects of our historicity, let alone as dimensions that we can experience and bear witness to. Thus, through works such as Sebald's and Morrison's, it may be that in witnessing someone else struggle with historical haunting, we become better able to recognize and respond to it in others or ourselves.

Therapeutic witnessing

In discussing these literary works, it is tempting to resort to psychological themes and concepts such as trauma, the unconscious, repression, denial, and dissociation to explain the effect of haunting and how the characters respond to it. This can be a fruitful endeavor, and has led to some convincing interpretations (Osborne, 2013, pp. 127–157; Krumholz, 1992). It is also an intriguing approach in general to make sense of historical haunting by way of psychological phenomena. Yet, one must be careful not to treat the psychological concepts employed here as a static explanatory framework. Haunting is not simply equatable with the classical concept of the unconscious, for instance. After all, a concept such as this is itself being reassessed in light of philosophical impasses like the memory crisis. It is just as fruitful, then, to wonder how psychoanalysis, broadly construed, can perform its own conceptual reassessment by way of engaging the phenomenon of haunting, and how it might accomplish this in a way that meets the ethical obligation of remembering well.

A major theme pervading the response to these questions is the recognition that historicity in general, and haunting in particular, is an embedded aspect of the world. Along these lines, we might begin by recalling that *Austerlitz* and *Beloved* do more than metaphorically portray haunting; in making it into a concrete experience for their protagonists, they capture an essential aspect of all memory, namely that it exists "out there, in the world." To cash this out psychoanalytically, it might help to return to the philosophical point, already noted above, that memory is not solely individual and mental; it is distributed and culturally sedimented, and it lurks in present practices, places, and relationships. It is more akin to a decentralized network than an internal, localized possession.

Transposing Gadamer's notion of horizons to the therapeutic setting, Philip Cushman (2009, pp. 134–135) notes that being situated together with another brings everything of their world along with them. To adopt the therapeutic stance is therefore not to engage in empathy, an interiorization that brackets the outside world and attempts to enter the client's mental space by remaining apolitical, ahistorical, and acultural. Rather, therapy always involves—at least implicitly—acknowledging our cultural and historical encumbrances. Cushman (2009) insists that "[w]hat hermeneutics supplies is exactly what empathy cannot: a good beginning, a purposefully historical, contextual, relational self in a non-Cartesian world" (p. 135).

Taking this stance in therapy is a way to make a "good beginning"—that is, a hermeneutically appropriate one—because instead of assuming a fully self-possessed initiation from either person, it attends to what is already there in both the client's and the therapist's ongoing historicities (and linguisticalities), while also recognizing that much of what is there is not possessed in full awareness. For something to be part of the client's world, it need not be explicitly formulated or named. To use Gadamer's terms, the opacity of inner infinity is intrinsically part of the encounter; it is present in the form of cultural inheritances, unreflected assumptions, faded memories, and the like. While no analysis could ever exhaust these, it can certainly bring them to one's attention.

A familiar way of describing this would be to speak of the unconscious meanings in the therapeutic encounter. In light of the hermeneutic dimensions just described, however, the concept of the unconscious has to undergo a radical inflection. It has to be revised from something hidden mentally within the person to something in a shared world, and with a less reified mode of existence. Donnel Stern (1997) has undertaken precisely this revision, reframing and externalizing the notion of the unconscious to reflect the dimension of "unformulated experience" that exists as part of the client's world (pp. 33–49). Rather than conceiving of the unconscious as "fully formulated thoughts simply waiting to be discovered, ready for exposition" (Stern, 1997, p. 36), Stern treats it as something very similar to the horizon that Gadamer described under the heading of "inner infinity."

For someone to engage with this dimension of their historicity is not to unpack a container of static information, but to recognize that something unformulated in their experience calls for understanding in the present, however difficult or even impossible that process of expounding might be. It is part of their historicity not by virtue of any internalization, but simply by living in a world of shared possible meanings. The unconscious is thus not within any one person, but is a distributed layer of intersubjective life upon which different people can have varying degrees of attention and focus. One of Stern's more recent insights is that this unformulated layer must not necessarily come to formulation through language: "both verbal *and* nonverbal meanings can be formulated" (Stern, 2010, p. xv, emphasis in original).

Combining Cushman's insight about the client's relational setting with Stern's reframing of unconscious meaning as unformulated experience, we can begin to grasp how historical haunting, if it aligns with something like the repressed or dissociated in the unconscious, need not be considered to exist mentally, but can pervade the discursive world in an unnoticed or unformulated manner. It can therefore, at least potentially, rise to intersubjective awareness. Much depends, as we noted above, on any given person's capacity to engage with historical haunting, and this entails an imaginative capacity to hear the silence that surrounds it.

Due to the distributed, intersubjective nature of haunting, it is not up to any one person to face and deal with it. It can certainly feel like an insurmountable individual burden to formulate something for the first time, but part of the purpose of the therapeutic relationship is to share that burden, to engage with historicity in a dialogical or narrative fashion that precisely uncovers its presently enacted structure and its ongoing potential for further response and understanding. Building on his insights concerning unformulated experience, Stern (2010) has thus described the process of witnessing as crucial to healing an individual's dissociation from the therapeutic relationship (pp. 107–129).

The role of the witness—someone who can hear and perhaps name that which has gone unnoticed, unexamined, or unclaimed—has in fact long held a significant role in individual therapeutic engagement (Felman & Laub, 1992, pp. 57–92). Given everything we have explored here concerning the intersubjective distribution of haunting as the unconscious, one ought to consider the role of witnessing beyond just the therapeutic dyad. It is quite possible to envision a type of witnessing taking place throughout social discourse, induced perhaps by works of narrative art such as those we considered above. Actively listening to that which haunts—for example, in the guise of historical shame—entails playing an ethical part in remembering, "recognizing our role in the moral construction and reconstruction of our cultural worlds" (Frie, 2014, p. 268).

This broadly social and ethical significance of witnessing is probably most obvious in the case of individual and collective trauma. Though one cannot simply equate it with haunting, the phenomenon of trauma is coming to be recognized as having similar features, and requiring a comparable engagement beyond the limits of the therapeutic encounter. To witness in this context is not only to listen for therapeutic insights; it is to make a place in the world for the traumatized person's history—indeed, to recognize that it already constitutes a hidden part of the world. Yet, this recognition, this task of making room for haunting, does not meet with universal agreement. Thus, one of the current debates around trauma mirrors much of the conceptual tension noted throughout this chapter. It centers on the very intelligibility and intersubjectivity of trauma.

When Catherine Malabou (2012) describes severe sufferers of post-traumatic stress disorder (PTSD) as dwelling in the meaninglessness of an "empty subjectivity" (p. 155), she may indeed be accounting for the affective and temporal rupture that trauma can cause, yet she is also thereby taking trauma to remove its victims "from any sociohistorical context" (Gammage, 2016, p. 405). In her view, PTSD is so damaging as to constitute "an impossibility of recovery, a nullification of sense, and therefore an impossibility of testimony" (Gammage, 2016, p. 411). An account such as Malabou's seems caught up in a conception of memory as linearly accumulated and individually contained. The traumatized person's isolation and unintelligibility would thus lie in the breaking of such a container and the severing of expressive connection to others. Yet, if one conceives of trauma by way of haunting and historicity, or if one allows the memory crisis to inform one's conception of what is dissociated in trauma, it no longer appears as such a destruction of the self.

The psychoanalysts Françoise Davoine and Jean-Max Gaudillière take exactly this approach, seeing trauma as existing in the world and framing their work as "research into uninscribed histories" to which their patients are witnesses (Caruth, 2014, p. 81). To hear those witnesses as testifying to something in the world is to recognize the opaque presence of historical haunting in these people's historicities: it is both an absence in the sense that it lacks overt historical sedimentation and may even have "no possibility of inscription" (Caruth, 2014, p. 83), and yet also a presence in the very madness that results from being haunted by uninscribed memories.

Davoine and Gaudillière insist that, despite this tension and in contrast to Malabou's claims, one can engage meaningfully with such madness. They speak of erased events being "in search of inscription," of enduring within the afflicted temporalities of the mad (Caruth, 2014, p. 93). Since encountering such affliction involves the type of unformulated experience elaborated above, following the course of this search means more than simply taking note of previously omitted historical details or events. To bear witness to the hauntings of the traumatized entails allowing something to emerge—possibly for the first time—with its penumbra of abyssal irretrievability, and this means that a particular "creative" and even "literary" sensitivity is required (Caruth, 2014, p. 98). One must to some degree follow along into the haunting.

The successes that Davoine and Gaudillière have had in their efforts, including the counter-transferential insights gleaned about their own historical "betrayals" (Caruth, 2014, p. 84), speak to the significance of framing trauma as meaningfully distributed in the world. Listening to the voices of the marginalized and hearing them as witnesses to uninscribed histories gives a concrete picture of what an engagement with historical haunting looks like. It also helps underscore why remembrance can be considered an ethical task—a debt owed to alterity.

More fascinating work remains to be done on this type of concrete engagement with historical haunting (Bilger, 2016). The constellation of philosophical and psychological concepts that can make sense of haunting has been aligning over the course of decades, and promises many future insights. Along with these theoretical developments, there appears to be a widening imagination concerning our involvement with the past, a growing sense of the inexhaustible alterity and receptivity within historicity.

References

Bilger, B. (2016, September 12). Ghost stories: Making peace with the dead in Germany. *The New Yorker*, *42*(28), 56–65.

Brockmeier, J. (2010). After the archive: Remapping memory. *Culture & Psychology*, *16*(1), 5–35.

Brockmeier, J. (2015). *Beyond the archive*. New York, NY: Oxford University Press.

Campbell, S. (2014). *Our faithfulness to the past: The ethics and politics of memory*. (C. M. Koggel & R. Jacobsen, Eds.). New York, NY: Oxford University Press.

Caputo, J. D. (1987). *Radical hermeneutics*. Bloomington, IN: Indiana University Press.

Caputo, J. D. (2000). *More radical hermeneutics*. Bloomington, IN: Indiana University Press.

Caputo, J. D. (2004). No tear shall be lost: The history of prayers and tears. In D. Carr, T. R. Flynn, & R. Makkreel (Eds.), *The ethics of history* (pp. 91–117). Evanston, IL: Northwestern University Press.

Caruth, C. (2014). *Listening to trauma: Conversations with leaders in the theory and treatment of catastrophic experience*. Baltimore, MD: Johns Hopkins University Press.

Cushman, P. (2009). Empathy—what one hand taketh, the other giveth away: Commentary on paper by Lynn Layton. *Psychoanalytic Dialogues*, *19*(2), 121–137.

Diedrich, L. (2007). Gathering evidence of ghosts: W. G. Sebald's practices of witnessing. In L. Patt (Ed.), *Searching for Sebald: Photography after W. G. Sebald* (pp. 256–279). Los Angeles, CA: The Institute of Cultural Inquiry.

Erll, A. (2008). Cultural memory studies: An introduction. In A. Erll & A. Nünning (Eds.), *Cultural memory studies: An international and interdisciplinary handbook* (pp. 1–15). New York, NY: Mouton de Gruyter.

Felman, S. & Laub, D. (Eds.). (1992). *Testimony: Crises of witnessing in literature, psychoanalysis, and history*. New York, NY: Routledge.

Frie. R. (2014). Limits of understanding: Psychological experience, German memory and the Holocaust. *Psychoanalysis, Culture & Society*, *19*(3), 255–271.

Gadamer, H.-G. (1976). *Philosophical hermeneutics*. (D. E. Linge, Trans.). Berkeley, CA: University of California Press.

Gadamer, H.-G. (1995). A conversation with Hans-Georg Gadamer. *Journal of the British Society for Phenomenology*, *26*(2), 116–125.

Gadamer, H.-G. (2000). *Truth and method* (2nd ed.). (J. Weinsheimer & D. G. Marshall, Trans.). New York, NY: Continuum.

Gadamer, H.-G. (2001). *Gadamer in conversation.* (R. Palmer, Ed. & Trans.). New Haven, CT: Yale University Press.

Gammage, J. (2016). Trauma and historical witnessing: Hope for Malabou's new wounded. *Journal of Speculative Philosophy*, *30*(3), 404–413.

Heidegger, M. (1962). *Being and time.* (J. Maquarrie & E. Robinson, Trans.). San Francisco, CA: Harper & Row.

Heidegger, M. (2009). *The Heidegger reader.* (J. Veith, Trans.). Bloomington, IN: Indiana University Press.

Hirsch, M. (1997). *Family frames: Photography, narrative, and postmemory.* Cambridge, MA: Harvard University Press.

Iser, W. (1978). *The act of reading: A theory of aesthetic response.* Baltimore, MD: Johns Hopkins University Press.

Krumholz, L. (1992). The ghosts of slavery: Historical recovery in Toni Morrison's *Beloved. African American Review*, *26*(3), 395–408.

Laub, D. (1992). An event without a witness: Truth, testimony and survival. In S. Felman & D. Laub (Eds.), *Testimony: Crises of witnessing in literature, psychoanalysis, and history* (pp. 75–92). New York, NY: Routledge.

Malabou, C. (2012). *The new wounded: From neurosis to brain damage.* (S. Miller, Trans.). New York, NY: Fordham University Press.

Morrison, T. (1987). *Beloved.* New York, NY: Vintage International.

Osborne, D. (2013). *Traces of trauma in W. G. Sebald and Christoph Ransmayr.* London: Legenda.

Risser, J. (2002). In the shadow of Hegel: Infinite dialogue in Gadamer's hermeneutics, *Research in Phenomenology*, *32*, 86–102.

Savoy, L. (2015). *Trace: Memory, history, race, and the American landscape.* Berkeley, CA: Counterpoint Press.

Sebald, W. G. (2001). *Austerlitz.* (A. Bell, Trans.). New York, NY: Modern Library.

Silverblatt, M. (2007). A poem of an invisible subject. In L. S. Schwartz (Ed.), *The emergence of memory: Conversations with W. G. Sebald* (pp. 77–86). New York, NY: Seven Stories Press.

Stern, D. (1997). *Unformulated experience: From dissociation to imagination in psychoanalysis.* Hillsdale, NJ: The Analytic Press.

Stern, D. (2010). *Partners in thought: Working with unformulated experience, dissociation, and enactment.* New York, NY: Routledge.

Terdiman, R. (1993). *Present past: Modernity and the memory crisis.* Ithaca, NY: Cornell University Press.

Veith, J. (2015). *Gadamer and the transmission of history.* Bloomington, IN: Indiana University Press.

Wachtel, E. (2007). Ghost hunter. In L. S. Schwartz (Ed.), *The emergence of memory: Conversations with W. G. Sebald* (pp. 37–61). New York, NY: Seven Stories Press.

Chapter 8

Changing societal narratives, fighting "crimes against humanity"

Doris Brothers

Sometimes, as Mark Freeman (2014) observes, it takes a shocking occurrence to "awaken us from the inattentive slumber" in which we tend to live (p. 14). I have little doubt that the 9/11 terrorist attacks on the World Trade Center in New York City provided just the sort of wake-up call Freeman had in mind. Since that fateful day, more and more of my patients spend time in their analytic sessions discussing calamitous events in our city, our country, and even distant parts of the world. The horrors of 9/11 seem to have played a weighty role in convincing them—and me—that we Americans are not exempt from the violence that roils our planet. By voicing their concerns about dramas on the world stage, my patients seem to be sending me a powerful message: their personal and familial narratives are shaped and re-shaped by what happens outside my door.

The traumatic residues of 9/11 are probably not the only reason that world events infiltrate my office. Turned into virtual cyborgs by smartphones and other technological devices that seem welded to our bodies, we receive news the moment it "breaks" anywhere in our world. And much of this news contains ominous threats to our survival.

As Koichi Togashi (2014) has astutely observed, it is often when our survival is gravely threatened that our experience of being human—which differs from a cognitive understanding that one is a member of the human species—may be lost or weakened. This "existential anguish," as he terms it, is most likely to overtake us when we face the loss of our intimate connections to others. The imminence of death (one's own or that of a loved one) is indisputably a context for this terrifying experience.

Trauma, in my view, is another. It constitutes the overarching context in which human connectedness, and consequently, the sense of being human, is imperiled. Although a specific trauma may not pose the threat of physical death to oneself or a loved one, I see trauma as always jeopardizing one's psychological survival. Forced to confront the unbearable uncertainty that others will join in the relational give and take upon which a sense of going-on-being (Winnicott, 1965) depends, the traumatized person feels exiled from the known, the familiar, and the meaningful (Brothers, 2008). Taking Togashi's insights into account, I would now add that, for many traumatized individuals, a previously unquestioned sense of being human is thrown into doubt.

We tend to think of people who have completely lost a sense of being human as suffering from psychosis. Patients like the man Victor Tausk (1933) described as suffering from the delusion of an "influencing machine" come to mind. However, many of my patients, including those who have none of the symptoms associated with psychosis, report feeling less than human. Many use words like "robot," "monster," and "zombie" to describe themselves. Indeed, if you accept my notion that trauma affects one's sense of being a human among humans, we may all be at risk of losing a sense of being human, especially when trauma involves our being treated inhumanely (Brothers, 2014b).

Although many courageous exceptions are to be found in historical literature, the truism that inhumanity breeds inhumanity appears to be well documented. The literature on the Holocaust abounds with examples. In his widely acclaimed book, *Night*, Elie Wiesel (1958/2006) describes acts of cruelty committed by concentration camp prisoners toward their fellow prisoners. Janice Gump (2010) convincingly argues that the brutally dehumanizing effects of slavery have been passed down from parent to child. The trauma of slavery, she suggests, still critically shapes the subjectivity of African Americans by means of the intergenerational transmission of what she calls slavery's "relationship of domination." And, describing the challenges he faces in his work with combat veterans, who are frequently both victims and perpetrators, Russell Carr (2014) observes that many of them "have lost a sense of being human, of being connected with the world" (p. 117).

Crimes against humanity

The term "crimes against humanity" is generally reserved for atrocious attacks committed on a large scale. As a result of the Nuremberg Trials, which were held soon after the end of World War II, murder, enslavement, deportation, and other inhumane acts committed against civilian populations before or during a war, or persecutions on political, racial, or religious grounds, were held to constitute such crimes. However, considering the horrific toll they take on all involved and the impact they have on future generations, we might feel justified in using this term in a broader sense to describe those contexts that give rise to an individual's loss of a sense of being human (Brothers, 2014b).

There is growing recognition that the beliefs and practices that operate within a society, and presumably give rise to these crimes against humanity, emerge in conjunction with what Jonathan Dawson (2014) has termed "grand societal narratives." He defines them as "clusters of beliefs and cultural norms that give shape and meaning to the human cultures within which we live." Dawson suggests that these narratives, which were forged in the Enlightenment and the Industrial Revolution and rest on Cartesian dualisms, are "so deeply rooted and so thoroughly embedded within a society's language, behaviour patterns, and rituals as to be all but imperceptible." Moreover, he observes that they are unconsciously accepted as universally true. For this reason, I think of grand societal narratives as strongly influencing the life stories whose themes I have described as "systemically emergent certainties" (Brothers, 2008, p. 36).

I find support for the idea that some of these grand societal narratives contribute to the emergence of crimes against humanity in the writings of Dawson, Mark Fairfield, and Marshall Ganz, among others. They suggest that today's dominant societal narratives contradict our fundamentally relational nature by portraying humans as standing apart from, and superior to, the rest of the natural world. Humans, so the narratives suggest, are compelled to fight for supremacy in a world marked by scarcity and the survival of the fittest. Under conditions that are undoubtedly complex and varied, they are organized into rationales for the domination, control, and destruction of other people, and the exploitation of the planet's resources.

So pernicious are the effects of these narratives that considering them has led me to question my work as an analyst. If our sense of being human is continually undermined by the myths of independent selfhood that pervade our society, can my therapeutic relationships with patients make a difference? I devote this chapter to an exploration of some possible ways in which the relational narratives that emerge within therapeutic encounters might serve to counter these dehumanizing narratives.

Creating relational narratives

Walter Fisher (1984) has been credited with calling our attention to the ubiquity and power of narrative in every aspect of life. Human communication, he contends, includes more than its rational form; it includes nonverbal and well as verbal dimensions and involves the cultural context in which it occurs. William Kirkwood (1992), who criticizes Fisher for focusing too exclusively on prevailing values and failing to emphasize the ways that narratives can promote social change, contends that when we accept new narratives that appeal to us, our values can change.

Narratives on the extremes of the political spectrum involving fundamentalism, nationalism, so-called "ethnic cleansing," the exploitation of the earth's resources, and other atrocities may seem particularly resistant to change. Massive social traumas that result from wars, terrorism, and genocide are often tragic testimonies to our failure to find political solutions. Moreover, some solutions themselves may inflict still more trauma. For example, a political alliance formed by a group of nations to protect against further aggression may inflame the hostile intentions of nations who have been excluded.

Yet, a number of prominent analysts have forcefully argued that psychoanalysis can transform politics. Andrew Samuels (2001), who has explored "the secret psychological life of politics" (pp. 1–14) as well as the secret politics of psychological life, is a persuasive proponent of this view. He observes that psychotherapy's contributions to transformational politics stem from its overall worldview that is reflected in its concept of "good-enoughness." This concept, according to Samuels, helps avoid over-idealizing or denigrating leaders. He also celebrates the psychoanalytic appreciation of ambivalence, and the acknowledgment of unconscious motivations.

Philip Cushman is another analytic writer who strongly believes in the power of relational psychoanalysts to transform the political landscape. He has urged psychoanalysts to integrate the postmodern focus on political power and oppression with the hermeneutic focus on moral understandings, historical traditions, and dialogue (Cushman, 2012). Writing about the transformational potential of relational psychoanalysis, he observes:

> Relationalists live out certain moral understandings that make political commitment possible: in their work they value honesty, fairness, collaboration, egalitarianism, freedom. Their commitments to

> compassion, self-reflection, and intellectual integrity make their analytic practices one of the few places where a resistance against the anti-intellectualism, militarism, racism, misogyny, classism, and homophobia of the far right come to light. It is that realization that has moved me to interpret relational psychoanalysis as a kind of quiet political resistance.
>
> (Cushman, 2012, p. 12)

Even the most superficial survey of current literature in a variety of other disciplines such as sociology, cultural anthropology, and religion suggests that new narratives involving our inescapably relational lives, our reliance on the land and other species, and our urgent need for care, community, and cooperation are emerging. But can these new stories replace the old ones that are so deeply entrenched?

Mark Fairfield (2015) suggests that nothing short of a social revolution is needed. Indeed, he has outlined a "relational movement" that involves the development of new narratives that concern our inescapably relational existence. Much of his work has been inspired by the writings of Marshall Ganz. Asserting that social movements are organized around identifying, recruiting, and developing leadership, Ganz (2009a, 2009b) contends that in addition to building relationships, leaders must learn the craft of what he calls "public narrative."

Ganz, in turn, acknowledges that his ideas about public narrative have been greatly influenced by developmental psychologist Jerome Bruner, who has studied narrative extensively. According to Bruner (1991), the narrative mode maps the world affectively, rather than analytically. It answers "why" questions, such as why we care and why we value one goal over another. Moreover, narrative is how we learn to exercise agency—choice in the face of uncertainty. And as Togashi (2014) has reminded us, a sense of self-determination, agency, is vital to one's sense of being human.

The "story of self"

Public narrative, for Ganz, contains three elements: a "story of self," which "communicates the values that call one to action;" a "story of us," which "communicates the values shared by those in action;" and a "story of now," which "communicates an urgent challenge to those values that demands action now" (Ganz, 2009a, p. 282).

It is probably obvious to most relational analysts that our dialogues with patients often contain aspects of the three elements of public narrative. For example, Ganz notes that "stories of self" allude to pain and hope and what philosopher Charles Taylor (1989) calls our "moral sources." Taylor contends that self and morality cannot be separated; who we are depends on what matters to us. Taylor conceives of one's sense of self as determined by those who constitute our "webs of interlocutors," those who live within "a defining community" (Taylor, 1989, p. 39). The moral and ethical choices we make both reflect and affect the kinds of stories we create within our defining communities, or to use the language I prefer, our interpenetrating relational systems. For this reason, "stories of self" tend to be constructed around choice points or moments when we faced a challenge and experienced an outcome.

It is often because they face a choice point in life that our patients come to us for help. A transgender adolescent I have recently begun to see needs to decide whether to undergo surgery; a highly successful lawyer must decide if she should abandon her law career in order to pursue life as a singer/songwriter; members of a couple need to decide whether, despite their fears, they should marry. Although they often do not explicitly mention it, my patients must also make what are often difficult decisions about the roles they play in society. For whom will they vote? How actively will they support the candidates of their choice? What causes will they support financially or through more active means? They may even have to decide whether to participate in a social movement.

But it is not only our patients who have profound choices to make; their analysts do as well. I have little doubt that one reason my patients talk more now about societal calamities than before 9/11 is that I am more willing to engage with them in these conversations. No longer believing that their reflections on world events represent "resistance" to their talking about themselves, I often choose to join them in discussing pressing cultural and/or political situations. In our talks, I not only learn more about the patient's experiential world but also my own. My own "story of self" centers around my hope that through the breadth, depth, and openness of my dialogues with patients and the mutual understanding we strive to reach, I am contributing to a world in which words rather than weapons are used to express sameness and difference.

The "story of us"

What we relational analysts find confirmed again and again is that every "story of self" also involves a "story of us." We feel convinced that our psychological survival depends on our relationships with others. Freeman (2014) notes that although personal narratives issue from a self, and "the story of my life is irrevocably mine, the forces that propel it forward derive from the Other" (p. 4). I find that my patients' "stories of us" often communicate the societal values they share with others, particularly insofar as every "story of us" implies a "them." Those who constitute "them" may be anyone whose race, religion, ethnicity, political affiliation, and sexual preference differs from one's own.

At times of traumatic stress, we may be tempted to employ very circumscribed definitions of "us" and to sharply differentiate ourselves from others whom we regard as "them." In recent writings, I have described my understanding of the reasons that trauma tends to reinforce the us–them binary (Brothers, 2012, 2016). Craving reassurance that they have not lost all connection to the familiar, meaningful world they inhabited before being flung into the lonely exile of trauma, trauma survivors may search for sameness with such intensity that it amounts to a denial of difference. At the same time, uncertainty about the continued availability of the relational exchange may threaten them with the loss of a sense of differentiated, unique selfhood. Finding differences, making sharp distinctions among that which is similar, tends to bring certainty to experience. Just as the search for sameness may become transformed into a denial of difference, the search for difference may be transformed into a denial of sameness.

Such denials rest on dissociative processes that blind us to the complexity of lived experience (Brothers, 2008). They tend to result in the black-and-white societal narratives that so often emerge in the aftermath of trauma. President George W. Bush's assertion about an "axis of evil" in the aftermath of the 9/11 terrorist attacks is a good example. Implicit in his slogan was a denial that differences existed among those who lived inside the so-called axis—that is, they were all evil—while at the same time it denied the sameness of Americans and inhabitants of the so-called axis countries.

Following wide-scale traumas, we may also be especially vulnerable to prevailing isolationist narratives insofar as they tend to be similarly simplistic and formulaic. They often involve denials of our shared humanity and our sameness and difference from one another. As patients solidify their sense of being complexly integrated humans in healing relationships, I find that their "stories of us" become increasingly inclusive.

The "story of now"

If we accept the idea that narratives organize experience into meaningful sequential episodes—that is, they flow forward over time—the idea of a "story of now" may seem like a contradiction in terms. At least, that would be the case if "now" is seen as a frozen snapshot that melts into non-existence a moment after it is taken. However, the duration of "now" changes according to the context in which it is invoked. "Now" may allude to a very long span of time, such as the present epoch or century, or any amount of time that is contrasted with the past and future.

Finding a "story of now" is often the challenge that patients bring to their therapeutic relationships. Some who have suffered grievous losses and traumas seem to dwell in nostalgic relation to times that preceded the loss. Nursing memories of moments (often more wished for than actual) of blissful contacts with lost others or personal triumphs, they express hopelessness about recapturing them in the present. Others seem to be so preoccupied with their ambitions for the future and are so driven to realize them that the present holds little appeal.

The development of narratives that address an urgent societal danger often depends on our openness to experience the political meanings in the present moment. One example is our pressing need as individuals and as members of society to face the crisis of climate change. Patients who are lost in nostalgia for the past or driven to realize their ambitions in the future are not likely to give much thought to the reduction of greenhouse gas emissions or the depth of their carbon footprints. Hopefully, however, as these patients find ways to live in the "now" of the therapeutic exchange, and as that capacity spreads to their other relationships, they will experience a greater capacity to consider societal situations that urgently require attention in the present.

The idea that we are capable of experiencing the present as completely free from the influence of the past and expectations about the future seems inimical to a relational systems perspective. Studies on the intergenerational transmission of trauma suggest that our life stories inevitably reflect the experiences of those who lived before us. A number of attachment theorists have described how enduring patterns of relating that infants develop in their early interactions with their parents reflect traumas experienced in earlier generations (Brothers, 2014a).

The "story of then"

While it does not figure in Ganz's schema (2009a), there is another element in the narratives that emerge between therapist and patient that seems to have the potential to change societal narratives that center around personal triumph, domination, and control: the "story of then." Mark Freeman (2010) is among a number of contemporary theorists who emphasize the importance of history and culture in the therapeutic process. Roger Frie (2012) is another. He contends that inherited traumatic memory is transmitted in family narratives that remain unconsciously organized and are guided by affective and dissociative processes. As Frie (2014, p. 651) puts it:

> just as the individual mind can never be fully separated from its social surround, personal memory is always related to the cultural contexts in which it unfolds. What I know or do not know, what I remember or forget, occurs in the interplay of cultural norms, social organization and family dynamics.

Building on Frie's work, Max Sucharov (2014, p. 307) refers to the "narrative turn" in psychotherapy. He notes that "story telling is a continuous unfolding in which we are active participants recreating and transforming history and culture." According to Sucharov, "The lens of reflective hindsight therefore constitutes a dialogic vehicle through which we can engage with the voices of our past and reconfigure our narratives into hopefully more humane forms" (p. 307).

Jamie's narrative

I believe ever more strongly that when I open myself to understanding the ways in which intergenerational traumas in my own life as well as that of my patient affect an ongoing relationship, new and healing narratives emerge between us. In a recent article (Brothers, 2014a), I described my work with a Native American man I called Jamie in which past familial traumas played a crucial role. I briefly review aspects of my relationship with him that show how our "stories of then" shaped what happened between us.

Jamie, who was conceived during a brutal rape, was adopted by a wealthy, upper-middle-class, white family shortly after birth. Burdened with severe learning disabilities and strikingly different in appearance from the light-skinned children in his upper-class neighborhood, he was the target of relentless bullying throughout his childhood. The "story of self" with which he entered therapy was filled with self-recriminations for his addiction to drugs and alcohol and for being a disappointment to his adoptive parents. His "story of us", which was almost entirely absent at first, came to include members of his biological family who live on a reservation (he was contacted by a half-sister on a social media site). His "story of now" was filled with his struggle to find meaning in a life he considered "a waste."

Crises in our relationship occurred when Jamie failed to return to therapy for long periods of time following my vacations. It was only after I arranged to phone him during my absences and assured him that I would welcome him back despite his resumption of drinking and drug use that he felt able to return. Explorations of the meanings of these disruptions led us to recognize similarities in our "stories of then." I realized that despite considerable differences in historical context, both Jews and Native Americans have been violently uprooted, forced into exile, and maligned by damning stereotypes. Many of our ancestors were victims of crimes against humanity.

Jamie eventually came to understand how his personal narrative, which involved feeling exiled from his people and his land, echoed the tragic history of his ancestors. My "story of then" involved immigrant grandmothers haunted by guilt over the friends and relatives left to perish in pogroms and in the Holocaust. I believe that their examples of self-sacrifice contributed to my having extended myself to Jamie in ways that kept our relationship alive when his hopelessness and despair had nearly ended it.

Not only did the similarities in our "stories of then" allow me to contact Jamie more empathically, but as our relationship has deepened, the narratives that are emerging between us now suggest that more profound healing is contingent upon our efforts to heal our wounded world.

Narratives of service to society

The results of a small qualitative research study that Koichi Togashi and I conducted on the long-term effects of the 9/11 terrorist attacks (Togashi & Brothers, 2015) suggest that survivors who develop a sense of commitment to society are better able to heal from wide-scale societal traumas than those who do not. One aim of our research was to describe how survivors integrate experiences of the uncertainty, irrationality, and absurdity of life that are often experienced in the aftermath of wide-scale traumatizing events. Our findings suggested that survivors who engaged in professional and/or personal activities they regarded as helping our wounded society were better able to integrate such experiences. For example, one participant, a news reporter who has covered every anniversary of 9/11, indicated that he believed that the role he plays solidifies his sense of purpose and meaning in life. Another participant, a lawyer, had devoted herself to helping family members of those who died in the attacks get the benefits to which they were entitled. While acknowledging that the senseless slaughter of innocent people still appalled her, these efforts have helped to alleviate an agonizing sense of helplessness and despair.

The "story of next"

A number of the narratives told by participants in our study about serving those who had been harmed by the 9/11 attacks contained messages of hope for a better world in the future. These messages might be thought of as constituting "stories of next." Developmental psychologists who study the earliest interactions between caregivers and infants have taught us that relational "expectancies" organize our lives from birth on (Beebe & Lachmann, 2002). What we expect to happen in the future, which is greatly influenced by our past experiences, profoundly influences the choices we make in the present. You might say that our "stories of then" play a crucial role in determining our "stories of next," which in turn influence our "stories of now."

I would like to think that when healing occurs in therapeutic relationships that have addressed past intergenerational traumas in the lives of the analytic partners, the actions they take in the present reflect their hopes for a better future. It strikes me as no coincidence that the most powerfully influential, forward-looking narratives in our society have been described as dreams.

"I have a dream"

At the historic March on Washington of August 28, 1963, Martin Luther King, Jr. described his dream that racism in America might end despite his painful acknowledgment that, even 100 years after Abraham Lincoln issued the Emancipation Proclamation, "the Negro is not free." As Jon Meacham (2013) observed, "With a single phrase, Martin Luther King joined Jefferson and Lincoln in the ranks of men who've shaped modern America."

What was it about King's speaking of his dream that has been so enduringly gripping? Perhaps one reason is that he drew on the power of dreams and the narrative form they take to affect the world in which we live. Understanding dreams and interpreting their meanings seems to have preoccupied humans from the dawn of history. There can be little doubt that dreams not only give expression to unconscious meanings in the lives of individuals but also to unconscious meanings in their societies as well. Moreover, the telling of the dream narrative to an other or others clearly has transformative potential.

In one of Jamie's dreams, he is searching for his biological mother but is unable to find her. After many difficult and dangerous encounters, he locates her in a palatial home (a far cry from her home on an impoverished reservation). She shows no surprise at seeing him but tells him that he has a lot of important work to do. She is wearing the headdress of a chieftain and he interprets her words to mean that he must assume a leadership role in his community. In recent months, Jamie has begun to speak out about racial bias at work and has come to the aid of younger men who have been unfairly treated.

Do the new narratives arising within therapeutic relationships neutralize or diminish the destructive power of the dominant societal narratives? Certainly not on their own. But I would like to think that, collectively, the relational narratives that are emerging in various therapeutic contexts around the world work in just this way. Even more, I hope they contribute toward what I see as a growing relational movement, one that creates a "story of next" that will allow us and those who come after us to live more peacefully, creatively, and lovingly together.

References

Beebe, B. & Lachmann, F. (2002), *Infant Research and Adult Treatment: Coconstructing Interactions*. Hillsdale, NJ: The Analytic Press.

Brothers, D. (2008), *Toward a Psychology of Uncertainty: Trauma-Centered Psychoanalysis*. New York: The Analytic Press.

Brothers, D. (2012), Trauma, Gender and the Dark Side of Twinship. *International Journal of Psychoanalytic Self Psychology*, 7(3):391–405.
Brothers, D. (2014a), Traumatic Attachments: Intergenerational Trauma, Dissociation and the Analytic Relationship. *International Journal of Psychoanalytic Self Psychology*, 9(1):3–15.
Brothers, D. (2014b), "Crimes Against Humanity" and the Societal Context of Trauma: Discussion of "A Sense of 'Being Human' and Twinship Experience" by Koichi Togashi. *International Journal of Psychoanalytic Self Psychology*, 9(4):282–289.
Brothers, D. (2016), "Screams and Shouts": Trauma, Uncertainty, and the Ethical Turn. In D. M. Goodman and E. R. Severson (Eds.), *The Ethical Turn: Otherness and Subjectivity in Contemporary Psychoanalysis* (pp. 117–124). New York: Routledge.
Bruner, J. S. (1991), The Narrative Construction of Reality. *Critical Inquiry*, 18(1):1–21.
Carr, R. B. (2014), Authentic Solicitude: What the Madness of Combat Can Teach Us About Authentically Being-With Our Patients. *International Journal of Psychoanalytic Self Psychology*, 9(2):115–130.
Cushman, P. (2012), Book Review: Why Resist? Politics, Psychoanalysis, and the Interpretive Turn. *DIVISION: A Quarterly Psychoanalytic Forum*, 4(3):11–13.
Dawson, J. (2014), Changing Stories: Using Narrative to Shift Societal Values. https://www.schumachercollege.org.uk
Fairfield, M. (2015), White Paper (unpublished manuscript).
Fisher, W. R. (1984), Narration as Human Communication Paradigm: The Case of Public Moral Argument. *Communication Monographs*, 51(1):1–22.
Freeman, M. (2010), *Hindsight: The Promise and Peril of Looking Backward.* New York: Oxford University Press.
Freeman, M. (2014), *The Priority of the Other: Thinking and Living Beyond the Self.* New York: Oxford University Press.
Frie, R. (2012), On Culture, History, and Memory: Encountering the "Narrative Unconscious." *Contemporary Psychoanalysis*, 48(3):329–343.
Frie, R. (2014), From Memorials to Bomb Shelters: Navigating the Emotional Landscape of German Memory. *Psychoanalytic Inquiry*, 34(7):649–662.
Ganz, M. (2009a), *Why David Sometimes Wins: Leadership, Organization, and Strategy in the California Farm Worker Movement.* New York: Oxford University Press.
Ganz, M. (2009b), Why Stories Matter: The Arts and Craft of Social Change. *Sojourners* (pp. 16–21). http://friendsofjustice.wordpress.com/2009/02/18/marshall-ganz-why-stories-matter.
Gump, J. (2010), Reality Matters: The Shadow of Trauma on African-American Subjectivity. *Psychoanalysis Psychology*, 27(1):42–54.
Kirkwood, W. G. (1992), Narrative and the Rhetoric of Possibility. *Communication Monographs*, 59(1):30–47.
Meacham, J. (2012), Martin Luther King Jr Architect of the 21st, Century. Content. time.com/time/magazine/article/0,9171,2149610,00.html.

Samuels, A. (2001), *Politics on the Couch: Citizenship and the Internal Life.* New York: Karnac.
Sucharov, M. (2014), Historical and Cultural Narratives: Confessions of a Diaspora Jew. *International Journal of Psychoanalytic Self Psychology*, 10(4):305–317.
Tausk, V. (1933), On the Origin of the "Influencing Machine" in Schizophrenia. *Psychoanalysis Quarterly*, 2:519–556.
Taylor, C. (1989), *Sources of the Self.* Cambridge, MA: Harvard University Press.
Togashi, K. (2014), A Sense of "Being Human" and Twinship Experience. *International Journal of Psychoanalytic Self Psychology*, 9(4):265–281.
Togashi, K. & Brothers, D. (2015), Trauma Research and Self Psychology: How 9/11 Survivors Integrate the Irrationality of Wide-Scale Trauma. Paper presented at the 38th Conference of the International Association of Psychoanalytic Self Psychology, Los Angeles, October 18.
Wiesel, E. (1958/2006), *Night*. New York: Hill & Wang.
Winnicott, D. W. (1965), *The Maturational Process and the Facilitating Environment: Studies in the Theory of Emotional Development.* New York: International Universities Press.

Chapter 9

Positioning self and other

How psychiatric patients, psychiatric inmates, and mental health care professionals construct discursively their relationship to total institutions

Branca Telles Ribeiro and Diana Souza Pinto

Introduction

This chapter discusses how psychiatric patients and psychiatric inmates construct discursively their relationship to total institutions (psychiatric and forensic hospitals). Specifically, it will focus on recurrent themes that emerge in patients' and inmates' narratives as they relate to location (how they index who they are and where they are, how much they long to be there, and where they would like to be) with the understanding that defining self (who we are construed as being) "changes with interactants and settings" (Lemke, 2008, p. 19). Perceptions of self and other emerge in patients' and inmates' narratives as they construct their relationship to a particular place. The last section of this chapter considers how mental health care providers view institutional settings regarding complex decisions in patient orientation.

In investigating the use of language in total institutions, this chapter discusses how individuals (participants engaged in an interaction) and settings (professional and institutional organizations) interact and work to create meaning in everyday face-to-face communication. We investigate how the social is constructed by language in interaction, and what informs it (Gumperz, 1982, 1999; Schiffrin, 1994, 1996; Tannen, 1986, 1993). We examine situated interactions: how these interactions constitute examples of the social and linguistic selves that participants display to one another. Specifically, we examine how language and communication constitute the tension between the social, the institutional, and the interactional self (Erickson, 2004; Sarangi & Roberts, 1999). For example, in total institutions such as psychiatric wards and prisons, how do participants co-construct a personal, professional, or institutional self or selves? How are these (re)presentations of self performed? How multifaceted can they be and what do they signal?

Our inquiry and analysis embrace specific concepts and methods. First, there is Goffman's concept of the social situation, which addresses the co-construction of interactional meaning by all participants present in a given interaction (1972, 1974); the question Goffman asks, "What is going on here?," is both semantic and pragmatic in nature, indicating that meaning and sense making are grounded within what is being metacommunicated by participants as they interact with one another. We focus on local meaning, the here and now, in face-to-face interactions with health care providers, patients, and researchers. A micro perspective such as this, as we will see, has implications for institutional and macro structures or systems.

Interactional constructs, in Goffman's (1974, 1981) and Schiffrin's (1996) notions of situated self and participant performance, help us understand subtle shifts in conversational footings, such as when a mental health care provider shifts from an authoritative to a caring position and provides guidance to a group of patients. Also, anthropological notions are of relevance, such as Erickson's concept of participation and performed social identities (Erickson, 2004; Erickson & Shultz, 1982), such as when a mental health care provider becomes the primary speaker in a focus group discussion, presenting clear professional positions for certain institutional decisions, or expressing—explicitly or implicitly—a lack of consistent policy. The analysis relies on the use of qualitative research methods: ethnographic observations in each institutional setting, research interviews with professionals and patients, and focus groups with health care providers and patients.

Our discourse approach derives from that of interactional sociolinguistics (Gumperz, 1982; Schiffrin, 1994; Tannen, 1986, 1993), a branch of communication studies grounded in contributions from linguistics and the social sciences. In analyzing situated interactions, this approach to discourse and narrative aims to focus on participants' situated interpretive processes ("How do I mean what I say and do when speaking to you?" and "How do I infer and respond to what you mean and do when speaking or listening to me?"), where macro social systems (which structure total institutions, such as hospitals and prisons) and micro interactional moves (which structure individual performances and face-to-face communication) are tightly interrelated. Schiffrin (1994) indicates that "speakers use language to provide continual indices of who they are and what they want to communicate" (p. 133). Such indices seem to be particularly relevant when voiced by psychiatric inmates, patients, and health care providers in institutional settings.

We consider the following questions for this discussion:

- How do inpatients and inmates refer to themselves and others in relation to where they are? What do such indexical processes capture in the dynamics of self and other, and identity performance? How do these shifts index personal, professional, and institutional selves as well as specific locations?
- How is location—a sense of place—referred to and assessed by patients/clients in a psychiatric and forensic hospital? How is location captured and used by health care professionals? Why is location an interesting marker to be examined when considering Goffman's notion of "total institutions"?

Indexicality, location, and identity

In order to understand language and communication in total institutions, particularly the notion of representation (how we represent a given location and present ourselves) and inferencing (how we understand what the interactants mean and do), we need to consider indexicality, and specifically what linguists call *deictic features*. Speakers produce talk in a given location. Thus, social identities and multifaceted roles are discursively constructed and embedded in these locations. Marmaridou (2000) reminds us that unless we know where speakers are, we will not be able to assign meaning to discourse markers expressed as a *locator*; for example, the use of the marker "here" as it relates to a hospital or a clinical ward (when a psychiatrist asks a patient "where are you, Ms. Jurema?" and she responds "I am here. HERE. HERE!"). What would "here" mean to the patient and the psychiatrist as a subjective locator—a psychological scene (Hymes, 1974)—as well as a geographical physical place?

Another essential characteristic of deixis is *egocentricity*, since it places the speaker (the self) as the center. Marmaridou (2000) states that a proper theory of deixis should account for the relationship between three parameters of communication: time (when did you arrive?), place (where are you now?), and person (who's speaking to whom?). Marmaridou claims that person and social deixis are mutually dependent since the first encompasses participants' social roles. In English, for instance, the pronoun "we" "encodes the roles of both speaker and addressee" (p. 75). It might be used in an inclusive invitation such as "Why don't we have coffee?" in which the speaker explicitly involves the hearer (other) in some co-membership activity.

Jacob Mey (2006) briefly defines *deictics* as

> words and expressions that directly refer to persons, objects, situations, etc. by "pointing" to them, using what is called *deixis* (Greek, for "pointing to," "indicating"). Thus, when I say *I* about myself, I point to the person that I am; *you* points to the person away from me, *viz.*, an actual or potential interlocutor.
>
> (p. 790)

Most languages have an elaborate system of such "pointers" that help us identify persons, locations, and situations in communication ("here," "there," "that," "this," etc.).

Deixis becomes more complex, as the process of indexicality and inferring can have many different forms and functions, which are often of a metaphorical nature. For example, a speaker's attitudes may be expressed by a deictic form when Mary indexes a class attribute by shifting to an academic register at an informal restaurant dinner by stating, "First and foremost, let us consider to whom we are speaking …"; or when Jane, a news reporter in the American Midwest, triggers some controversy by indexing her Spanish ethnic linguistic background (by rolling her Rs), challenging the standard American cultural assumption that a newscaster would deliver the news in standard American English. Mey (2006) states that "such 'indexing' can happen with and without my knowing or willing; when not consciously monitored, such cases reveal a speech which 'betrays' the speaker—the language I speak reveals (or 'indexes') my social or local roots" (p. 790).

An intricate (and sometimes elusive) characteristic of talk in interaction relates to particular shifts in *positioning* (Davies & Harré, 1990)—that is, when participants take on different alignments or stances in interaction, displaying different positionings, and can themselves be positioned by others. These subtle enactments of self relate to participants' display in identity performance (Goffman would name such moves a shift in footing, alignment, position, or stance). In our discussion, linguistic deixis—a marker for self or an indicator for a location—helps signal, and may constitute, a positioning. For example, at the closing of doctor–patient interviews at the Institute of Psychiatry, a patient would frequently try to assess her credibility status as narrator or patient ("Do you believe me? Do you really believe me?"). Concerns about trust and veracity (i.e., "Can I be seen as truthful and therefore 'sane'?") seem to be prominent when the narrative has been constructed in such a location and produced by a psychiatric patient. This type of question would rarely surface or be expected in a clinical (rather than a psychiatric) environment. Hence, the notion of deixis points to the dynamic and reflexive nature of discourse and its relation to social and interactional context (Goffman, 1981).

Thus, it is not simply context that is of interest, but mostly the *processes of contextualization* (Gal, 2009, p. 525). Analyzing the use of deixis (specifically its linguistic tokens) reveals how contextualization develops in communication: how interactants point to self or other in talk exchanges or refer to settings in various communicative acts. John Gumperz (1982, 1999) calls such linguistic expressions "contextualization cues." These may be subtle cues (such as a shift in tone, pitch, or voice quality, among other prosodic features of speech) as well as changes in reference (topics) or participants' activities (speakers' acts of requesting, apologizing, complimenting, or even more subtly, claiming a type of identity, shifting decision power, etc.). Schiffrin (1989) points out that these contextualization cues not only signal changes in context but also constitute these very contexts (p. 260). In this chapter, we discuss specifically cues for locating self and other in a given spatial relation.

Background: the data

Our data derives from clinical and research interviews in a psychiatric hospital and a forensic psychiatric institution in the city of Rio de Janeiro, Brazil. We conduct ethnographic field observations and tape, transcribe, and analyze talk in interaction in these institutional settings (Pinto, 2011; Pinto, Ribeiro, & Lopes Dantas, 2005; Ribeiro, 1994, 2002; Ribeiro & Pinto, 2015). Ethnographic descriptions of the particular interview contexts and its participants inform our analysis of discursive practices. Both institutions are what Goffman (1961) referred to as "total institutions": "a place of residence and work where a large number of like situated individuals cut off from the wider society for an appreciable period of time together lead an enclosed formally administered round of life" (p. xiii). According to the American sociologist, one of the main features of such institutions is the mortification of the self, an inevitable and inescapable result of from long-term institutional incarceration. Conformity to a regimented pattern of life subjects the whole being of the individual by capturing his/her time and existence. The data analysis presented in the second section of this chapter, however, points out how inmates engender strategies that might open up other perspectives regarding self and total institutions (Clough, 1990). Such strategies capture some mobility and patient agency (De Fina, 2003), as well as ongoing changes in the institution itself.

Heitor Carrilho Forensic Hospital is a custody and treatment institution that admits mentally ill patients who are charged with or convicted of crimes ranging from misdemeanors to major felonies. Founded in 1921, Heitor Carrilho is the first forensic psychiatric hospital in Latin America. In 2013, following a process of de-institutionalization of the mentally ill in accordance with Act 10.216/2001 (Hirdes, 2009), the State of Rio de Janeiro renamed it Heitor Carrilho Medical Examination Institute, charged with providing psychiatric medical examinations for all convicted criminals in the State of Rio de Janeiro. For six years, Pinto and colleagues (Pinto, 2011; Pinto & Nascimento, 2012; Santos, Farias, & Pinto, 2015) have coordinated an interdisciplinary research project on the construction of narrative at this institution, entitled "Heitor Carrilho Hospital: Narrative and Memory (2009–2015)." This project investigates the social memory of the hospital by focusing on the narratives of inmates, reports from the management team, and the analysis of institutional documents so as to understand how the institution has been perceived and portrayed by its users and the public at large. The discussion presented in this chapter is directly related to this project.

In terms of its setting, the forensic institution has three main buildings: the administration, and the male and female wards. There is also a cafeteria, a small soccer court, and two renovated one-bedroom houses that have served as shelters for a couple of male and female former inmates. In terms of its main roles, it is a hybrid institution whose main social functions are to treat and to confine inmates. Yet, it also has to fulfill another institutional role: to shelter a few ex-inmates who lack social support and structure for basic care, safety, and independence. As the data indicates, the institution offers such support and provides some flexibility and adaptation to a semi-independent life. Nevertheless, what has prevailed is the culture of imprisonment with its practices. As such, the sheltered inmates have to comply with unstated rules and norms, which once again order their daily lives. As a consequence, they need to constantly negotiate adjustments with the staff pending on institutional requirements, once more reminding us of Goffman's definition of a total institution.

The second setting, the Institute of Psychiatry (Federal University of Rio de Janeiro) founded in 1938, is considered a model school for the study of mental health in Brazil. It is a teaching hospital and fosters academic research and professional training. Since the 1980s, work policy has been grounded in inter- and cross-disciplinary research, learning, and clinical assistance. Research programs flourish in rich partnerships with major academic centers in Brazil and abroad. A permanent commission of Brazilian researchers routinely participates at the World Health Organization (WHO). The Sistema Unico de Saude (SUS)—Unified Health System—of the Ministry of Health together with the Councils of Health and the Brazilian scientific community rely on the institute as a prominent research and training center. Admittance to the psychiatric wards, the daycare hospital, and the outpatient clinic are institutional resources available to all patients. As a federal hospital, the institute serves the working and lower middle classes. It is located in a historical site in the city, with colonial buildings and open spaces decorated by small gardens, rubber trees, and flowering shrubs that are tended daily by the patients. At the time of the interviews (Pinto et al., 2005; Ribeiro, 1994; Ribeiro & Pinto, 2010), the institute still preserved a somewhat lush and rural environment, with chickens as well as domesticated cats on the many outdoor patios. While ward policies have shifted over the last 40 years (from strictly male/female to mixed wards and then back to separate wards), today the separate wards for men and women treat a small number of inmates (around 110, between 18 and 70 years old).

Data discussion

The taped interactions occurred during observations, interviews, and conversations in the field. Pinto, Lopes Dantas, and Ribeiro have developed research in both institutions since 1995 (Ribeiro & Pinto, 2006a, 2006b;

Pinto, 2011). Ethnographic observations informed interviews, (video) recording, and transcription. For this discussion, the first two segments took place in the psychiatric forensic hospital. They are part of a 20-minute research interview between Glaucia (a 40-year-old clinical psychologist) and Maria (a single, 50-year-old, working-class woman) who has been living at the institution for over 35 years. The interaction took place in 2012, when the forensic hospital was still a custody and treatment institution, and also worked as a shelter for a few former inmates.

Maria had a long history of hospitalization in different mental institutions that started when she was 18. Among her many stories of violence and seclusion, the loss of her baby boy more than 30 years ago stands out. At that time, she became pregnant at the forensic unit; she was then sent to a public maternity hospital to deliver her baby. Although clinical records attest that the baby died soon after birth, Maria believed that he had been given up for adoption. For over a year after giving birth, she was referred to by staff as troublesome, "causing deep trouble," by returning often to the maternity hospital, where she would yell in the halls, asking everyone "Where's my baby?" After throwing stones at the parked cars at the institution, she eventually injured a nurse with a knife and was then sent back to the forensic hospital. More serious criminal offenses followed after this event.

Maria was a frequent participant in the Heitor Carrilho research project that was developed at the institution over the course of almost six years (2009–2015). She would constantly approach the researchers and engage in conversations when she would recurrently introduce her missing baby boy as a topic. More often than not, she would cry while she repeatedly asked "Where's my boy? I want my boy." In Freud's terms (Freud, 1894), Maria had faced a traumatic experience. Trauma involves an individual and how he/she experiences a given situation; it is deemed to be an "excess of experience" with an intense affective component. The individual cannot convey the experience in words and articulate it (thereby creating a narrative and some sort of reasoning). Thus, it remains unexpressed in language and the individual keeps insisting on trying to find a way to provide some kind of explanation and express his/her pain. The traumatic reminiscences attest to the dynamic quality of memory; such memories cause pain and return every now and then.

At the time of the interview from which the following excerpts were taken, Maria was no longer an inmate. However, given her lack of family ties and social support, she decided to stay and was cared for by the institution, which had built a one-bedroom house at the back of the hospital to function as a temporary shelter. Maria and a couple of other female former inmates, who were in a similar situation, were hosted by the institution. While they had a place of their own where they would cook, wash their clothes, and watch their own TV, they were still subjected to a set of institutional rules and norms. For instance, they were allowed to leave the small area where their house was and spend some time at the open patio as long as the other inmates were also there under surveillance. Here we are faced with institutional practices that challenge the definition of total institution, as the sheltered females were partially controlled but also allowed some mobility.

Perception of location: ambivalent positionings and contradictory wants

In addressing a research interview, an inmate may have ambivalent responses about her confinement in a psychiatric forensic hospital (is it a place for treatment or for custody?). *Ambivalent positionings* indicate that the institution can be seen as "good" ("one can eat, one can sleep, one has everything") and it can also be viewed negatively ("[crying] but I'm hoping I can leave"). This was often the case for Maria. After she had been discharged, she spent some time wandering around the city, mainly the neighborhood where she used to live before being imprisoned. However, she voluntarily asked to return. As she would tell the team of researchers afterwards, "that is the place I belong to." This episode illustrates the extent to which the institutional space is crucial to her understanding of who she is and to her sense of belonging. The perception of herself co-constructed along with the others (staff and inmates) and the memory of the institution seems to be closely intertwined.

In our data, certain markers, such as the pronoun "here," encode not only the spatio-temporal location in relation to where participants are, but also capture processes of identity shift. In the interview, the marker "here" is reiterated by both interlocutors, but "here" can assume different interactional meanings. Also the recurrent use of such deictics conveys a sense of involvement (Tannen, 1989) and sometimes intense emotions felt by the interviewees/patients:

Segment 1 At the outset of a research interview—Glaucia (interviewer) and Maria (inmate):

1. Glaucia: and how do you like it here?
2. Maria: here it's good for me,
   one can eat, one can sleep, one has everything but (not audible), [she cries]
3. Glaucia: um hum, today you have here **a place of your own**, isn't?
4. Maria: [crying] but I'm hoping I can leave.

In Turn (1), Glaucia asks Maria an open question (and introduces a new topic) "and how do you like it here?" where the deictic "here" may have several meanings: a hospital, a shelter, and a home. Maria responds by juxtaposing a sequence of actions that enables us to interpret "here" as home. She first evaluates "here" positively ("it's good for me") and then explains her previous assessment by describing very basic needs ("one can eat, one can sleep") being fulfilled by the institution. She closes with an encompassing statement that reinforces how good "here" is: "one has everything" (shelter, care, and food).

Two aspects need to be discussed in her response. First, Maria uses a third-person indefinite reference "one" instead of the first-person pronoun, signaling detachment, as if she were an observer on this scene, rather than a true participant. Second, she shifts to a contrastive position ("but") and uses a semiotic sign of distress (crying).

In this sequence, the interviewer uses "here" a third time in a yes/no question followed by the expression "a place of your own," a reference that adds a personal and emotional connection to the location. Contextual information helps us better understand this reference. In 2010, the hospital leadership approved the construction of a shelter to house former inmates who did not have family ties or any other social support structure, and needed to remain at the institution. Maria was the first to live in this small one-bedroom house, along with other female inmates, as we mentioned earlier in this chapter. Ethnographic observations indicate that Maria was extremely happy to have "a place of her own," as she used to tell anyone at first. She was particularly proud of how tidy everything was. In Turn (3), the interviewer echoes Maria's prior positive assessment, as Maria was known to be helpful and thoughtful: she was sympathetic to others, frequently asking how they were; if people (selected staff and inmates) were upset, she would ask them why; she would be eager to help and participate in celebratory events (Christmas, birthdays, etc.) and joint repair efforts at the institution. In discussing the forensic institution as "location," we notice how social and cultural sources of selfhood provide room for the allocation and the performance of identities: Maria as empathetic, as resourceful, and interested in the institution and others' wellbeing.

However, in Turn (4), Maria reassesses her present situation by crying (signaling a lament or complaint) and closes the conversation stating that she hopes she could leave. Although implicitly acknowledging that she has a place of her own, it seems that having such a place is no longer enough. She reframes the location as a place she hopes to leave, connoting a painful reference to the hospital where she has been kept away from the world—where she has been imprisoned for all of her adult life.

In the next segment, the interviewer reminds Maria how popular she is in this institution. In this instance,"here" refers to the place where Maria has co-constructed her identity with many others over the years and where she has been ratified, accepted, and appreciated by many others.

Segment 2 Glaucia and Maria, ten minutes into the interview:

1. Glaucia: now there's something,
   I've noticed that **everyone** knows you around here, Maria,
   everyone kids you when they see you,
   everyone likes you,
   you are very much liked around here, right?
2. Maria: they like me ... I don't wanna leave (from) here any more.
3. Glaucia: don't wanna (leave) any more?
4. Maria: **don't** wanna [crying]

Maria answers affirmatively ("they like me") and concludes after a brief pause "I don't wanna leave here any more." Once again, she expresses an ambivalent position toward her location. It seems that recognizing herself as the object of the attention and care of others gives her some comfort and provides her with a positive assessment of self, which shifts her position: "I don't wanna leave here any more." Being reminded of the many others in her life triggers a shift from a position of pain to a position of some comfort. Closing with an emotional statement (crying) works as a contextualization cue of her ambivalence and distress in recognizing her objective and subjective locations: how misplaced she might feel as a former inmate for whom "here"—the forensic hospital—has been the sole location where she can truly relate and construct herself; and while staying in this location she can be appreciated by many others. Conflicting social and psychological interpretations take place: both the isolation of an inmate (removed from world affairs), and the appreciation of many others who co-created important relationships in this specific location.

Perception of location: credibility and assessment by a psychiatric patient

Next, we turn to perceptions of self and place by a psychiatric patient in an acute psychotic crisis. The patient, a 61-year-old lower-middle-class Brazilian woman, was hospitalized under an acute crisis. The psychiatrist, a young female resident, has been assigned to oversee her case. The following segments are taken from the second half of the admitting interview (Ribeiro, 1994). They portray how the patient, Dona Jurema, views herself and others at the hospital. In spite of her psychotic discourse and behavior, appropriate contextual references for place, time, and self are presented by Jurema at different moments in this interview.

Halfway through the interview, Jurema says emphatically that she is "here, at the hospital." Then, the patient holds the floor for a long stretch of talk, during which she says that she has to get going, that she is very tired, and that one could not make any noise "here." This is followed by the doctor asking a question.

Segment 3 Psychiatric interview—halfway into a 15-minute interview:

1. Doctor: HERE **where**, Dona Jurema?
2. Jurema: here, **here, here**.
   [bends over, looks down, speaks into microphone]
3. Doctor: **where are you**?
4. Jurema: **HERE**!
5. Doctor: **mmm**?
6. Jurema: **here**!
7. Doctor: what place is this "here" you're at?

8. Jurema: I am in a hospital.
[moves torso and head backward, raises head slightly, both hands on armchair, looks down]
9. Doctor: which hospital?
10. Jurema: I thought I'd be going to another hospital,
11. Doctor: mmm
12. Jurema: and I ended up in a very beautiful hospital.

Jurema was going to be taken to a psychiatric emergency hospital (a location with which she was familiar). However, she ended up going to the Institute of Psychiatry at the Federal University, which she assessed quite positively. By using the deictic "here," Jurema identifies coherently her present locations (the ward, the hospital, and the emergency hospital).

Jurema also relates a clear perception of her own disability, which she introduces halfway through the interview. Prior to this segment, the doctor had asked questions trying to establish common referential ground with the patient. She asks Jurema what she had seen on her way from her ward to the office.

Segment 4 Doctor–patient interview—halfway into a 15-minute interview:

1. Doctor: DID YOU SEE SOME LITTLE ANIMAL OUT THERE, WHEN YOU CAME ON YOUR WAY HERE?
Uhm, Dona Jurema?
[singing]
2. Jurema: I saw a little ant!
3. Doctor: a little **ant**?
[singing]
4. Jurema: I saw a little ant!
5. Doctor: what about the other animal you showed me outside?
[baby talk; lower tone]
6. Jurema: the otherotherother **animal**?
7. Doctor: what was it?
[baby talk; lower tone]
8. Jurema: it's a grown-up. we cannot talk about grown-ups.
9. Doctor: mmm.
[baby talk; lower tone]
10. Jurema: we can only talk about little people.
and me, since I am a little midget—

It seems that perception of location (and consequently unfolding relationships within this location) indexes one's sense of self in a psychiatric hospital: I am a little midget" (not a child; possibly a partially developed adult) and everyone else here (at the hospital) are "grown-ups," says Jurema to her doctor. Jurema adds that "we cannot talk about grown-ups" and that "we can only talk about little people." She embeds a sense of self ("I") in the group ("we") probably made up of inmates and/or patients who are part of the "little people" community.

At the close of this interview, the patient inquires whether she is credible: "Do you believe me? You really believe me?" A psychiatric patient's doubtful credibility emerges as related to her sense of self and of how she assesses herself in this particular location. In a reflexive move, she asks her doctor whether she is credible in her eyes (possibly the "grown-up eyes").

These excerpts capture sharp contrasts related to the process of hospitalization: the hospital can be "very beautiful," but it houses a "little midget" who can only see and talk about "little ants." Strong differences in power relations are expressed by this psychiatric patient (who can neither talk about nor address "grown-ups"). Indexicality points to how a psychiatric hospital can be a place for sharp contrastive interpretations of self and other, often contradictory in nature.

Mental health care professionals: ambivalent responses to inmates' sexual practices

Finally, we turn to mental health care professionals (MHCPs) who work at the Institute of Psychiatry—doctors, psychologists, social assistants, nurses—to discuss their ambivalent positioning vis-à-vis the psychiatric hospital. Is it a place to provide treatment, a place to control inmates' desires and emotions, or a place for counseling? We briefly focus on MHCPs' perception of patients' sexuality and how they relate to inpatients' well-documented and recurrent sexual practices in a mental hospital (Krumm, Kilian, & Becker, 2004; McCann, 2010; Wainberg et al., 2007; Wainberg et al., 2016). Ribeiro, Pinto, and Mann (2014) investigated MHCPs voice their perceptions and positions regarding the sexuality of psychiatric patients, particularly when they have to deal with sexual activities in the institutional context. In a multidisciplinary focus group discussion in 2003, 13 MHCPs discussed how they view issues of sexuality, mental health, and HIV/AIDS.

Such focus groups were part of an umbrella research project, the Interdisciplinary Project in Sexuality, Mental Health, and Aids (PRISSMA), that anchored the creation of a Brazilian provider-delivered HIV prevention program for the severely mentally ill (Pinto, Mann, Wainberg, Mattos, & Oliveira, 2007; Wainberg et al., 2007; Wainberg et al., 2016). Between 1997 and 2003, the institution had mixed-gender wards, following psychiatric guidelines upheld in Europe, specifically in Italy. The MHCPs often expressed a variety of positionings and feelings regarding mixed-gender wards and sexuality among patients, ranging from caring to perplexity, from a duty to repress and enforce the prohibition of sex on the wards, to counseling clients/patients on HIV prevention. MHCPs stated that there was confusion as to what the goal of the institution is and how their professional positions should adjust to these goals.

Indexing location attests to a shifting relationship, which ultimately has implications for who the MHCPs is as he/she takes on different identities as a caregiver, a counselor, or a guardian. In the following segment, a nurse technician narrates an event, which attests to her conflicted position regarding sexual practices "here."

Segment 5 Focus group discussion among MHCPs—Nilma (psychiatric nurse):

Nilma: I got in the ward, not thinking much, two patients were having sex . . . . .
then I put my hands up and said "what's happening here?"
(laughter) (...)
but that was the only reaction I had.
then they left and I didn't know what to say,
either "you can't do this" or "you can do this but not (here)."
you're not ready when it happens, you know it happens,
yet you don't expect to see it [here].

Faced with two patients having sex on a mixed-gender psychiatric ward, she inquires, "What's happening here?" She admits to having been unsure whether she should tell the patients they could or could not have sex; acknowledging how location indexes meaning and displays contradictory orientations. She also acknowledges how unprepared MHCPs are to cope with such scenes: "you know it happens, yet you don't expect to see it [here]."

Nilma's first reaction is to gesture ("put my hands up") and then shout "What's happening here?," both expressions pointing to her shock. On the one hand, she has unwittingly become a witness to a very private relationship. On the other, sexual practices among inpatients are not accepted in Brazilian clinical institutions. Thus, in the rhetorical question she puts forward ("What's happening here?") the deictic highlights the inappropriateness of such activities in a place where individuals' existences are fully controlled (Foucault, 2014), where a system of explicit formal rules is superimposed upon individuals' desires and wishes. Following Goffman (1961), the total institution defines contexts where all human activities (sleeping, eating, showering) become visible to one another and are conducted under the same single authority.

Nilma presents her personal and professional self as lacking the interactional competence to deal with the unprecedented situation ("I didn't know what to say"). Her ambivalence is then reinforced when she links two alternative statements ("either ... or") that point to the prohibition of sexual practices at the hospital [("here") ("You can't or can but not here")]. Thus, by repeating the deictic, she affirms the logic of the institution, which historically forbids and punishes such activities; she also presents herself as ambivalent, perplexed, and not competent.

Lastly, Nilma moves from the self ("I") and uses the general, indeterminate "you" to acknowledge that despite ongoing sexual activities in the institution, MHCPs lack the expertise to cope with it. She constructs herself and her peers as perplexed and sometimes frustrated professionals unable to cope and understand such complex topics and activities.

This focus group discussion illustrates perspectives seldom explored when it comes to the investigation of total institutions. First, it brings to light sensitive topics related to psychiatric patients' sexuality and sexual practices within the institutional space. In Goffman's terms, the staff are a small class that supervises and controls the patients. It is also socially integrated with the outside world and in general conceives the other members—the inmates or patients—in a stereotyped way. Moreover, the staff tend to feel righteous and knowledgeable. However, prior analysis (Ribeiro et al., 2014) and our discussion in this chapter portrays MHCPs whose discourses point to an alternative perception and understanding of the institutional context. Sexual practices among inmates in the institutional space are acknowledged and could be interpreted not as acts of disobedience but as resistance strategies against the so-called stripping process that results from the mortification of the self (Goffman, 1961; Foucault, 2006). Furthermore, while reflecting upon the function of the institution, these MHCPs do question themselves on what their responsibilities and duties are in such a hybrid institutional context (is it a place of treatment or is it an imprisoning location?). Reflections and different perceptions of one's professional self abound. Moreover, they acknowledge their lack of interactional skills to cope with these challenges, positioning themselves often as lacking competence in decision making in such difficult matters. Instead of relying on their assured institutional and official authority, they express their anxiety, distress, and discomfort by assuming a rather perplexed position that reinforces how at a loss they feel and how human they are in their uncertainties.

Conclusion

This chapter focuses on how psychiatric patients and inmates construct discursively their relationship to psychiatric and forensic hospitals. We also examine how MHCPs refer to these locations as guardians, counselors, or caretakers and how they position (or frame) patients/inmates in specific ways. Linguistic deixis is used to understand how interactants mark their location, their shifting identities, and their relationship to these settings. Marmaridou (2000) reminds us that deixis is a rich and variable linguistic phenomenon, as it locates participants and discourse in particular psychological, social, and cultural worlds. Not only does deixis depend on contextual parameters but it is also almost never neutral. With regard to the relationship between the self, the others, and the institution, the specific use and frequent repetition of the marker "here" signal the degree of emotional involvement with the places they refer to, which contributes to the construction of the speaker and the others' various positionalities.

A few common themes emerge when looking at location as it relates to self and other in total institutions. First, location may be a private place, a "place of one's own" (where one keeps it tidy for one's own use and is proud of that space). For Maria, it is the place where she spent all of her adult life, her home and shelter where she feels protected and cared for. For Jurema, it's a "very beautiful hospital" with gardened grounds cared for by patients and with many diverse types of life. It is also a place one does not want to leave, as Maria acknowledges by crying about the many others in her life at the hospital.

This private space of care and safety, relationships and beauty is, however, contrasted with the public space, our second theme. In public locations such as total institutions, there are physical barriers, as Foucault (2014) and Goffman (1961) attest, and separation as a system of social norms is imposed on individual freedom. There is loneliness (Maria cries) and smallness (Jurema feels diminished) as many powerful others (MHCPs) control and limit time, practices, and habits. They are the adults in a world of midgets, as Jurema says. And one cannot speak to adults. Therefore, we see how contrastive positions clearly emerge in how a patient and/or an inmate index location. Having a sense of the private space (a room, home) vs. the public space (a ward, the hospital) provides for very different positionings of self and other. In such cases, it seems that it is not one position versus another, but rather both or sometimes contrasting positions at the same time (one is sad and happy, as Maria cries out of sadness and happiness in her processes of institutionalization and de-institutionalization, as well as one wishes to leave and stay at the same time).

Ambivalent and contradictory positionings are also present among MHCPs, mostly when they relate to practices that have yet to be fully examined and regulated, such as patients' rights to exert their sexuality within hospital settings (Ribeiro et al., 2014). We see that MHCPs shift positionings according to their perception of the hospital. Is "here" a place for treatment and care or is it a place where patients should obediently subscribe to a set of rigid rules? Is it a public or a private place? How much privacy can patients/inmates have within a public space? MHCPs often display a lack of interactional competence, ambiguity, and perplexity in their relationship to inpatients and to themselves when indexing location as it relates to practices that are not yet fully accepted.

Thus, investigations grounded in microanalysis of interactions among inmates, caretakers, and researchers contribute to a better understanding of the complexity of total institutions such as forensic and psychiatric hospitals. These studies help bring to the surface hidden meaning and complex institutional layers that have not been sufficiently investigated. While forensic and psychiatric hospitals undoubtedly create a system that controls and disciplines inmates' existences, they are also a social unit where human beings (re)create their selves, where they co-construct themselves in everyday activities, and where they learn how to affect and be affected by others.

Goffman (1961) explored the implications of total institutions upon the construction of self for patients and inmates. Degrading procedures and reduced opportunities for interactions with others in the outer world were his focus. However, in both institutions under investigation in this discussion, some of the "adjustment strategies" have played a distinct role. Interactions among MHCPs and patients in the psychiatric hospital challenge the expected and homogeneous values of the staff, as well as the set of attitudes and knowledge that the staff take for granted. Professional teams face institutional dilemmas of their own. As for the Heitor Carrilho Forensic Hospital, its long de-institutionalization process came to an end in February 2016 in accordance with Act 10.216/2001, which established new collective mental health psychosocial rehabilitation for all types of psychiatric patients—convicts included. Since 2009, the multidisciplinary teams in the State of Rio de Janeiro have fought for a more humanitarian treatment for its population. On the one hand, they fully complied with referring inmates to sentence reassessments, a procedure that would generally take much longer than the two years stated by Brazilian law. On the other hand, they were struggling to find alternative forms of psychosocial rehabilitation for the sheltered population, like Maria, who lacked social support for basic care, safety, and independence and thus had stayed at the institution. MHCPs' and sheltered patients' interviews and stories attest to the dynamics of this hybrid institution where there had also been sufficient room for subjective practices.

Finally, it is worth highlighting the Brazilian social and political context and noting that the process of de-institutionalization—which started in the 1980s and was regulated in 2001—has not been fully implemented (Hirdes, 2009). The current public policy for the mental health sector endorses an interdisciplinary health care model that aims for the social rehabilitation of patients. Substitute services, such as daycare hospitals, centers of psychosocial care (CAPs), and therapeutic residences, are strategic and essential for the de-institutionalization process of patients who spend most of their lives in psychiatric institutions. However, the Brazilian public mental health care system has yet to provide enough of such services, often leaving users, family members, and MHCPs in a vacuum. MHCPs find themselves still shifting from more traditional positions (as guardians) to more contemporary positions (as counselors). While Brazilian social norms dictate that patients' rights as full citizens need to be respected, the psychiatric hospital is still an isolated and enclosed system whose primary aim is also to control all aspects of patients'/inmates' lives, including their sexuality.

Appendix A: original interview segments in Brazilian Portuguese

Segment 1 At the outset of a research interview—Glaucia (interviewer) and Maria (inmate):

1. Glaucia: e o que que você acha daqui?
2. Maria: aqui pra mim é bom,
   que tem o que comer, tem onde dormir,
   tem tudo, mas (impossivel), [cries]
3. Glaucia: um hum, hoje você aqui tem seu **cantinho**, é isso?
4. Maria: [crying] mas eu tô com esperança de ir embora.

Segment 2 Glaucia and Maria, ten minutes into the research interview:

1. Glaucia: agora uma coisa,
   eu observei que **todo mundo** aqui dentro conhece a Maria,
   todo mundo passa e brinca com você,
   todo mundo gosta de você,
   você é muito querida aqui, né?
2. Maria: gostam ... eu não quero mais ir embora daqui não.
3. Glaucia: não quer mais não?
4. Maria: quero **não**. [crying]

Segment 3 Psychiatric interview—halfway into a 15-minute interview:

1. Doctor: AQUI **aonde**, Dona Jurema?
2. Jurema: aqui, **aqui**, **aqui**.
   [bends over, looks down, speaks into microphone]
3. Doctor: **a senhora está aonde**?
4. Jurema: **AQUI**!
5. Doctor: **mmm**?
6. Jurema: **aqui**!
7. Doctor: que lugar é esse "aqui" que a senhora está?
8. Jurema: eu tô num hospital.
   [moves torso and head backward, raises head slightly, both hands on armchair, looks down]

9. Doctor: qual hospital?
10. Jurema: eu pensava que ia ficar noutro hospital,
11. Doctor: mmm
12. Jurema: e fiquei num hospital muito bonito.

Segment 4 Doctor–patient interview—halfway into a 15-minute interview:

1. Doctor: A SENHORA VIU ALGUM BICHINHO LA FORA, QUANDO PASSOU POR AQUI?
   uhm, **Dona Jurema**?
   [singing]
2. Jurema: eu vi uma formiguinha!
3. Doctor: **formiguinha**?
   [singing]
4. Jurema: eu vi uma formiguinha!
5. Doctor: e o outro bicho, que a senhora mostrou lá fora?
   [baby talk; lower tone]
6. Jurema: o outrooutrooutrooutro **bicho**?
7. Doctor: qual foi?
   [baby talk; lower tone]
8. Jurema: é gente grande. a gente não pode falar de gente grande.
9. Doctor: mmm.
   [baby talk; lower tone]
10. Jurema: só pode falar de gente pequena.
    e eu como sou anãozinho—

Segment 5 Focus group discussion among MHCPs—Nilma (psychiatric nurse):

Nilma: Eu entrei de bobeira na enfermaria, dois pacientes transando. . . . .
aí eu botei a mão na cintura e falei "que que é isso?" (risos) (...)
mas foi a única reação que eu tive.
aí eles saíram e eu não sabia o que dizia,
ou "não pode fazer isso" ou "faz isso mas não (aqui)."
na hora você não espera, você sabe que acontece,
mas você não espera ver.

Appendix B: transcription conventions

.	Sentence final falling intonation
,	Sentence final rising and fall intonation; more to come
?	Brazilian Portuguese question pattern
...	Pause (length of time was not assigned)
.....	Short text omitted
bold	Emphatic stress
CAPS	Very emphatic stress
(not audible)	Transcription impossible
(words)	Uncertain transcription
( )	Unclear referent
[ ]	Description of nonverbal behavior indicated one line below the talk

References

Brazil, Act 10.216/2001. www.planalto.gov.br/ccivil_03/leis/LEIS_2001/L10216.htm.

Clough, P. (1990). Reading Goffman: Toward the deconstruction of sociology. In S. Riggins (Ed.), *Beyond Goffman: Studies on communication, institution, and social interaction* (pp. 187–202). New York, NY: Mouton de Gruyter.

Davies, B. & Harré, R. (1990). Positioning: The discursive construction of selves. *Journal for the Theory of Social Behaviour*, *20*(1), 43–63.

de Fina, A. (2003). *Identity in narrative: A study of immigrant discourse.* Philadelphia, PA: John Benjamins.

Erickson, F. (2004). *Talk and social theory.* Cambridge: Polity Press.

Erickson, F. & Shultz, J. (1982). *The counselor as gatekeeper: Social interaction in interviews.* New York, NY: Academic Press.

Foucault, M. (2006). *Psychiatric power. Lectures at the Collège de France, 1973–1974.* New York, NY: Palgrave Macmillan.

Foucault, M. (2014). *Wrong-doing, truth-telling: The function of avowal in justice.* Chicago, IL: University of Chicago Press.

Freud, S. (1894/2001). The neuro-psychoses of defence. *The standard edition of the complete psychoanalytic works of Sigmund Freud. Vol III (1893–1899).* London: Vintage.

Gal, S. (2009). Linguistic anthropology. In J. L. Mey (Ed.), *Concise encyclopedia of pragmatics* (2nd ed.) (pp. 519–533). Oxford: Elsevier.

Goffman, E. (1961). *Asylums.* New York, NY: Anchor Books.

Goffman, E. (1972). The neglected situation. In P. P. Giglioli (Ed.), *Language and social context* (pp. 61–66). Baltimore, MD: Penguin.

Goffman, E. (1974). *Frame analysis*. New York, NY: Harper & Row.

Goffman, E. (1981). *Forms of talk*. Philadelphia, PA: University of Pennsylvania Press.

Gumperz, J. (1982). *Discourse strategies*. Cambridge: Cambridge University Press.

Gumperz, J. (1999). On interactional sociolinguistic method. In S. Sarangi & C. Roberts (Eds.), *Talk, work and institutional order: Discourse in medical, mediation and management settings* (pp. 453–471). New York, NY: Mouton de Gruyter.

Hirdes, A. (2009). The psychiatric reform in Brazil: A (re)view. *Ciência & Saúde Coletiva, 14*(1), 297–305.

Hymes, D. (1974). *Foundations in sociolinguistics: An ethnographic approach*. Philadelphia, PA: University of Pennsylvania Press.

Krumm, S., Kilian, R., & Becker, T. (2004). Psychiatric inpatient care and sexuality. *Psychiatrische Praxis, 31*(4), 212–217.

Lemke, J. L. (2008). Identity, development, and desire: Critical questions. In C. R. Caldas-Coulthard & R. Iedema (Eds.), *Identity trouble: Critical discourse and contested identities* (pp. 17–42). New York, NY: Palgrave.

Marmaridou, S. S. A. (2000). *Pragmatic meaning and cognition*. Philadelphia, PA: John Benjamins.

McCann, E. (2010). The sexual and relationship needs of people who experience psychosis: Quantitative findings of a UK study. *Journal of Psychiatric and Mental Health Nursing, 17*(4), 295–303.

Mey. J. L. (2006). Pragmatics overview. In J. L. Mey (Ed.), *Concise encyclopedia of pragmatics* (2nd ed.) (pp. 786–797). Oxford: Elsevier.

Pinto, D. (2011). Discourse analysis, the use of images and the health field: Theoretical-methodological aspects. *Revista Eletrônica de Comunicação, Informação & Inovação em Saúde, 5*(2), 8–15.

Pinto, D. & Nascimento, U. (2012). Caminhos da memória social do hospital de Custódia e Tratamento Heitor Carrilho: uma investigação filosófica. *Psicanálise & Barroco em Revista, 10*(1), 1–22.

Pinto, D., Ribeiro, B. T., & Lopes Dantas, M. T. (2005). "Let the heart speak out": Interviewing practices by psychiatrists from two different traditions. *Communication & Medicine, 2*(2), 177–188.

Pinto, D., Mann, C. G., Wainberg, M., Mattos, P., & Oliveira, S. B. (2007). Vulnerability to HIV, and mental health: An ethnographic study of psychiatric institutions. *Cadernos de Saúde Pública*. FIOCRUZ, *23*(9), 2224–2233.

Ribeiro, B. T. (1994). *Coherence in psychotic discourse*. Cambridge: Cambridge University Press.

Ribeiro, B. T. (2002). Erotic discourse strategies in powerless women: Analyzing psychiatric interviews. In L. Litosseliti & J. Sunderland (Eds.), *Gender identity and discourse analysis* (pp. 193–219). Philadelphia, PA: John Benjamins.

Ribeiro, B. T. & Pinto, D. S. (2006a). The psychiatric interview: An insider's perspective. In M. Gotti & F. Salager-Meyer (Eds.), *Advances in medical discourse analysis: Oral and written contexts* (pp. 155–175). Bern: Peter Lang.

Ribeiro, B. T. & Pinto, D. S. (2006b). Medical discourse, psychiatric interview. In F. Salager-Meyer (Ed.), *Encyclopedia of language and linguistics* (pp. 658–664). Oxford: Elsevier.

Ribeiro, B. T. & Pinto, D. S. (2010). Psychotic discourse. In L. Cummings (Ed.), *Routledge pragmatics encyclopedia* (pp. 370–374). London and New York: Routledge.

Ribeiro, B. T. & Pinto, D. S. (2015). *Positioning self and other: How psychiatric patients and psychiatric inmates construct discursively their relationship to total institutions*. Paper presented at the Psychology and the Other Conference, Cambridge, MA. October.

Ribeiro, B. T., Pinto, D. S., & Mann, C. G. (2014). Mental healthcare professionals' role performance: Challenges in the institutional order of a psychiatric hospital. In E. H. Hamilton & S. Chou (Eds.), *The Routledge handbook of language and health communication* (pp. 389–406). New York, NY: Routledge.

Santos, A. L. G., Farias, F. R., & Pinto, D. S. (2015). Por uma sociedade sem hospitais de custódia e tratamento psiquiátrico. *História, Ciências, Saúde-Manguinhos*, *22*(4), 1215–1230.

Sarangi, S. & Roberts, C. (1999). *Talk, work and institutional order: Discourse in medical, mediation and management settings.* New York, NY: Mouton de Gruyter.

Schiffrin, D. (1989). Conversation analysis. In F. J. Newmeyer (Ed.), *Linguistics: The Cambridge survey. Volume 4: Language: The socio-cultural context* (pp. 251–276). Cambridge: Cambridge University Press.

Schiffrin, D. (1994). *Approaches to discourse*. New York, NY: Blackwell.

Schiffrin, D. (1996). Narrative as self-portrait: Sociolinguistic constructions of identity. *Language in Society*, *25*(2), 167–203.

Tannen, D. (1986). *That's not what I meant! How conversational style makes or breaks your relations with others.* New York, NY: William Morrow, Ballantine.

Tannen, D. (1989). *Talking voices: Repetition, dialogue and imagery in conversational discourse*. Cambridge: Cambridge University Press.

Tannen, D. (1993). *Framing in discourse.* New York, NY: Oxford University Press.

Wainberg, M., Cournos, F., Wall, M., Norcini Pala, A., Mann, C. G., Pinto, D., Pinho, V., & McKinnon, K. (2016). Mental illness sexual stigma: Implications for health and recovery. *Psychiatric Rehabilitation Journal*, *39*(2), 1–7.

Wainberg M., Gonzalez, A., McKinnon, K., Elkington, K., Pinto, D., Mann, C. G., & Mattos, P. (2007). Targeted ethnography as a critical step to inform cultural adaptations of HIV prevention interventions for adults with severe mental illness. *Social Science & Medicine*, *65*(2), 296–308.

Chapter 10

"I am not myself, but I am not an other"

Self-dissolution narrative in medical rehabilitation psychotherapy

Orin Segal[1]

Introduction

Coping with acquired chronic medical-physical conditions: overview

The purpose of this chapter is to explore *self-dissolution*, as a common and major psychological phenomenon following acquired chronic medical-physical conditions (ACMC) and as a key feature in self-illness narratives that follow these conditions.[2] Through the exploration of different aspects of this experience, I suggest a theoretical and practical inter-disciplinary self-illness narrative framework to further understand the subjective experiences of individuals coping with ACMC.

Before I present the self-illness narrative model and the key role that self-dissolution plays within it, we should start with the rationale and importance of further understanding and exploring the psychological effect of ACMC. Examining various websites, books, and publications that deal with general health, public health policy, welfare rights, or the physical-socio-psychological impact of ACMC, one realizes that chronic medical conditions are ubiquitous. For example, in OECD (Organisation for Economic Co-operation and Development) states and in the USA, about 10 to 15 percent of the population is coping with serious physical disability, congenital or acquired (Brault, 2012; Carrol et al., 2014). These physical conditions may include coping with a vast range of physical and mental changes and challenges, such as dealing with: limitation in hearing, vision, cognition, or mobility; chronic or acute pain or physical discomfort; loss or lack of ability to perform or participate in normative tasks in a normative fashion; and disfigurement of the body or an apparent uniquely different body from a perceived norm.

These long-term challenges have an emotional toll. Persons with physical disability and chronic illness tend to seek emotional help and are frequently diagnosed with emotional distress. For example, in 2012 the Israeli Ministry of Health published a survey showing that in Israel, 60 percent of persons with chronic illness were also diagnosed with depression or anxiety (Israeli Ministry of Health, 2012).[3] Furthermore, research literature describes the traumatic experience of the subjective perception of profound and unexpected changes in one's self, amongst the unique psychological effects of acquired medical conditions (Katz & Florian, 1986–1987; Livneh & Martz, 2007).

Intuitively, it is not surprising that the traumatic physical experience is interrelated to an experience of traumatic change of self. This connection is theoretically supported; both philosophers and psychologists argue that the physical body and the psychological self are phenomenologically and theoretically entwined. The former emphasize cognitive and ethical aspects of this self–body bond, and the latter emphasize emotional and relational aspects (Bermúdez, 1998; Butler, 2004; Gubb, 2013; Neisser, 1993; Stern, 2000; Winnicott, 1966). Viewing this bond from a cognitive stance, our body—through its sensations, perceptions, and actions—is a primary source of self-knowledge, both implicit and explicit (Neisser, 1993). But more importantly in relation to my argument, the physical body does not only serve as a tool for acquiring knowledge of the self, it is a primary constituent of the self—on a cognitive, emotional, interpersonal, and social level.[4]

Hence, as our bodily experience fundamentally and abruptly changes following ACMC, we are confronted by a twofold psychological toll. We have to cope not only with a painful, weak, and limited body, but also with the disruption to the foundations of our self-knowledge and self-constitution.

Regarding this last point, it is important to refer to the analytic and linguistic philosopher Ludwig Wittgenstein, who had an influential role in what is referred to as the "linguistic turn" of the twentieth century in philosophical thought (Rorty, 1992, p. 373). Amongst other linguistic investigations, Wittgenstein was concerned with how self-knowledge and accessibility to individual private experiences are shaped and limited by the mechanism of language, which is publicly constructed (Wittgenstein, 1953, 1969). Going back to the issue of self-foundations, Wittgenstein believed that in order for us to make meaning of our experience, we have to hold certain beliefs, or a belief system, as indisputable. A disruption to this belief system, such as the disruption following self-dissolution, which I will further elaborate on, is so dangerous to our cognitive and psychological self-assurance that Wittgenstein asked whether such a "'revision' would amount to annihilation of all yardsticks?" (1969, Para. 492).

Self-dissolution and complicated grief following ACMC

It is important to note that during the last few decades, health and rehabilitation psychology literature has focused on the sense of loss of self. In most cases, this has been achieved through the empirical study of the targeted ACMC population, i.e. the sense of loss following spinal cord injury, head injury, chronic heart disease, etc. These studies usually focus on the effect that specific ACMC have on a particular sense of loss, as I will describe.

Yet, few studies and writings have attempted to consolidate this empirical knowledge into a systematic, theoretical framework. Even fewer have attempted to tie this sense of loss of self to psychoanalytic and philosophical theories regarding the concept of self. Moreover, the majority of studies concerned with perceived loss of self focus on this experience following acquired brain injuries. This narrow focus has reduced the attention given to self-dissolution experienced following other acquired conditions, even giving rise to the Kohutian understanding that "[t]he loss of a limb can therefore be mourned, like the loss of a love object; a defect in the realm of our mental functions, however, is experienced as loss of self" (Kohut, 1972, p. 383).

Following the idea that traumatic change to self is the main consequence of all ACMC, two common psychological sequelae are viewed in this chapter as key concepts, generating self-illness perceptions or narratives. These concepts are *self-dissolution* and its common (but not necessary) companion, *complicated grief*.

In short, self-dissolution is the experience behind common expressions such as "I am another person" or "I am not my-self," expressed by many persons experiencing sudden onsets of disabling and distressing long-term physical conditions. The feeling of self-dissolution is a feeling of shattered or split self. It is a feeling of split and disintegration between a previously known and seemingly stable self, and a present unknown and unpredictable self. If persistent over time, self-dissolution can cause profound distress.

As self-dissolution consists of a clash between a present and past sense of self, a major part of self-dissolution is the experience of vague loss of self. In light of the postmodern conceptualization of the self as a multitude of states, this loss of self should be better described as a mourning reaction to a subjective sense of irreversible or overwhelming change in specific self-domains or self-states (Bromberg, 1998; Orange, 2001; Stern, 2000).

As mentioned earlier, many of the rehabilitation and health psychology studies are concerned with this sense of loss. Usually, these studies target specific senses of loss. One such loss described in the psychological literature is the loss of control and knowledge of one's body and world (Van de Velde et al., 2012). Another is the loss of previously achievable functions and goals. This is frequently accompanied by shattered beliefs about one's own capabilities and self-expectations, and the need to alter previously held goals for one's life (Yeates, Gracey, & McGrath, 2008). A third is the perception of a profound social change. This includes a real or perceived change in social status, social opportunities, feeling of social worth, and sense of togetherness and belonging (Davis, 1995; Wright, 1983).

These experiences account for the "twinning," mentioned earlier, between self-dissolution and the agonizing complicated grief. "Complicated grief" is a term that refers to a continuous and unresolved feeling of loss.[5] Robert Neimeyer and colleagues (Neimeyer, Pennebaker, & Van Dyke, 2009), who write about and work with people coping with loss and bereavement, define complicated grief as "a crisis in meaning that simultaneously deprives the survivor of a significant past, a comprehensible present and a purposeful future" (p. 457). They add that the effect of this is feeling stuck in a non-developing and limited narrative.

Respectively, this chapter attempts to tie together the varied empirical knowledge we have on the psychological outcomes of ACMC, mainly the different senses of loss, in a conceptual and theoretical framework. I believe that self-dissolution, referring to perception of change and not just loss, can serve as a macro-concept, linking together the empirical phenomenology and the interdisciplinary theory of self. Furthermore, as I understand the link between body and self to be inseparable, this chapter emphasizes that self-dissolution is an experience shared by many individuals coping with various ACMC.

We see that coping with ACMC alters life immensely. It forces one to re-re-cognize oneself. It forces one to reconcile and mourn the lost aspects of a previously known self, and yet still identify continuous aspects of a recognizable self. This is an ongoing, confusing, and ambiguous mourning process, not always understood by the social milieu, demanding resolution and adjustment.

I would like to illustrate the sense of self-dissolution and the negotiation of complicated grief in the following blog text, written eloquently by Christina Symanski, referred to on her blog as Chrissi.[6] Chrissi was a young woman who had suffered a severe spinal cord injury when she was in her mid-twenties, a few years prior to writing this blog. Following her injury, Chrissi was left quadriplegic, able to control only her facial muscles. She had learnt to use a mouth brush to paint and a mouth pointing device to use a computer. Using her mouth, she expressed her emotional experience in writing and painting. Chrissi writes about her sense of self-dissolution:

> It's difficult to keep it together. At times I feel myself going crazy, or just feel like I've had enough and want to give up. It's a challenge finding balance, and finding reasons to move forward with the life I have now and to the person I've become. The person I was no longer exists. She was taken away and replaced with the person I am today.
>
> Almost every aspect of my life changed overnight, and although I'm the same person in some aspects, my physical state impacts my mental and emotional well-being. My entire perspective on life has changed; my priorities, my coping skills, my abilities, my personality, my desires and motivation are all directly impacted by paralysis ... Even if I were to be miraculously cured, I'd never be the same person as I was before, because I'm not ... My paralysis has forced me to change, and grow, in many ways, both positively and negatively.
>
> (Chrissi, 2007)

Self-dissolution in a narrative framework

Following the notion that self-dissolution is one of the major psychological sequelae following ACMC, I would like to refer to postmodern psychoanalytic concepts of self. Postmodern approaches view the self not as an entity to be found in our minds, but more as a mental construct. One way of conceptualizing the self, according to this view, is as an active mental construct through which the individual achieves a sense of continuity over time, and through which he/she perceives the world, organizes and selects information about it, and grants it meaning and sense (Mitchell, 1991; Stern, 2000).

Narrativists and constructivists add to this idea that humans make meaning and organize their life experiences through narratives (Roos & Neimeyer, 2007; Schafer, 1980a). The self, or self-narrative, is viewed as a "'macro-narrative' that consolidates our self-understanding, establishes our characteristic range of emotions and goals, and guides our performance on the stage of the social world" (Neimeyer, Herrero, & Botella, 2006, p. 129). Based on this view, the self is conceptualized as a contingent mental narrative construct serving a twofold purpose: to gain a sense of continuity in a non-continuous experience, and to organize and make sense of a chaotic and non-organized world. This mental function is performed effortlessly and in most cases without conscious deliberation.

Using this conceptualization, if self or self-narrative serve as a function of meaning-making, then experiencing ACMC can alter this meaning in a fundamental way. "[A] somatic disorder—which might be enduring or short lived," writes Marilia Aisenstein (2006), a psychoanalyst from the Paris Psychosomatic School, "must later be integrated into the chain of psychic events which make up a life" (p. 670). Until this is done, the "chain of psychic events" can be meaningless and feel unconnected, hence causing dissolution of meaning when meaning is most needed.

Looking at self-dissolution this way, it becomes clearer why the emotional reaction is linked to complicated grief. Not only does self-dissolution invalidate meaning, as does complicated grief, it also captures one in a restricted and non-developing narrative. Roughly speaking, this is a rigid narrative in which there is a former self, recognized as a previously organized construct, and a new sense of self, which is not totally meaningful. The two are split by an illness, a physical injury, or an ongoing acquired impairment. The relationship between the two selves is an ambiguous one, simultaneously causing an unsettling sense of familiarity and estrangement. In many ways, this strangeness is the Freudian "Unheimliche" (Freud, 1919). It is that "crazy" feeling that Chrissi describes in her blog—the feeling of being "replaced with the person I am today" that she finds so distressing and unresolvable in her experience.

A self-illness narrative model

The self-dissolution concept that is presented here is embedded in a wider *self-illness narrative model*, which I will not describe in depth, as the scope of this chapter is limited. In short, two main parts roughly divide the features of the self-illness narrative told, the "text and context" or *structure* and *author–listener* (Neimeyer & Raskin, 2000; Zilber, Tuval-Mashiach, & Lieblich, 2008, p. 1048).

The textual or structural features are the intrinsic, independent features, and include in the suggested self-illness narrative model the more formal narrative concepts, such as *theme* and *form*. The context or author–listener field refers to the social, cultural, and relational features, interdependent with the listener's experience. In my model, the relational features include the interpersonal context in which the story is being told, such as the interaction and the role interplay between narrator and listener, and the way the narrative itself serves as a purposeful action in the world and shapes a self-state accordingly. When discussing self-narratives, the narrative fields also correspond to current psychoanalytic theory, in which narrative structure can be compared to intra-personal psychology, while author–listener can be compared to interpersonal and relational psychology (Aron, 2006; Jopling, 2000).

As I will soon discuss more comprehensively, the focus of this chapter is to discuss self-dissolution as it presents itself in the structural field of self-illness narratives, both as a thematic component, and as a formal one. I suggest that it can shape the narrative and be interpreted through: (1) theme, as manifested in *dissolution dominance* or (2) form, as manifested in *coherence disruption*.

Before I do so, it is important to note that by emphasizing the intrinsic "intra-psychological" characteristics of self-dissolution, I do not mean to imply that this experience is not relationally embedded as well. I believe that human experiences, including experiences of ACMC, are rooted in inter-subjective and social contexts, thus affecting self-constitution accordingly. This is in agreement with current psychological relational thought, and current philosophical discussions regarding the role of interactions with others on self-knowledge and self-constitution (Atwood, Orange, & Stolorow, 2002; Butler, 2004; Jopling, 2000; Neisser, 1993; Stern, 2000; Stolorow & Atwood, 1994). However, as the scope of this chapter is limited, I will not further discuss the effect of the author–listener/inter-personal field on self-dissolution or other self-illness aspects.

Dissolution dominance: self-dissolution as a thematic feature

Describing the contribution of theme and form to the sense of self, Neimeyer (2000) writes: "A biographical sense of identity becomes consolidated as one tacks back and forth between tacit participation in the plot structure of one's life (the experiencing me) and the explicit attribution of thematic meaning to these episodes (the explaining I)" (p. 223). Following this idea, the theme deals with the "*why*" behind a narrative, the explanations and connections between different experiences or aspects of the experiences. This explanatory or binding system grants an overall meaning to experiences.

In this sense, themes can function as "micro-themes," giving meaning and significance to an isolated experience, like an episode in our life story. Alternatively, they can also function as "macro-themes," as an overall meaning for life experiences, or, as Schafer (1980a) puts it, "one or another systematic account of them" (p. 36). The self, as an organizing construct, serves as a macro-theme, tying together past, present, and future, and different emotional, physical, and interpersonal experiences.

As described earlier, when traumatic experiences affect the core theme of the self, self-dissolution takes place. This sense of dissolution corresponds to the self-aspects that are challenged by the traumatic experiences, such as social competence or physical self-image, thus creating a *dissolution dominance*, functioning as a temporary or chronic macro-narrative.

Dissolution dominance keeps a constant sense of an unstable, fundamentally changed self, a feeling of estrangement from self-states or perceptions. As long as dissolution dominance continues to dictate the self-illness theme, the narrative is fixated on the clash between the previously known me, and the estranged and unwanted new me.

Three major dissolution dominance themes can be extrapolated out of clinical cases and research in the field of health and rehabilitation psychology. The first two correspond to the basic philosophical subject–object debate. The third is usually described as a core feature of the self in most definitions of self.

Dissolution dominance: dissolution of self as physical object

The first dissolution dominance I will focus on is of the self as a physical object. This relies on the sense of change to the known physical or physically related attributes of the self, "the physical *me*" (James, 1892, p. 292). Before discussing the dissolution of the self as a physical object, I will briefly describe the sense of self as an object, and, specifically, as a physical object.

Following William James, Ludwig Wittgenstein (1958) describes in *The Blue and Brown Books* this sense of self as the knowledge I have about myself that identifies me as a person and that enables me to talk and think about myself (p. 91). It includes my biography, abilities, and traits, my physical attributes, and the objects that belong to me. To these characteristics, which were also described by James, Wittgenstein adds an important characteristic of self as object, which is the possibility of making an identity error (De Gaynsford, 2006, p. 54; Wittgenstein, 1958, p. 97). This means that as with all objects, if we perceive the self as an object, we can make judgment errors when doing so. This is not the case when the self is perceived as a subject. As the identification of self as subject is not based on empirical attributes, but rather on a first-person sense of I-ness, there is immunity to error, according to Wittgenstein.

The idea of identity error in self-as-object perception could have several implications for self-dissolution. Possibly the most prominent one is the sense of not knowing who one is because physical attributes that were previously used to construct a personal identity have changed due to illness or injury. This raises a question frequently asked by persons coping with ACMC: Is this me? Is this really me?

Following the comparison between perceptions of objects in general, and perception of self as physical object, Jean-Paul Sartre (1943) further suggests that "I exist therefore for myself as known by the Other – in particular in my very facticity" (p. 351). That is, the cognition of self as object is essentially no different from the cognition of other factual objects in the world, thus causing a sense of distance from myself while doing so. Sartre does not imply that the perception of self as object is the only ontological stance one can have in the world, but he argues that there are conditions that trigger this kind of self-consciousness.

One of the main conditions he suggests, highly relevant to this chapter, is the perception of the body. When one perceives one's body—for example, by observing one's hand, looking in the mirror, or being aware of pain—self as object becomes automatically dominant in one's consciousness. Following this idea, if experiencing a physical medical condition tends to attract our attention to our physical attributes, this affects a domination of a sense of self as object and, accordingly, dissolution dominance of self as object. In many cases, this dissolution dominance is expressed through a sense of merger between self and illness. The illness becomes me.

Dissolution dominance: dissolution of self as autonomous subject

The second dissolution dominance described in my narrative model is dissolution of the self as an autonomous subject. Generally speaking, both in psychoanalysis and in philosophical discussions of self, the sense of self as subject is described as the sense of an active self, capable of making choices (Gertler, 2011; Kohut & Wolf, 1978).[7] This is a self that is perceived as a core of mental actions, such as knowing, thinking, sensing, perceiving, and deliberating.

As opposed to the sense of self as a physical object, perceived in the second or third person, this core self is felt within the body, as situated in it and perceiving from it. As Sartre (1943) describes it: "I exist my body" (p. 351). This is the reason why we are "immune to errors" (i.e. cannot make mistakes), nor can we or should we try to validate this sense of self empirically (Wittgenstein, 1958, p. 98).

A major aspect of the self as subject, which received abundant attention in the noughties, is the sense of self as an autonomous agent, as a "center of initiative" (Kohut, 1979, p. 452; Korsgaard, 2009). This includes being intentional (being able to make everyday and life choices), being deliberate (acting purposefully to achieve choices), and feeling a sense of efficacy (managing to achieve these life goals and choices). Other concepts expressing an active self, such as self-control, omnipotence, and self-action, are all functions related to this sense of self. This is the perception of oneself as "a tool machine" (Sartre, 1943, p. 320).

The perception of oneself following physical illness, injury, or disability can challenge any of these aspects of self as autonomous agent, thus contributing to dissolution dominance. These challenges to self as autonomous may include not being able to make everyday and life choices, and losing a sense of intentionality and deliberation. They might also include not being able to act purposefully, not managing to achieve these life goals and choices, or losing a sense of efficacy and self-control.

Dissolution dominance: dissolution of self as continuous and united

The third sense of self, which is frequently the focus of self-dissolution following ACMC, is the continuous and united sense of self. Although philosophy and postmodern psychology have had a long and ongoing debate about the possibility of the self being a single entity or mental construct, it is accepted that the self is usually perceived by the individual as unitary and continuous. Part of this dialectical debate is summarized eloquently by Philip Bromberg (1998), a relational psychologist, who describes the self as "defined by nonlinear, discontinuous states of consciousness that attain a coherence that overrides the awareness of discontinuity and leads to the experience of a cohesive sense of personal identity and the healthy illusion of being 'one self'" (p. 228).

According to philosopher Christine Korsgaard (1989), this perception of united self is directly linked to the sense of self as autonomous. In order for us to achieve autonomy, we must act and make choices between alternative actions, "and you have only one body with which to act" (p. 111).

As self-dissolution emphasizes a conflict between a previously known self and a present "ill" self, such that the body and the characteristics of self are frequently perceived as different to a pre-morbid body and self, one must unwillingly experience the debate of multiplicity vs. unitary self. When experiencing this forced multiplicity of self, the illusion of a united self is shattered.

Interpreting dissolution dominance in clinical texts

The following two texts are taken from therapy sessions with Leviah, a 30-year-old woman. By means of these texts, I would like to demonstrate the interpretation of dissolution dominance. The first text is from a session that took place a few weeks after Leviah was diagnosed with the first remission of her cancer, four months after the end of a seemingly successful reaction to a previous treatment. The second text is from a therapy session that occurred after Leviah had just received confirmation of her fear that her cancer was back again, for the third time. All of Leviah's previous treatments were stopped temporarily and her prognosis was unclear.

> It's all a question of how good my story is and how much you believe in it. That is what I say to future clients when I try to promote my work, and I think it is also what I think I am doing when I am talking about myself. Last week, when I met you, my story was a tragic one. I was confused and devastated. In my story, everything was going wrong. The cancer was back for the second time, my career wasn't doing as well as I'd hoped, and even my newborn nephew, whom I love with all my heart, felt more like a threat. The fact that I would not see him grow up was devastating. That added up to a story of a successful, artistic young woman, who lost it all because of a rapid growing cancer. This week, my story is a different one. It's a story of a girl who will beat it and win.

> This has changed my life in a profound way. Not so much in a good or bad way, just profoundly. I am more sensitive, probably friendlier and more outgoing than I used to be. On the other hand, I have never thought so much about death in my life. I always felt like I had a strong network of people who love me and whom I can trust. I don't have that feeling today … I don't know …
>
> Even if this is over, and the cancer is gone, which I doubt, how will I ever be able to change this state of mind? After two years of this being my life, how will I be able to return to a life where cancer isn't a huge part of it? All the bureaucracy and the practical day-to-day dealing with it—insurances, treatments, doctors … and the way I perceive life. I don't know … How can that change again? ...
>
> Sometimes, such as lately, I feel so alone. It is as if I am the only one in the world. No one understands me. No one can really help … I can't help myself either. It's all such a mess. I'm a mess. All I need is to be understood, to let the guard down. I tell my husband that, but he doesn't understand. He can't or he won't, because that, for him, would be admitting that things are all wrong. That I really, really might be dying … I don't know ….

Reading Leviah's texts, we can see two kinds of dissolution dominances. The first is dissolution of the self as continous and united. This is expressed through her comparisons between who she is now and who she was before coping with cancer. In the second text, she compares herself on a characteristic level, through comparative adjectives describing who she is now as opposed to previously, such as being now "more sensitive, probably friendlier …" than she was before she experienced cancer. Another expression of dissolution of continuity is Leviah's perception of changes in her real and believed social networks and ties. This is emphasized through her feeling she has lost the trust she once held in her social networks and support. A third expression of dissolution of continuity is Leviah's perceived change in "state of mind," which we could view as a perceived change in self-state. She feels that, as opposed to who she used to be, her state of mind is now "cancerous."

This dissolution of self is further enhanced by autonomy dissolution, apparent in both of Leviah's texts. In the earlier text, this is expressed through her negotiation between feeling her story is "a tragic one … a story of a successful, artistic young woman, who lost it all because of a rapid growing cancer" (being a self-story of passivity and helplessness), and perceiving her self-narrative as "a story of a girl who will beat it and win" (being a self-story of autonomy and control over her life). While in the first text she is negotiating between two narratives, not being able to determine which narrative she identifies with, in the later text her experience is dominated by a sense of loss of autonomy, helplessness, lack of control, and emotional despair and fear in the face of her rapidly recurring cancer.

One of the prominent expressions in Leviah's second text is "I don't know." This expression reflects the fundamental effect of self-dissolution on theme, which is the stripping away of meaning to a self-narrative. As much as the self serves as a macro-theme, tying together experiences and thus granting them sense, dissolution does the opposite. It can paradoxically still serve as a macro-theme, but it fractures the links between experiences, making the story of self a confusing and nonsensical one.

Coherence disruption: self-dissolution in narrative form

The narrative form roughly refers to the "*what*" in the narrative: what and who are included and excluded in the story; how the events are organized; what language is used; what the genre and style of the story is, etc. Although there are many formal characteristics in a narrative that one can take into account, for the purpose of reducing a confusing overload of interpretative categories and concepts, my self-illness narrative model follows Neimeyer's description of narrative form. This includes three main components of the self-narrative form: plot, setting, and characters. Neimeyer et al. (2009) summarize this view of form in the following sentence: "People spontaneously segment their experience into identifiable episodes, organizing these into stories with intelligible plots, populated by motivated characters, enriched by descriptions of relevant settings, exemplifying underlying themes, and targeted toward abstract goals" (p. 456).

When our psychological goal in a self-narrative gives an overall meaning to our chaotic and scattered life experience, one of the main purposes of form is to achieve narrative coherence. "What we are after, it seems, is a narrative account that provides a coherent picture of the events in question," writes psychoanalyst Donald Spence (1982, p. 180). He adds that not only do we seek coherence and organization through our narratives in order to make sense of our un-ordered experience, but our narratives are also judged as plausible and even real on the basis of their coherence. The clearer the thread between the different experiences, the greater an overall feeling of connectedness and a sense of core sameness between the experiences, and the more coherent a narrative account seems. This feeling of self-narrative coherence is probably what William James refers to in his description of "self-warmth" and "continuity" as the essential features of the sense of self (1892, p. 335).

Given the importance of coherence as a formal feature of the self-narrative, I propose that self-dissolution can influence the narrative form through its effect on narrative coherence. To describe this, I draw on Kaethe Weingarten's concept of *illness narrative coherence*, and Neimeyer's idea of *narrative disruptions* (Weingarten, 2001; Neimeyer, 2012; Roos & Neimeyer, 2007).

The way form-related narrative aspects, such as characters, setting, and plot, are assimilated into a self-illness narrative will affect the sense of coherence and integration. On the level of character, coherence is attained or disturbed through the perceived continuity, discrepancy, or dissociation amongst different relationships held between the self and other characters included in the illness narrative. These may include relationships with 'medical characters' (doctors, nurses, psychologists, other patients, etc.) or 'non-medical characters' (family and friends), or the comparison between current relationships and relationships prior to ACMC experiences. The perception of different illness-related and non-illness-related settings (such as hospitals, clinics, and home environments) before and after ACMC as sharply different or on a continuum also contributes to the construction of a coherent or disrupted narrative. Similarly, on the plot level, the way different illness-related and non-illness-related experiences are plotted, juxtaposed, or opposed affects the overall integration, disintegration, or dominance of an illness experience in relation to other past, present, and future experiences.

Three self-illness narrative disruptions

Neimeyer describes three ways in which the experience of loss is integrated (or disintegrated) into the overall self-narrative (Neimeyer, 2012). He suggests that this conceptualization can also be relevant to the experience of a loss of self following chronic illness, thus accounting for what I referred to here as a sense of self-dissolution (Roos & Neimeyer, 2007).

I would like to further suggest that the concepts of narrative assimilation and narrative disruption described by Neimeyer are specific forms of narrative coherence. Viewed in this way, they reflect the self-dissolution effect on form, which is somewhat different from the dissolution of the theme-specific sense of self that was my focus when discussing the thematic aspects. In other words, the ways one integrates loss or illness experiences into the macro-narrative of self determine *how* the self-narrative is organized, thus affecting the narrative form. This complements *what* is the focus of the self-experience, thus affecting the narrative theme.

Neimeyer describes three kinds of narrative disruptions: *narrative disorganization*, *narrative dominance*, and *narrative dissociation* (Neimeyer, 2012, p. 378). He describes narrative disorganization as a state in which "the story of one's life-altering injury, trauma or bereavement may give rise to a chaotic story that resists clear 'emplotment' in a coherent account" (2012, p. 378). When this is experienced, illness experiences and non-illness experiences, as well as past and present narratives, seem not to share meaningful connections. Ultimately, this kind of disorganized narrative does not feel like a narrative at all. If a macro-narrative is a means to organize an experience, narrative disorganization reflects a dis-ordered sense of the overall experience. To an extent, it is a macro-non-narrative. Arthur Frank (1998) and Kaethe Weingarten (2001), who both write about narrative therapy in the face of chronic illness, describe the chaos illness narrative that I believe is an expression of narrative disorganization. They describe this as an unintelligible account of the experience, thus related to a sense of social isolation. This is exacerbated by real anxiety, helplessness, and frequent lack of acceptance by the social environment. As meaning is lost, so are the words to describe it. Accordingly, this feeling of internal chaos is difficult to express to others and to the self and one is left in a sense of confusion, senselessness, and isolation.

The second kind of disruption, narrative dominance, is described by Neimeyer as "an oppressive fixation in a hopeless story that 'colonizes' the life of its protagonist" (2012, p. 378). In this case, the ACMC narrative is the macro-narrative, dominating the individual's whole experience. Events, settings, and characters that are unrelated to the medical or impairment experience are filtered out of the main self-narrative. As I understand this narrative form, it can be one that is governed by medical and clinical language, with a hope for physical restitution or despair over lack of physical progress. At the same time, all other hopes, wishes, and life contexts are abandoned. In this narrative form, self-dissolution is continuously experienced, as the ill self and the previous self one hopes to return to are perceived as totally dichotomous and estranged.

Neimeyer describes the third narrative disruption, narrative dissociation, as "a 'silent story' that cannot be acknowledged in its essential details—perhaps not even to oneself" (ibid). We suggest that the effect of this dissociated and silent illness narrative on the self is similar to what Bromberg describes as a "not-me" state (Chefetz & Bromberg, 2004, p. 421). Bromberg argues that through this dissociation, "traumatic experiences 'elude' our knowledge," yet continue to exist as non-symbolic, mental constructs. More than just being a "not-me" experience, these dissociated experiences, when transformed into a dissociated mental construct, form a confusing "silent me" that is "not-me."

Viewing narrative dissociation in this way, it is easier to see the connection to self-dissolution following ACMC. As opposed to narrative dominance, in which the "ill me" has dominated the self-illness narrative, silencing other self-narratives, in narrative dissociation the "ill me" awaits in the shadows. In both cases, the different self-narratives do not interact and are dissociated from each other, thus maintaining a self-dissolution narrative form.

However, not all ACMC experiences fundamentally disrupt the self macro-narrative. In many cases, the experiences are eventually assimilated into the overall story of self. This does not mean that these experiences do not alter the narrative, but that they do not necessarily continue to disrupt the narrative coherence. Neimeyer argues that achieving a renewed coherence offers "a meaningful explanation for identity-transforming life events, capturing the complexity of lived experience, and advancing socially valued action" (Neimeyer et al., 2009, p. 7). In line with this idea, we would like to think that the main purpose of the self-illness narrative model, partially presented in this chapter, and one of the main purposes of rehabilitation psychotherapy, is to help reduce narrative disruptions, which cause distress and agony, and facilitate processes of narrative integration, leading to a multitude of different self-narratives and experiences.

Interpreting narrative disruptions in clinical texts

Interpreting Leviah's texts from the perspective of narrative coherence, it seems that there are two main apparent disruptions. In the first text, Leviah is trying to assimilate her illness experience into the macro-narrative of her life experience. This draws upon a pre-morbid perception of omnipotence and self-control, expressed in previous therapy sessions. She had perceived herself as a well-experienced winner of battles and challenges up to that point in life. Leviah's attempt to hold a coherent self-narrative started to fail when she became aware of the shift in her self-narratives between sessions. She was aware that she was shifting between a new, tragic self-illness narrative and a previous winner self-illness narrative. For the time being, the two narratives could not be tied together in Leviah's mind.

In the later text, this clash has become much more prominent and there is a strong sense of narrative disorganization. For Leviah, previous experiences do not now seem to resemble present ones. She feels previous standpoints and beliefs are useless and not helpful in making her current state more intelligible or tolerable. Past and present experiences and narratives feel felt disconnected and scattered, leaving her with a constant feeling of "I don't know," which she repeats again and again throughout the second text.

Alongside narrative disorganization, both texts are dominated by the cancer experience. Everything is viewed in light of this experience: her body, sense of self, family ties, and work and life aspirations. In the second text, cancer is dominant in her overall experiences to such an extent that she asks "how will I be able to return to a life where cancer isn't a huge part of it?" As I have stressed in this chapter, one of the major consequences of self-dissolution, which also ties it with complicated grief, is the "thinning down" of meaning. When Leviah's narrative becomes a narrative dominated by her cancer, the rest of her self becomes vacant and inaccessible.

Obviously, one could argue that this narrative dominance is a result of the fact that Leviah required therapy for the purpose of coping emotionally with cancer. She talks about cancer, because that is what she expects to talk about in the therapeutic context. Of course, this argument is true, but does not detract from the fact that cancer does actually dominate her self-illness narrative in therapy. I believe that it is dominant out of therapy as well, influencing her initial decision to seek therapy. Furthermore, even in therapy, one can see how gradually cancer has become more dominant in Leviah's overall narrative. This is a result of her experience with another return of cancer, longer and more painful treatments, and an accumulation of different life experiences during this long period of coping with cancer.

Nevertheless, the contextual criticism is an important one, and we should be cautious of generalizing our interpretation regarding Leviah's self-illness narrative. This was her narrative in the context of therapy and at a specific point in time. This caution and restriction of my narrative interpretation emphasizes the importance of paying careful attention to the contextual aspects of a narrative.

Discussion

The conceptual role of self-dissolution

I would like to end this chapter with a text describing the feeling of estrangement following self-dissolution. The text is taken from a therapy session with a young man coping with a severe acquired head injury:

> I don't know exactly what this feeling is. How to describe it? It is like I am in a desert and there is nothing around me, nothing is stable. You can't really grab or perceive anything, not my feelings too. I am not my-self anymore, but I am not an other either. How can I make sense of it all? How can I know who I am again?

I believe that the experience of confusion, isolation, and dissociation described above is common following ACMC. Moreover, I have stressed throughout this chapter the idea that self-dissolution following ACMC is a key factor, if not the most important one, contributing to emotional distress. As a theoretical idea, self-dissolution ties together different aspects of coping and adjusting to different life challenges, described in literature as influencing the existence and preservation of a sense of loss and enduring complicated grief. As a narrative idea, self-dissolution and its affects shape the illness experiences, diluting and reducing meaning and sense.

Self-dissolution in a self-illness narrative framework

This chapter suggests that through the construction of a diverse yet integrative narrative framework, clinicians and theoreticians can establish a thorough working model for the interpretation of different effects of self-dissolution on the self-illness narrative. Specifically, we have discussed the way self-dissolution can affect the narrative theme and form.

First, I have described three kinds of dissolution dominance affecting the narrative theme: dissolution of the self as a physical object, dissolution of the self as an autonomous subject, and dissolution of the self as continuous and united. The conceptualization and mapping of these dominances was established using an interdisciplinary method, connecting self-knowledge discussion on the one hand and rehabilitation psychology research concerning the sense of loss and change of self on the other (Gertler, 2011; Livneh & Martz, 2007).

Second, I have described three kinds of self-dissolution disruptions to narrative coherence: narrative disorganization, narrative dominance, and narrative dissociation. The ideas of coherence and coherence disruptions draw heavily on narrative theories, stressing the importance of coherence both as a self-narrative goal and as a measure of judging the plausibility of a narrative account (Neimeyer, 2000; Spence, 1982). All three disruptions of narrative form presented in this chapter limit the meaning of the self-illness narrative.

By means of the discussion of narrative coherence and coherence disruptions, I considered the psychological importance of the integration of illness experiences into a broad and multifaceted self-narrative. I emphasized the importance of this as a major goal of rehabilitation psychotherapy. Stressing this point, it is important to note that although the focus in this chapter is on presenting the interpretive role of the self-illness narrative model, this is a means to an end, which is building a therapeutically helpful bridge to mitigate against self-dissolution, and integrate the sense of present self and the sense of past self, perceived as an other. This can hopefully help the patient to "know who I am again."

Limitations and further research

It is important to note that the model presented here is not a definitive one. First of all, we have elaborated on the intrinsic, structural field of the self-illness narrative, leaving out the contextual field. Moreover, even in the structural field, we have focused on specific thematic and formal characteristics, leaving out many other narrative characteristics described in narrative and self-narrative theory and in philosophical and psychological literature regarding the self.

Obviously, the self-illness narrative model can be made "thinner," to give a more minimal and robust interpretation of a narrative, or more comprehensive, adding more factors such as changes to narratives over time and over contexts, specific medical conditions narratives, other dissolution dominances referring to other self-attributions, and pre-morbid perceived strengths and vulnerabilities that mediate self-dissolution, etc.

Although in this chapter the application of the self-illness narrative model is an interpretive one, the model is intended to serve as a therapeutic tool as well. This can be done by using narrative and therapeutic techniques that focus on elaborating and generating new narratives and accounts. These can include highlighting and elaborating on alternative self-narratives or self-experiences, "re-storying loss" and identifying strengths and lessons learnt through the experiences, and creating a dialogical space between different self-states (Carey, Walther, & Russell, 2009; Neimeyer, 2006; Raggatt, 2006).

The self-illness narrative model can add to these methods by focusing on the areas where one is caught "in the spaces," as Philip Bromberg phrases it, unable to get out of a fixated, distressful state (Bromberg, 1996). By emphasizing these areas of rigidity, reduction, silence, and many times chaos—in which self-estrangement is felt and is dominant—therapy can help reconstruct sense and meaning.

Notes

1 This manuscript is based on a chapter in my PhD dissertation, under the supervision of Dr. Dorit Lemberger. I would like to thank Dr. Lemberger for guiding and supporting me throughout this journey, with her warmth, intelligence, curiosity, and vast knowledge. I would further like to thank Dr. Aner Govrin, Head of the Hermeneutics and Psychoanalysis Track and the whole unique ensemble of lecturers in the Culture and Hermeneutics Program. Finally, I would like to thank my mother, Jill Segal, for her careful and loving line editing.

2 I will use "ACMC" as a general term describing a multitude of acquired impairments, such as chronic illness, acquired physical injuries, and other acquired medical conditions that result in physical impairments. For example, this can include illnesses, such as multiple sclerosis or rheumatic diseases; physical injuries, such as head injuries, spinal cord injuries, or traumatic amputations; and acquired impairments in hearing, seeing, cognition, or emotional regulation. Using ICF (International Classification of Functioning) language, the term "ACMC" solely refers to the physical impact of an acquired condition.

3 For the purposes of the survey, "chronic illnesses" included heart illnesses, respiratory illnesses, diabetes, kidney illnesses, cancer, neurological illnesses, thyroid illnesses, and chronic pain.

4 As different theoretical disciplines emphasize different aspects of the self, the role of the physical body is described differently, accordingly. For example, the existential philosopher Jean-Paul Sartre argues that we are who we are through and because of our unique, subjective experiences with our own bodies and the unique perspectives that are shaped by our bodies (Sartre, 1943). Psychoanalyst Donald Winnicott and developmental psychologist Daniel Stern emphasize the importance of the physical interactions we have with our caregivers. These interactions shape our emotional regulation, our ability to establish a sense of separate self, our understanding of others and ability to establish meaningful relationships, and our ability to move between an internal, private reality and an external, objective reality, or between an emotional and a somatic reality (Stern, 2000; Winnicott, 1965, 1966). Philosophers and social theorists such as Michel Foucault and Judith Butler emphasize the role that interactions with the bodies of others or with the control or limitations others apply to our bodies have on the way we constitute our sense of self (Butler, 2004; Foucault, 1963, 1976, 1977, 1997a, 1997b; Tremain, 2008).

5 Other concepts that are used in a similar fashion are "chronic sorrow" and "ambiguous loss" (Boss & Carnes, 2012; Burk, Eakes, & Hainsworth, 1999). I have decided to adopt the term "complicated grief" for two main reasons: (1) much of the narrative framework in this chapter elaborates on Robert Neimeyer's ideas, therefore using "complicated grief" keeps a coherent linguistic lineage; (2) I suggest that there are a few characteristics shared by the terms "complicated grief" and "self-dissolution," such as the reduction of sense of meaning and the feeling of being trapped in time. This will be further elaborated later in this chapter. Although these two concepts share characteristics, they are also different, thus creating a richer understanding of the experiences following ACMC. While grief emphasizes the psychological sequelae of loss, dissolution emphasizes the psychological sequelae of a sense of split and self discrepancy.

6 During the course of this chapter, I will illustrate various points by using case descriptions, emphasizing contributions of different aspects of the presented theoretical account to the understanding of the experience. In agreement with narrative line of thought, I argue that, like self-narratives, self-dissolution narratives are told in many different contexts (Neimeyer et al., 2009; Schafer, 1980a; Spence, 1982; Weingarten, 2001). Hence, the cases presented in this chapter are taken from different sources, such as blogs, interviews, and therapeutic encounters.

7 It is difficult to draw the line regarding the differences between philosophical and psychological theories of self. Roughly speaking, philosophical discussions, such as those of Gertler (2011), Korsgaard (2009), or Sartre (1943), or Wittgenstein's (1958) account of self as subject, emphasize their concern with the cognitive aspects or the ethical implications of this self-consciousness. Psychoanalytic or psychological theorists dealing with this issue, such as Aron (2000), Kohut (1979), Kohut & Wolf (1978), and Schafer (1980b), emphasize the connections between self as autonomous subject and emotional well-being, self-esteem, sense of identity, and interpersonal relatedness.

References

Aisenstein, M. (2006). The Indissociable Unity of Psyche and Soma: A View from the Paris Psychosomatic School. *International Journal of Psycho-Analysis*, 87: 667–680.

Aron, L. (2000). Self-Reflexivity and the Therapeutic Action of Psychoanalysis. *Psychoanalytic Psychology*, 17: 667–689.

Aron, L. (2006). Analytic Impasse and the Third: Clinical Implications of Intersubjectivity Theory. *International Journal of Psycho-Analysis*, 87: 349–368.

Atwood, G. E., Orange, D. M., & Stolorow, R. D. (2002). Shattered Worlds/ Psychotic States: A Post-Cartesian View of the Experience of Personal Annihilation. *Psychoanalytic Psychology*, 19: 281–306.

Bermúdez, J. L. (1998). Self-Consciousness and the Body: An Interdisciplinary Introduction. (J. L. Bermúdez, Ed.) *The Body and the Self* (pp. 1–28). Cambridge, MA and London: MIT Press.

Boss, P. & Carnes, D. (2012). The Myth of Closure. *Family Process*, 51: 456–469.

Brault, M. W. (2012). Americans with Disabilities: 2010. *US Census Bureau*, available at www.census.gov/prod/2012pubs/p70-131.pdf.

Bromberg, P. M. (1996). Standing in the Spaces: The Multiplicity of Self and the Psychoanalytic Relationship. *Contemporary Psychoanalysis*, 32: 509–532.

Bromberg, P. M. (1998). Staying the Same While Changing: Reflection on Clinical Judgment. *Psychoanalytic Dialogues*, 8: 225–236.

Burk, M. L., Eakes, G. G., & Hainsworth, M. A. (1999). Milestones of Chronic Sorrow: Perspectives of Chronically Ill and Bereaved Persons and Family Caregivers. *Journal of Family Nursing*, 5: 374–387.

Butler, J. (2004). *Precarious Life. The Powers of Mourning and Violence*. New York: Verso.

Carey, M., Walther, S., & Russell, S. (2009). The Absent but Implicit: A Map to Support Therapeutic Enquiry. *Family Process*, 48: 319–331.

Carroll, D. D., Courtney-Long, E. A., Stevens, A. C., Sloan, M. L., Lullo, C., Visser, S. N., Fox, M. H., Armour, B. S., Campbell, V. A., Brown, D. R., & Dorn, J. M. (2014). Vital Signs: Disability and Physical Activity. *Morbidity and Mortality Weekly Report*, 63: 407–413, available at www.cdc.gov/mmwr/preview/mmwrhtml/mm6318a5.htm.

Chefetz, R. A. & Bromberg, P. M. (2004). Talking with "Me" and "Not Me": A Dialogue. *Contemporary Psychoanalysis*, 40: 409–464.

Chrissi. (2007). The Sketchbook Project. Retrieved August 10, 2014, from "Life – Paralyzed," https://www.sketchbookproject.com/library/4604.

Davis, L. J. (2006 [1995]). Constructing Normalcy: The Bell Curve, the Novel, and the Invention of the Disabled Body in the Nineteenth Century. (Davis, L. J., Ed.), *The Disability Studies Reader*, Second Edition (pp. 1–16). New York: Routledge.

de Gaynesford, M. (2006). *I: The Meaning of the First-Person Term*. Oxford: Oxford University Press.

Foucault, M. (1963). *Naissance de la clinique* (Hebrew Version 2008). Tel-Aviv: Resling Publishing.
Foucault, M. (1976). *The History of Sexuality I* (Hebrew Version 1996). Israel: Hakibbutz Hameuchad Publishing House.
Foucault, M. (1977). *Discipline and Punish: The Birth of the Prison.* New York: Vintage Books.
Foucault, M. (1997a [1970–1974]). The Abnormals. (Rabinow, P., Ed.), *Ethics: Subjectivity and Truth* (pp. 51–58). Trans. R. Hurley et al. New York: New Press.
Foucault, M. (1997b [1982]), Technologies of the Self. (Rabinow, P., Ed.), *Ethics: Subjectivity and Truth* (pp. 223–252). Trans. R. Hurley et al. New York: New Press.
Frank, A. (1998). Just Listening: Narrative and Deep Illness. *Families, Systems & Health*, 16: 197–212.
Freud, S. (1925 [1919]). *The Uncanny*. (J. Strachey, Ed. and Trans.), *The Standard Edition of the Complete Psychological Works of Sigmund Freud. Vol. XVII* (pp. 217–256). London: Hogarth Press.
Gertler, B. (2011). *Self Knowledge*. New York: Routledge.
Gubb, K. (2013). Psychosomatics Today: A Review of Contemporary Theory and Practice. *The Psychoanalytic Review,* 100: 103–142.
Israeli Ministry of Health (2012). *Anxiety and Depression Disorders in Israel*, available at www.health.gov.il/publicationsfiles/depression_anxiety_israel.pdf.
James, W. (2007 [1892]). *The Principles of Psychology*. Cambridge, MA: Harvard University Press.
Jopling, D. (2000). *Self-Knowledge and the Self.* New York: Routledge.
Katz, S. & Florian, V. (1986–1987). A Comprehensive Theoretical Model of Psychologcial Reaction to Loss. *International Journal of Psychiatry in Medicine*, 16: 1986–1987.
Kohut, H. (1972). Thoughts on Narcissism and Narcissistic Rage. *Psychoanalytic Study of the Child*, 27: 360–400.
Kohut, H. (1979). Four Basic Concepts in Self Psychology. (Ornstein, P. H., Ed.) *The Search For the Self: Selected Writings of Heinz Kohut: 1979–1981. Vol. 4* (pp. 447–470). London: Karnac Books.
Kohut, H. & Wolf, E. S. (1978). The Disorders of the Self and Their Treatment: An Outline. *International Journal of Psycho-Analysis*, 59: 413–425.
Korsgaard, C. M. (1989). Personal Identity and the Unity of Agency: A Kantian Response to Parfit. *Philosophy & Public Affairs*, 18: 101–132.
Korsgaard, C. M. (2009). *Self-Constitution: Agency, Identity and Integrity*. Oxford: Oxford University Press.
Livneh, H. & Martz, E. (2007). An Introduction to Coping Theory and Research. (Livneh, H. & Martz, E., Eds.) *Coping with Chronic Illness and Disability: Theoretical, Empirical, and Clinical Aspects* (pp. 3–28). New York: Springer.
Mitchell, S. A. (1991). Contemporary Perspectives on Self: Toward an Integration. *Psychoanaytic Dialogues*, 1: 121–147.

Neimeyer, R. A. (2000). Narrative Disruptions in the Construction of Self. (Neimeyer, R. A. & Raskin, J. D., Eds.) *Constructions of Disorder: Meaning Making Frameworks for Psychotherapy* (pp. 207–242). Washington, DC: American Psychological Association.

Neimeyer, R. A. (2006). Re-Storying Loss: Fostering Growth in the Posttraumatic Narrative. (Calhoun, L. & Tedeschi, R. G., Eds.) *Handbook of Posttraumatic Growth: Research and Practice* (pp. 68–80). Mahwah, NJ: Lawrence Erlbaum.

Neimeyer, R. A. (2012). Reconstructing the Self in the Wake of Loss: A Dialogical Contribution. (Hermans, H. J. M. & Gieser, T., Eds.) *Handbook of Dialogical Self Theory* (pp. 374–389). New York: Cambridge University Press.

Neimeyer, R. A. & Raskin, J. D. (2000). On Practicing Postmodern Therapy in Modern Times. (Neimeyer, R. A. & Raskin, J. D., Eds.) *Constructions of Disorder: Meaning Making Frameworks for Psychotherapy* (pp. 3–14). Washington, DC: American Psychological Association.

Neimeyer, R. A., Herrero, O., & Botella, L. (2006). Chaos to Coherence: Psychotherapeutic Integration of Traumatic Loss. *Journal of Constructivist Psychology*, 19: 127–145.

Neimeyer, R. A., Pennebaker, J. W., & van Dyke, J. G. (2009). Narrative Medicine: Writing through Bereavement. (Chochinov, H. M. & Breitbart, W., Eds.), *Handbook of Psychiatry in Palliative Medicine*, Second Edition (pp. 454–469). New York: Oxford University Press.

Neisser, U. (1993). The Self Perceived. (Neisser, U., Ed.), *The Perceived Self: Ecological and Interpersonal Sources of Self-Knowledge* (pp. 3–25). New York: Cambridge University Press.

Orange, D. (2001). From Cartesian Minds to Experiential Worlds in Psychoanalysis. *Psychoanalytic Psychology*, 18: 287–302.

Raggatt, P. T. F. (2006). Multiplicity and Conflict in the Dialogical Self: A Life-Narrative Approach. (McAdams, D. P., Ruthellen, J., & Lieblich, A., Eds.) *Identity and Story: Creating Self in Narrative* (pp. 15–35). Washington, DC: American Psychological Association.

Roos, S. & Neimeyer, R. A. (2007). Reauthoring the Self: Chronic Sorrow and Posttraumatic Stress Following the Onset of CID. (Livneh, H. & Martz, E., Eds.) *Coping with Chronic Illness and Disability: Theoretical, Empirical, and Clinical Aspects* (pp. 89–106). New York: Springer.

Rorty, R. M. (1992). *The Linguistic Turn: Essays in Philosophical Method.* Chicago, IL University of Chicago Press.

Sartre, J.-P. (1995 [1943]). *Being and Nothingness: An Essay on Phenomenological Ontology*. Trans. H. E. Barnes. London: Routledge.

Schafer, R. (1980a). Narration in the Psychoanalytic Dialogue. *Critical Inquiry*, 7: 29–53.

Schafer, R. (1980b). Action Language and the Psychology of the Self. *Annual of Psychoanalysis*, 8: 83–92.

Spence, D. P. (1982). *Narrative Truth and Historical Truth: Meaning and Interpretation in Psychoanalysis*. London and New York: W.W. Norton & Company.

Stern, D. N. (2000). *The Interpersonal World of the Infant: A View from Psychoanalysis and Developmental Psychology*. New York: Basic Books.
Stolorow, R. D. & Atwood, G. E. (1994). The Myth of the Isolated Mind. *Progress in Self Psychology*, 10: 233–250.
Tremain, S. (2008). Foucault, Governmentality, and Critical Disability Theory: An Introduction. (Tremain, S., Ed.), *Foucault and the Government of Disability* (pp. 9–26). Ann Arbor, MI: University of Michigan Press.
Van de Velde, D., Bracke, P., van Hove, G., Josephsson, S., Devisch, I., & Vanderstaeten, G. (2012). The Illusion and the Paradox of Being Autonomous, Experiences from Persons with Spinal Cord Injury in Their Transition Period from Hospital to Home. *Disability & Rehabilitation*, 34: 491–502.
Weingarten, K. (2001). Making Sense of Illness Narratives: Braiding Theory, Practice and the Embodied Life. *Working with the Stories of Women's Lives*, available at www.dulwichcentre.com.au/illness-narratives.html.
Winnicott, D. W. (1965). Communicating and Not Communicating Leading to a Study of Certain Opposites (1963). (Winnicott, D. W., Ed.) *The Maturational Processes and the Facilitating Environment: Studies in the Theory of Emotional Development* (pp. 179–192). London: Hogarth Press and the Institute of Psycho--Analysis.
Winnicott, D.W. (1966). Psycho-Somatic Illness in Its Positive and Negative Aspects. *Journal of Psycho-Analysis*, 47: 510–516.
Wittgenstein, L. (1958 [1953]). *Philosophical Investigations*. Oxford: Basil Blackwell.
Wittgenstein, L. (1958). *The Blue and Brown Books* (Hebrew Version 2006). Tel-Aviv: Resling Publishing.
Wittgenstein, L. (1969). *On Certainty*. (Anscombe, G. E. M. & von Wright, G. H., Eds.). Trans. D. Paul and G. E. M. Anscombe, available at www.edtechpost.ca/readings/Ludwig%20Wittgenstein%20-%20On%20Certainty.html.
Wright, B. A. (1983). *Physical Disability: A Psychosocial Approach*, Second Edition. New York: Harper & Row.
Yeates, G. N., Gracey, F., & McGrath, J. C. (2008). A Biopsychosocial Deconstruction of "Personality Change" Following Acquired Brain Injury. *Neuropsychological Rehabilitation*, 18: 566–589.
Zilber, T. B., Tuval-Mashiach, R., & Lieblich, A. (2008). The Embedded Narrative: Navigating Through Multiple Contexts. *Qualitative Inquiry*, 14: 1047–1069.

Chapter 11

The idealized "other"

A reparative fiction

Amira Simha-Alpern[1]

It seems that we achieve a sense of identity and social belonging partially through the process of marking similarities and differences between ourselves and other people: we are who we resemble and we are not who we differ from. In a sense, identity has little meaning without defining the "other"; and the process of "othering"—conceiving that which is not "self" (Beville, 2010)—is an essential part of identity formation. Unfortunately, we often not only identify differences but also privilege sameness over difference. The cognitive processes of othering often propel the experience of disgust and abjection in relation to the other who is not only different but also inferior to us (Benjamin, 1995; Beville, 2010). Frequently, these identified differences are imagined rather than real and are sustained through distortions and misattributions. I would like to suggest a different approach to othering, one in which the other is idealized rather than debased. In this process, the other is attributed ultimate standards of perfection and is contrasted with the imperfect, inferior self. The binary opposite demarcation between self and other still holds but the other is altered by aggrandizement and exaltation rather than denigration (Freud, 1914/1957; Spruiell, 1979).

Since its inception, psychoanalytic theory has recognized idealization as an important developmental need and a central psychological process. What is important to this chapter is the idealization of the other, or what Freud (1914/1957) referred to as object-libido. The general understanding is that creating an idealized other facilitates personality formation and protects oneself against psychopathology. Freud used *idealization* and *overvaluation* interchangeably and positioned them at the center of the Oedipal drama and love relationships. In Freud's theory, idealization of the father is essential for proper resolution of the Oedipal struggle and the emergence of psychic structure. It is vital for the inhibition and sublimation of drives and the emergence of the superego. Failure to transform primary narcissism and relinquish the grandiosity of the self in favor of—and submitting oneself to—the superiority of a paternal idealized figure or a loved other results in a developmental arrest in pregenital objects (Chasseguet-Smirgel, 1974; Spruiell, 1979).

A similar idea is reflected in Benjamin's (1995) notion of *identificatory love*. Although Benjamin proposes it for the understanding of gender identity, I believe that it can be applied to identity formation in general. Identificatory love is in essence identification with a different idealized other who is unlike the self. This process offers the potential for internalizing attributes that are not naturally or readily available to one's self and, by doing so, expands the possibilities of one's character. If the differences between self and other are not put in polar opposition to one another and the other does not become the repository of all that cannot be owned by the self, good or bad, complementarity can actually expand and enrich the self. In the specific example of feminine identity formation, the girl's identification with the loved and admired father fosters her autonomy—a quality she cannot easily internalize through her symbiotic attachment to the mother, an object similar to herself.

In love relationships, idealization of the partner—overvaluation of the love object by holding him or her above criticism and above all others who are not loved, and often above the self—is necessary for falling in love (Freud, 1914/1957). Accepting one's own limitations and loving the different object as an outside figure who embodies what the self does not might be seen as the road to object love. Consequently, being loved by an idealized object is essential for healthy self-esteem and mitigates malignant narcissism (Benjamin, 1995).

Idealization of a parent as an other holds a special meaning in human experience. The traditional psychoanalytic understanding of idealization of a parent is that it reflects either a developmental need or a defense against object-instinctual investments. As a developmental need, idealization is instrumental for structuring internal personality agencies. It is an essential, growth-promoting process that furthers ego development by facilitating identification with a benign ego ideal. In Freud's formulation, identification and internalization of an idealized parental figure ushers the development of the superego—the unity of conscience and ego ideal. For Kohut (1971), the developmental need for an idealized and idealizing other is rooted in the human need to be loved and admired. We therefore tend to idealize others from whom we expect narcissistic supplies. The parent as an idealized self-object becomes a source of narcissistic sustenance or a mirror for one's own grandiose wishful self. Actual contact with an idealized parent precludes fragmentation of ego functions. Parent idealization in the context of the longing for parental care seems to provide an "omnipotent reassurance" (Klein, 1952/1975, p. 70) that we will be cared for and loved.

Inflexible parent idealization lingering beyond its years results in developmental arrests, potentially leading to psychopathology. *Defensive idealization* of parental figures is viewed as a protection against one's own aggression toward the parent or fear of the parent's destructive and retaliatory power. Turning a parent into an all-powerful figure puts the parent beyond the reach and destructive power of the self. It is often an expression of a conflictual need for the parent coupled with a warded-off rage and envy toward him or her. In this context, idealization serves to deny the real qualities of the parent because the latter is associated with instinctual conflicts—unbearable frustration with a depriving, or terrifying, persecuting bad object. When the real qualities of the parent cannot register, defensive idealization signals a failure in separation and internalization resulting in a developmental arrest (Lachmann & Stolorow, 1976).

Freud (1914/1957) identified two anaclitic prototypes of idealization: a nurturing/feeding maternal archetype and a protective paternal one. The longing to be cared for and protected like a young child by a maternal figure who is nurturing, responsive, and attuned is ever-present throughout life (Fromm, 1964; Jung, 1911–1912/1956, 1928/1966) and seems to be at the heart of personality formation, childhood fixation, and psychopathology. The pre-Oedipal attachment to the mother and the yearning for what Fromm called "paradisiacal bliss"—a symbiotic relatedness to a loving mother who makes one feel safe and secure—is the cause of developmental arrests. In extreme cases, this attachment is expressed as a longing to return to the womb.

The profound need to remain connected to parental figures facilitates psychological maneuvers that aim at assuring sustainability to these ties, at times at a great psychological cost. Fairbairn (1963/1994) recognized those processes by observing how abused children remain attached to their abusive parents. He concluded that "the earliest and original form of anxiety, as experienced by the child is separation-anxiety" (p. 155), and that the dread of social isolation is a major motivating force in human development. In the absence of "real," secure, satisfying caretaking, and in an effort to avoid the pain and disappointment of rejection while keeping the attachment figure close, involved, and invested, the human mind internalizes and alters the parental object. The internalized object is split: the rejecting (i.e., antilibidinal) aspects are split off from the exciting (i.e., libidinal) aspects of the object and repressed, leaving a kernel of idealized internal images that are often distorted images of the real other.

It seems, however, that the need for an omnipotent parental figure prevails beyond the childhood years and is an inseparable part of well-being, not only psychopathology. Bowlby (1958), the father of attachment theory, elaborated on—and actually put at the center of human development—humans' lifelong fundamental need for safety, security, and a sense of being cared for by a sensitive and responsive caretaker. Psychic life is organized around the individual's repeated attempts to achieve safety from threat and to connect to others who offer protection and security (Slade, 2014). As Spitz's (1946) studies of orphanage babies and Harlow's (Harlow, Dodsworth, & Harlow, 1965) isolated monkeys experiments clearly showed, this basic need is for more than mere physical minding. Primates need warmth and a subjective sense of "felt security" (Srouf & Waters, 1977) rather than the "objective" availability of a caretaking other for their psychological, and even physical, survival. What matters is the subjective feeling of safety, which is much more than merely the absence of discomfort and anxiety. Imagoes of mother and father are universal, "real but subjective phenomenon" (Jung, 1911–1912/1956, p. 86); and much of normal behavior as well as many clinical phenomena, such as those observed in neurosis, psychosis, and addiction, can be understood as the ego's attempts to preserve a sense of safety (Sandler, 2003).

What is embedded in all the above-mentioned perspectives of our need for an ideal parental figure is the idea that the self transforms through an external other who adapts one's external world. A core tenet of attachment theory is the premise that the development of the infant's immature self is facilitated through an external other with a mature self who modifies the environment to provide for the infant what he or she cannot provide for the self (Schore, 2001). The various aspects of "holding"—provision, the experience of being understood without words, attunement, and mirroring—are part of the maternal functions that facilitate the transformation of the self from preverbal, affective experience to more mature, organized thoughts and from dependency to self-reliance. In that vein, Bollas

(1978/2011) believes that we have a lifelong pursuit of an idealized parent as a "transformational object": an external medium or an other that promises to transform the external world and, in turn, the self or the ego's state. We look for "the mother as the other who alters the self" (p. 11) and we need to re-experience an external holding object similar to the one we experienced in our early years. Bollas writes:

> The search for transformation and for the transformational object is perhaps the most pervasive archaic object relation, and ... this search arises not out of desire for the object per se, or primarily out of craving or longing. It arises from the person's certainty that the object will deliver transformation; this certainty is based on the object's nominated capacity to resuscitate the memory of early ego transformation. The ego experience of being transformed by the other remains a memory that may be re-enacted ... in a wide range of culturally-dreamed-of transformational objects ... that promise total change of internal and external environment.
>
> (pp. 10–11)

Often the search for the transformational object generates from the need for ego repair—a search for health.

The deep-rooted need for an ideal parental approach is reflected in common myths throughout history and across all cultures. The word "mother" evokes a universal feminine archetype of a caretaking stance characterized by nurturance, warmth, sensitivity, attunement, and unconditional love or acceptance. This matriarchal principle translates into universality, equality, peace, tenderness, humanness, and concern for the world's welfare and happiness (Bachofen, 1992). In Greco-Roman myths, when one does find a maternal figure, she is often portrayed as someone who will do anything to save her children. To mention just a few: the goddess Gaia— the all-powerful Mother-Earth whose motherhood was challenged by giving birth to deformed children—does everything she can to free and nurture her children when their own father, Uranus, tries to hide them and forbids her to see them; Rhea saves her baby from being eaten by her husband Cronus, who attempts to avoid the prophecy that he would be dethroned by his own child by swallowing his newborn children; and Demeter, the goddess of agriculture and fertility who nurtures and protects livestock and agricultural products, endlessly wanders the earth disguised as an old woman in search of her daughter Persephone after Persephone was abducted to marry her father's brother Hades, the god of the dark underworld. In her agony, Demeter lets the earth perish; only when her daughter is returned does she allow the earth to flourish again. Since Persephone has already been claimed by the underworld, Demeter is forced to agree that Persephone will spend four months each year in the underworld. During these months, Demeter grieves her daughter's absence and withdraws her gifts from the world, creating winter. Persephone's return brings the spring.

Judaism and Christianity glorify mothers. In Judaism, the Divine Presence of God (the *Shechinah*) is feminine. The *Shechinah* is often portrayed as a loving mother who is present at times of personal need and distress. She suffers along with her children Israel in exile; she toils at their side while they are slaves in Egypt; and she protects them in the wilderness after they are liberated. She is there for the individual as well as for the collective; the Talmud states that she "dwells over the head side of the sick man's bed" (Talmud, Shabbat 12b, Epstein, 1972).

In Christianity, Mary, the desexualized mother of the Messiah, is perceived as the dominant parent of Jesus. She is venerated and considered to be the most meritorious saint of the Church, the mother of all mothers. Mary's devotion to her son is characterized as unwavering even when he refuses to see her—when he is surrounded by followers and announces that his disciples are his family members. She tolerates with great agony his loss to the temple and his crucifixion and insists on participating in his burial. The Virgin Mary is believed to bestow seven graces upon her devotees, which are extensions of the maternal functions: peace to their families, enlightenment, consolation of their pains, provision of as much as they ask for, defense and protection in every instant of their lives, help in the moments of their death, and provision of eternal happiness, consolation, joy, and forgiveness of sins (Cameron, 2010).

Similarly, the word "father," often associated with God as a supreme being or human religious clergymen, connotes protection, wisdom, concern for people, and indestructible power (Jung, 1911–1912/1956). God's otherness as an omnipotent entity unlike the self, free of human constraints and cultural norms—the embodiment of alterity and transcendence—has been discussed in the literature (Goodman & Freeman, 2015). Psychoanalytic thinkers recognized a universal lifelong need to experience a good and powerful godlike figure (Jung, 1911–1912/1956) and theorized that God signifies the ultimate ideality (Mills, 2017). Mills (2017) suggests that "the idea or notion of God is the manifestation of our denial and response to our being-in-relation-to-lack, and hence the longing to replace natural absence with divine presence" (p. 2). Without entering the religious debate on the existence of God, and regardless of one's position in this complex discourse, it is acknowledged that "if God did not exist, it would be necessary for us to invent Him" (Voltaire, 1768). God's entity promises peace, happiness, and eternal salvation. Even the ambivalent notion of God as an external object or an other that is both protecting and punishing, merciful and merciless, and providing salvation and damnation generates from its idealized qualities as the ultimate caretaker and the epitome of a moral ideal. The latter provides a sense of order and justice (Mills, 2017).

A dramatic illustration of the need to idealize a powerful paternal figure as a way of coping with loss and despair is the Jewish prayer, the Mourner's Kaddish, one of the most important and central elements in the Jewish liturgy. The Kaddish, which means "holy" in Aramaic, is a hymn recited by the mourner who has lost a close family member—first at the burial, then daily throughout the initial mourning period, and finally at each death anniversary. In this prayer, there is no mention of loss, death, or emotional pain that reflects the actual mental state of the mourner. Instead, it is a string of superlatives that magnifies and sanctifies God's power and reiterates his eternality (Nulman, 1996). It is hard to understand the relevance of this prayer to the occasion without incorporating the idea that we need to assure ourselves of an all-powerful, protective other when we face our own helplessness and mortality (Berman, 2015).

Our need for a benevolent caretaking parental figure is so profound that if we do not experience nurturing and protective figures in our real-life relationships, we often invent them in our minds. This idealization of a parental figure is a *reparative idealization*—a necessary reparatory fiction that is essential for our psychological survival. Because the most convenient way of heightening feelings of safety is through the modification and control of perception, the real rejecting, abandoning, or unavailable parent is neglected in favor of a phantasmic, idealized one whose image is colored by wish fulfillment—a "magical helper," an omnipotent and omniscient figure who provides everlasting care and gives comfort. This type of fantasy depicts a magical world, a scenario in which the limitations of our physical universe no longer hold. We become attached to this internal image that our fantasy created and gain reassurance through an "*intrapsychic role relationship*" (Sandler, 2003, p. 19, emphasis in source): an internal dialogue with this inner object where the object plays our longed-for role vis-à-vis the self. This internal compensatory, phantasmic, ideal object and the ongoing internal dialogue relieve the individual from anxieties and provide unlimited, immediate, and everlasting gratification, as well as security and protection from persecutory objects. It is a "potent assurance" rather than "omnipotent reassurance" (Alvarez, 1992, p. 119), guaranteeing everlasting security.

Current research confirms the human tendency to idealize parental figures as an attempt to cope with the devastating realities of loss, neglect, and a subjective sense of being uncared for. Main (2000), a linguist and attachment researcher, studied internal parental representations through analyzing the narration of the parents in the Adult Attachment Interview. Subjects were asked to describe early relationships with their parents and to evaluate the effects of these relationships and experiences on their present functioning. Subjects were also asked for five adjectives to describe each parent as well as memories that supported their choice of each adjective. Analyses of parental narration of individuals who had neglectful parents earlier in their lives and were subsequently classified as *dismissing* adults indicate that their discourse appeared to minimize the importance of attachment-related experiences. At the same time, the parent tends to be described in highly positive terms. In one of her case illustrations, Main quotes a dismissing woman who stated regarding the effects of her relationship with her mother: "I didn't have any of these traumatic experiences people talk about. I had a good childhood" (p. 1085). She also selected exclusively positive, idealistic adjectives to describe her mother as "caring, loving … and supportive" (p. 1084). However, when asked for memories that would illustrate why she chose these adjectives, she had difficulty recalling concrete incidents of being comforted when distressed. On the contrary, she recounted: "I didn't tell her I broke my arm; she would have been really angry" (p. 1083). Concrete episodes of being rejected were not recalled either, suggesting a strong need to suppress negative experience with the maternal caretaker. In contrast, secure-autonomous adults tend to describe their parents in more realistic and balanced terms, acknowledging both positive and negative events and attributes.

There is a distinction between the traditional psychoanalytic conceptualization of idealization as a developmental need or a *defensive idealization,* and what I am proposing to be a *reparative idealization.* Reparative idealization is not necessarily a transient developmental need. Rather, it is a lifelong longing to experience a protective and nurturing other outside of the self. Phantasmic reparative idealization facilitates well-being in adulthood just as much as in childhood. Jung's "prospective function" (1916/1960), Freud's (1920/1955) *Nachträglichkeit*; ("afterwardness"), Kohut's (1971) "forward moves," and Bion's (1991) "memories of the future" represent the idea that fantasy can facilitate future growth, development, and well-being throughout the life span. It carves a path out of dissatisfaction with the real world and creates an opening to the impossible object and inaccessible enjoyment. "Fantasy is above all the creation of possibility out of impossibility" (McGowan, 2007, p. 24), ultimately offering us the power to change fate into destiny (Aron & Atlas, 2015). In this respect, phantasmic idealization and holding on to an idealized created image may be a key for adaptation—creating a transitional object that secures attachment by sustaining parental comfort, affectional bonds, soothing and warding off of anxieties during absences, as well as channeling destructive fantasies (Mills, 2017). This in turn facilitates a healthier developmental trajectory and allows one to transcend a reality of parental deprivation. As a transitional object, an idealizing fantasy can be viewed as a form of imaginative play, a mental activity designed to overcome pain rather than deny it and to foster growth rather than arrest it. It fills gaps in reality in order to make the parental absence more bearable by way of gaining mastery and confidence in the accessibility of a parental object. Through this process, a deprived individual who is susceptible to desolation and emptiness may learn "not about the properties of the absentable objects, but about the property of the objects which return, and about his own capacity to make them return" (Alvarez, 1992, p. 168). It can become a safe base from which to explore the world and a safe haven to return to when distress and disappointment permeate real life. Engagement with this fantasy can in turn shift psychic structures (Bonovitz, 2004).

As psychoanalysts, we often rush to force historical narrative and deconstruct what we believe to be an overly cathected and idealized phantasmic internal parental object. Our assumption is that a distorted internal image is somehow malignant, contributing to fixation, and that mental health must be governed by the reality principle. It is also true that attachment to an idealized parental image can impinge on one's life. When no flawed human can measure up to a rigidly idealized vision of a caring other, relationships with real human beings are doomed to be experienced as depriving, and establishing a loving relationship is almost impossible.

Similarly, a secure sense of one's good self is also unattainable when it is constantly checked against an idealized internal object. However, premature recognition that the imagined good parent is only a phantom of the patient's imagination can throw the patient into a panic or disorganized state. When there is a loss of sense of safety and security, the outside world is likely to be experienced as toxic and persecutory. In that vein, idealized fantasy can enhance one's ability to love. Loving feelings toward another person, at times, can only become possible if one can connect with an internal good and loving object, real or imagined (Lieberman, Padrón, Van Horn, & Harris, 2005; Mitchell, 2000).

In a paper entitled "Passion (or Past Shunned): The Use of Fantasy to Recreate Past Loving and Sexual Self-Experiences in the Present," Braucher (2014) unfolds his personal history of two psychoanalyses. His first analyst emphasized the domineering attributes of his mother, who had stifled his growth. As accurate as his analyst's perception was, this analysis pathologized his relationship with his mother and did not promote Braucher's ability to establish a loving adult relationship with a partner. It was only through his second analysis, where the analyst "loved" Braucher's mother and allowed him to love her distorted idealized image of her, that he was able to move on and find his own loving relationship.

The following clinical example, taken from my own clinical therapeutic work, attempts to illustrate the importance of idealized internal parental representations as means of psychological survival. Failure to create and invoke an idealized image may result in repeated failures to establish loving and nurturing relationships or to become a nurturing object for others. Conversely, the ability to create a real or imagined internal nurturing object is essential for one's ability to survive parental deprivation and for becoming a nurturing figure for others.

Clinical illustration

Molly, a woman of natural beauty and grace, was 49 years old when she began therapy with me. She had made numerous failed attempts to start therapy but was never able to stick with one therapist because she felt unsafe and easily criticized. Molly was the first girl born after five boys. She lost her father at the age of five and her life became hellish soon after when her mother, a dependent woman, married an abusive man to whom she devoted all her attention. Molly not only had to defend herself from this man but also had to run to the rescue of her older brothers, who were repeatedly abused by this man when the mother was not around. After giving birth to another daughter, the mother's second marriage dissolved and Molly was accused of causing this breakup. In addition, Molly was repeatedly abused by her older brothers and had no one to turn to—no one to believe her story and no one to fend for her. She grew up with a chronic sense of threat and danger.

Molly's recollection of her maternal grandmother is of a loving and nurturing caretaker. However, based on Molly's own narrative, there is good reason to believe that the grandmother was far from a perfectly attuned and protective caretaker. Yet the full meaning of the grandmother's digressions did not register in Molly's mind. For example, it appears that the grandmother knew about the repeated abuse but failed to stop it. Molly recalls an incident where her grandmother hit her brother with a shoe saying: "I know what you are doing!" Molly sees this as evidence of her grandmother's protectiveness and devotion and derives a sense of affirmation that her experience of abuse was real. At the same time, she ignores the fact that the grandmother did nothing to fully stop it. She is also unable to connect her chronic sense of being unattractive with her grandmother's message that she had big unattractive lips, rather than recognizing and celebrating her noticeable beauty.

Except for her grandmother, who took her into her own room to shield her from the abuse, the only benign parental holding object in Molly's life was God. She is a devout Catholic who deeply believes in a protective, providing, and just God. She prays often and resorts to prayer at times of profound helplessness when resources are not available or human assistance and care are not accessible. Her deep religious belief in God has always been her saving grace, a guiding beacon that has helped her hold on to a sense of being cared for throughout her life. It provides her with a psychological sense of safety when human caretakers neglect their duty to protect and comfort her. It offers order, justice, reassurance, and hope in a world of chaos and confusion where protectors are perpetrators and caretakers are self-serving.

During her treatment, Molly developed an unyielding idealized transference to me. She saw me as a competent, "brilliant," "generous," and resilient clinician, "beautiful in and out." On the one hand, the idealization was problematic since it was repeatedly contrasted with her own inadequate self. However, it was the very thing that allowed Molly to trust and seek help from me in spite of repeated betrayals and breaches of trust by important people in her life. Over three years of treatment, attempts were made to work through many issues and deconstruct many misconceptions. However, as her therapist I never punctured her idealized vision of her grandmother, recognizing that this was the only benign internal object Molly relied on. Without it, Molly could have felt defenseless, despondent, and alone in an unsafe world full of perpetrators lurking to take advantage of her vulnerability. In spite of being deprived of parental care herself, Molly has been able to nurture three daughters who are now growing up to become adaptive adults, drawing from the love of her idealized grandmother and the sense of safety and hope provided by her profound belief in a protective and just God.

Discussion

It is important to note that our universal parental imagoes are more ambivalent and complex than unidimensional. Our cultural myths and, unfortunately, our societal realities also include parents who commit the unthinkable: hurting and abandoning their own children. Similarly, God's imagoes are both protective and dangerous. Discussing the primordial need to vilify parental imagoes is beyond the scope of this chapter. Suffice it to say that it is partly generated from the same intense longing for a protective parent who oversees the social order.

This chapter discusses a process of othering in which the alterity of the other is preserved through attributes of ultimate standards of perfection that are contrasted with the imperfect, inferior self. The binary opposite demarcation between self and other still holds, but the other is altered by aggrandizement and exaltation rather than denigration. In other words, through idealization the object is kept as an image unlike the self. This chapter introduces the notion of *reparative idealization* and contrasts it with the traditional psychoanalytic notion of *defensive idealization*. The argument in the chapter is that our need for a caretaking parental figure is profound and everlasting. In the absence of nurturing and protective figures in our real-life relationships, we idealize and alter parental internal representations in our minds in order to, at least symbolically, experience the longed-for parental functions. We are attached to these internal representations. These idealized parental figures are reparative fictions essential for our psychological survival and the lifelong sense of security.

Holding on to an idealized created image—a transitional object that facilitates a healthier developmental trajectory and allows one to transcend a reality of parental deprivation—may be a key for adaptation. This is a growth-promoting process, not just a defensive mental maneuver, which seems to be a universal phenomenon.

Note

1 This chapter is an elaboration on a paper originally published in *Other/Wise: The Online Journal of the International Forum for Psychoanalytic Education*, Issue 3, Winter 2015, located at https://ifpe.wordpress.com. Published with permission.

References

Alvarez, A. (1992). *Live company: Psychoanalytic psychotherapy with autistic, borderline, deprived and abused children.* London: Routledge.

Aron, L., & Atlas, G. (2015). Generative enactment: Memories from the future. *Psychoanalytic Dialogues*, *25*(3), 309–324.

Bachofen, J. J. (1992). *Myth, religion, and mother right.* (R. Manheim, Trans.). Princeton, NJ: Princeton University Press.

Benjamin, J. (1995). Sameness and difference: Toward an "overinclusive" model of gender development. *Psychoanalytic Inquiry*, *15*(1), 125–143.

Berman, N. (2015, October). The dragon in the abyss: The "other side" of Kabbalistic myth and the paradoxes of abjection. Paper presented at Psychology and the Other Conference, Cambridge, MA.

Beville, M. (2010). Introduction. *Otherness: Essays & studies 1.1.* Aarhus: Centre for Studies in Otherness, Aarhus University. Retrieved from www.otherness.dk/journal/vol_1.

Bion, W. R. (1991). *A memoir of the future: Books 1–3*. London: Karnac.

Bollas, C. (2011). The transformational object. In *The Christopher Bollas reader* (pp. 1–12). New York: Routledge. (Original work published 1978.)

Bonovitz, C. (2004). The cocreation of fantasy and the transformation of psychic structure. *Psychoanalytic Dialogues*, *14*(5), 553–580.

Bowlby, J. (1958). The nature of the child's tie to his mother. *International Journal of Psychoanalysis*, *39*, 350–373.

Braucher, D. (2014, July). Passion (or past shunned): The use of fantasy to recreate past loving and sexual self-experiences in the present. Paper presented at The Seventh Joint International Conference: Passion, Florence, Italy.

Cameron, P. J. (2010). *Mysteries of the Virgin Mary: Living our Lady's graces.* Cincinnati, OH: Servant Books.

Chasseguet-Smirgel, J. (1974). Perversion, idealization and sublimation. *International Journal of Psycho-Analysis*, *55*, 349–358.

Epstein, I. (Ed.) (1972). *The Soncino Hebrew-English Talmud: Tractate Shabbat.* London: Soncino Press Inc.

Fairbairn, W. R. D. (1994). An object relations theory of the personality. In E. Fairbairn-Birtles & E. D. Scharff (Eds.), *From instinct to self: Selected papers of W. R. D. Fairbairn: Vol. I. Clinical and theoretical papers* (pp. 155–156). Northvale, NJ: Jason Aronson. (Original work published 1963.)

Freud, S. (1955). *Beyond the pleasure principle.* In *The standard edition of the complete psychological works of Sigmund Freud, Vol. XVIII* (pp. 159–215). (J. Strachey, Ed.). London: Hogarth Press. (Original work published 1920.)

Freud, S. (1957). *On narcissism.* In *The standard edition of the complete psychological works of Sigmund Freud, Vol. XIV* (pp. 67–102). (J. Strachey, Ed.). London: Hogarth Press. (Original work published 1914.)

Fromm, E. (1964). *The heart of man.* New York: American Mental Health Foundation Books.

Goodman, D., & Freeman, M. (Eds.). (2015). *Psychology and the other.* New York: Oxford University Press.

Harlow, H. F., Dodsworth, R. O., & Harlow, M. K. (1965). Total social isolation in monkeys. *Proceeding of the National Academy of Sciences of the U. S. A., 54*(1), 90–97.

Jung, C. G. (1956). *The collected works of C. G. Jung, Vol. 5. Symbols of transformation: An analysis of the prelude to a case of schizophrenia* (2nd ed.). (G. Adler & R. F. C. Hull, Eds. & Trans.). Princeton, NJ: Princeton University Press. (Original work published 1911–1912.)

Jung, C. G. (1960). General aspects of dream psychology. In *The collected works of C. G. Jung, Vol. 8. The structure and dynamics of the psyche* (pp. 237–280). (G. Adler & R. F. C. Hull, Eds. & Trans.). New York: Pantheon. (Original work published 1916.)

Jung, C. G. (1966). *The collected works of C. G. Jung: Vol. 7. Two essays on analytic psychology* (2nd ed.). (G. Adler & R. F. C. Hull, Eds. & Trans.). Princeton, NJ: Princeton University Press. (Original work published 1928.)

Klein, M. (1975). Some theoretical conclusions regarding the emotional life of the infant. In *The writings of Melanie Klein, Vol. 3* (pp. 61–93). London: Hogarth Press. (Original work published 1952.)

Kohut, H. (1971). *The analysis of the self.* Madison, CT: International Universities Press.

Lachmann, F. M., & Stolorow, R. D. (1976). Idealization and grandiosity: Developmental considerations and treatment implications. *Psychoanalytic Quarterly, 45*(4), 565–587.

Lieberman, A. F., Padrón, E., van Horn, P., & Harris, W. W. (2005). Angels in the nursery: The intergenerational transmission of benevolent parental influences. *Infant Mental Health Journal, 26*(6), 504–520.

Main, M. (2000). The organized categories of infant, child, and adult attachment: Flexible vs. inflexible attention under attachment-related stress. *Journal of the American Psychoanalytic Association, 48*(4), 1055–1095.

McGowan, T. (2007). *The real gaze: Film theory after Lacan.* Albany, NY: SUNY Press.

Mills, J. (2017). *Inventing God: Psychology of belief and the rise of secular spirituality.* New York: Routledge.

Mitchell, S. A. (2000). *Relationality: From attachment to intersubjectivity.* Hillsdale, NJ: The Analytic Press.

Nulman, M. (1996). *The encyclopedia of Jewish prayer: The Ashkenazic and Sephardic rites.* Northvale, NJ: Jason Aronson.

Sandler, J. (2003). On attachment to internal objects. *Psychoanalytic Inquiry, 23*(1), 12–26.

Schore, A. N. (2001). Effects of a secure attachment relationship on right brain development, affect regulation, and infant mental health. *Infant Mental Health Journal, 22*(1–2), 7–66.

Slade, A. (2014). Imagining fear: Attachment, threat, and psychic experience. *Psychoanalytic Dialogues, 24*(3), 253–266.

Spitz, R. A. (1946). Anaclitic depression: An inquiry into the genesis of psychiatric conditions in early childhood, II. *The Psychoanalytic Study of the Child, 2*, 313–342.

Spruiell, V. (1979). Freud's concepts of idealization. *Journal of the American Psychoanalytic Association, 27*(4), 777–792.

Srouf, L. A., & Waters, E. (1977). Attachment as an organizational construct. *Child Development, 48*(4), 1184–1199.

Voltaire (1768). Epistle to the author of the book, *The Three Impostors*. (J. Iverson, Trans.). Retrieved from https://www.whitman.edu/VSA/trois.imposteurs.html.

Chapter 12

Foucault and Derrida on interiority and the limits of psychoanalyzing sexuality and madness

Peter Capretto

Introduction

A cursory understanding of Freud's allegiance to Darwinism and the ideas of unconscious repression and libidinal energy already makes clear why there is an adversarial relationship between Michel Foucault and psychoanalytic thought. Put simply, Foucault's *histoires* on madness and sexuality do not play well with psychoanalytic understandings of subjectivity. For psychoanalysis, it is the cultural repression of unconscious forces and the internalization of group mentalities that create cultural neuroses and hinder sexual expression. For Foucault, the power of political, religious, and cultural regimes is more complex than the picture painted by Freud's analyses of cultural and sexual repression; these biopolitical powers not only harness and produce repression, but also proliferate and manage sexual speech and discourse through biopower. At stake in this dispute is nothing less than deciding what drives personhood, subjectivity, and their histories. If there are in fact narratives on sexuality in modernity to be gleaned from Foucault and psychoanalysis, they are unquestionably at odds with one another in significant ways.

Despite the force and persuasiveness of his claims, Foucault clearly has his detractors. A complex apologist for psychoanalysis, Jacques Derrida has responded to Foucault in ways that make it hard to simply read psychoanalysis as passé in its understanding of modern sexuality and its visions of psychic interiority. Foucault's claims on repression do more than offer a different narrative of modern sexuality; they make specific claims on the structure of modern subjectivity, agency, and interiority, which strike at the roots of modern psychology and, to a similar degree, phenomenology. In short, biopower as something derivative of but not reducible to the structures of subjectivity—insofar as power is not only possessed but possesses—does not fit well into modern phenomenological and psychoanalytic understandings of interiority, observation, and introspection. Derrida's many responses to Foucault on psychoanalysis intend, at least in part, to resist the tides that threaten to wash away Freud and the central concepts that psychoanalysis contributes to modern theories of sexuality and identity.

Tracking and interrogating Foucault's criticisms of psychoanalysis in his discourses on sexuality, madness, and the abnormal, this chapter argues that the dispute between Foucault and psychoanalysis is best understood as a disagreement over drive, desire, and *différance*. By this, I mean that a close interrogation of the arguments between Foucault and psychoanalysis—largely represented by Derrida—reveals various impasses that are less a matter of theoretical superiority and more a matter of methodological intent. Most central for Foucault and Derrida is the issue of theoretical limits vis-à-vis psychoanalysis: Madness, sexuality, and subjective interiority present countless limits to philosophical interrogation as well as to genealogy. While a number of psychoanalytic and queer theorists have tried to synthesize the insights of Foucault and Freud under the rubric of a "Freudo-Foucauldianism," Foucault's analytics of power and Freud's analyses of the psyche are irrevocably pointed in different directions (Huffer, 2009, p. 131). More specifically, they differ in both their views on where the limits of philosophical discourse analysis lie, and on whether to transgress them, as in Foucault, or to work *at* their limits, as in Freud and Derrida.

Given its task, this chapter is in part a theoretical narration of the controversy and response to Foucault's criticism of psychoanalysis, primarily through his conversation with Derrida, and Derrida's critical analysis after Foucault's death in 1984. Yet through this narration, a central claim I make is that their conflict cannot be resolved merely by championing one thinker's theory of subjectivity over the other's. Contrary to approaches that synthesize Foucauldianism and psychoanalysis—thereby trivializing or obfuscating their differences—I instead argue that partisan and synthetic readings neglect the ways that their conflict emerges from differing methodological decisions at the outset of their analyses. While these decisions on the limits of madness, sexuality, and interiority must be treated critically on their own regard, they must also be used to situate larger and more tertiary disputes between Foucauldian and psychoanalytic analyses of subjectivity and identity. To make this case, this chapter is divided into four sections.

In the first section, I lay out Foucault's case against the psychoanalytic formulation of sexuality both in the repressive hypothesis of *The History of Sexuality, Volume I* (Foucault, 1976/1990) and in the ways that psychiatry silences unreason within *History of Madness* (Foucault, 1961/2006). Citing figures in queer theory (Butler, 1990/2006; Huffer, 2009) and contemporary antipsychiatry (Strozier, 2002; Yeng, 2010), I outline the way that, for Foucault, psychoanalytic understandings of subjective interiority claim to liberate through its ideas of interiority and confinement, but in truth enact a technological regime of biopower that represses sexual expression.

In the second section, I present the counter position that refutes Foucault's critiques of psychoanalysis. Looking primarily to Derrida (1968/1978, 1992/1994), but also to Judith Butler (1990/2006) and Joel Whitebook (2005), I present a many-fronted resistance to Foucault's claims that psychoanalysis silences madness and confines sexuality in an authoritarian way. Most directly, this section argues that Foucault's criticisms of psychoanalysis operate on an unstated and ill-supported assumption of the inherent violence of introspection and the gaze of interiority. Subsequently, contra Foucault, it contends that psychoanalysis is more receptive to the insights of madness and criticism than Foucault suggests, and that Foucault's analysis of madness is less receptive to the voice and resistances of madness than it believes itself to be.

In the third section, I consider though ultimately reject attempts to synthesize or develop a dialectical relationship between Foucault and psychoanalysis. Looking to several theorists who attempt develop what Lynn Huffer (2009, p. 131) describes as "Freudo-Foucauldianism," I endorse Huffer's contention that these attempts either water down, modify, or ignore essential features of either Foucauldian or psychoanalytic forms of analysis.

In the fourth and final section, I temper Huffer's claim by noting that the irreconcilability of Foucault and psychoanalysis does not lead to the triumph of Foucauldian analyses of sex and identity as naturally as she suggests. Turning to their most trenchant and nearly ad hominem attacks on one another, I argue that the dispute between Foucault and Derrida over psychoanalysis is best understood as a disagreement over whether philosophical and conceptual limits themselves are to be respected when it comes to hearing madness and sexuality. While psychoanalysis and the concept of psychic interiority might help people express various forms of repression, Foucault decides that the philosophical limits of psychoanalysis ultimately silence and manipulate subjectivity to such a degree that it would be better to have no *oeuvre* or concept of madness and sexuality at all. Yet alongside Derrida, I argue that by eschewing the limitations of interiority, Foucault neglects the potential ways that psychoanalysis actually critiques discourse on madness and sex through interiority, which in turn resists the ideological silencing of madness and sexuality. Turning to Butler's (1997) analysis of Freud and Foucault as well as her own reflections on the endurance of interiority in performance theory, I contend that the psychoanalytic resources offered by Derrida actually enable a conversation about this impasse, whereas Foucault's do not.

While I am tempted to conclude with the undecidable and impenetrable attitude that each figure offers their own strategic efforts of resistance against power and oppression, I end my argument less modestly than Derrida does. Psychoanalysis' anticipation and reception of criticism and suspicion toward its understanding of sexuality and interiority not only make it more resilient and less ideological than Foucault's analytics of power in sexuality and madness, but its abidance within the limits of philosophy—even if through a double strategy that aims to exceed it—makes it more receptive to interiority and alterity not as silence, but as difference. Despite its many shortcomings, the psychoanalytic perspective challenges critical dissent through receptive dialogue, not through a wholesale rejection of theoretical legitimacy.

Foucault's critique of psychoanalysis on sexuality and psychic interiority

For Foucault, the concern with psychoanalysis is closely tied to psychiatry's unique location in the late nineteenth century at the meeting place of medicine, psychology, and legal authority. This location positions it in a perfect and, therefore, dangerous relationship with the political regulation of bodies. In his 1976 work, *The History of Sexuality, Volume I*, Foucault (1976/1990) argues that the technique of psychoanalysis depends on pathologizing behavior in order to relieve it, which means that, despite its appeals to science, psychoanalysis cannot help but devolve into a legalistic theory. In particular, the narrative Foucault develops at the outset of his critique is about narrative itself, or the discourse that is generated in the modern West around sex.

Foucault foregrounds a more explicit critique of psychoanalysis and psychiatry by first explaining,

> This is the essential thing: that Western man has been drawn for three centuries to the task of telling everything concerning his sex; that since the classical age there has been a constant optimization and an increasing valorization of the discourse on sex; and that this carefully analytical discourse was meant to yield multiple effects of displacement, intensification, reorientation, and modification of desire itself.
>
> (ibid., p. 23)

While Foucault is intent on critiquing the power wielded by psychoanalytic discourse in particular, he notes that locating the influence of medicalization as late as Freud would be wrongheaded. Psychoanalysis may be a high point of the medicalization of regulatory discourse on sex, but regulatory speech about sex was already built into late modernity (ibid., p. 35). The ways that sex has been regulated have varied greatly, shifting the landscape through which discourse on sex has been proliferated in a public way. Before psychoanalysis, it was canonical law, pastoral power, and civil law that provided less overt but equally successful ways of managing sexuality prior to the end of the eighteenth century (ibid., p. 37).

Yet Foucault's case is that psychoanalysis emerged at the ideal moment as the perfect technique and technology of biopower for taking the regulation of sexuality into a new epoch. He makes it clear on several occasions that he does, in fact, view psychoanalysis as a technology of biopower (ibid., p. 113). "Psychoanalysis comes in at this juncture: both a theory of the essential interrelatedness of the law and desire, and a technique for relieving the effects of the taboo where its rigor makes it pathogenic," Foucault explains (ibid., p. 129). "In its historical emergence, psychoanalysis cannot be dissociated from the generalization of the deployment of sexuality and the secondary mechanisms of differentiation that resulted from it" (ibid., p. 129). That is, psychoanalysis succeeds in alleviating sexual suffering by confining sexual speech to the doctor's office and then setting the rules for judging sexual speech, acts, and bodies. Its hypotheses about pathology through sexual repression are ultimately about power and control, often unbeknownst to or implicitly wielded by the physicians themselves. By combining classical concepts of the familial alliance within the therapeutic dyad, psychoanalysis develops its own narrative of repression, claiming among other things that if one's sexual partners or families cannot offer the outlets for expressing one's desire, then psychoanalysis is the medicalized technique available for talking through this otherwise unspoken repression.

Fifteen years earlier, Foucault (1961/2006) in *History of Madness* characterizes this myth of repression with particular attention to the way that psychoanalysis shapes bodies, sexuality, and subjectivity through apparatuses of confinement. Foucault sees that "psychoanalysis understood that all forms of madness have roots in troubled sexuality" and subsequently that "[s]ince time immemorial, and probably in all cultures, sexuality has been governed by systems of constraint" (ibid., pp. 88–89). The true genius of psychoanalysis is that, under the guise of medico-legal authority, it succeeds in convincing or duping persons that this confinement of discourse in a public yet regulated way actually helps them with their liberation. It is for this reason that "[c]onfinement was thus to be a space of truth as much as a space of restraint, and had to be the latter only to be the former" (ibid., p. 436). It is within the confines of the doctor's office, the therapeutic alliance, and psychoanalysis that one might finally be free and that one's identity might be mirrored back to oneself. This also enables and reifies structures of narcissism predicated on a desire to undo oneself through a strangely "self"-imposed confinement.[1]

Foucault does not believe that the West finally experiences power enforcing itself on the life of sex in culture with the advent of Freud; the problem of the regulation and biopower of sexual bodies is not limited to psychoanalysis (ibid., p. 377). But there is, still, a qualitative distinction in psychoanalysis as the harbinger of a form of biopower that far exceeds the regimes that preceded it. Particularly in his 1974–1975 lectures on the *Abnormal*, Foucault (1999/2003a) clarifies the extent to which "expert medico-legal opinion is not deployed in a field of opposition, but in a field of gradation from the normal to the abnormal" (p. 42). More specifically, the discourse of psychoanalysis is one that has an infinitely looping effect and relation to sexuality and normality, a feature that theorists (Butler, 1990/2006) use to argue for the inherent heteronormativity of psychoanalysis. It is the authority of psychoanalysis into the social, the legal, the familial, and the biomedical that allows it—and situates itself in a way that society demands of it—to make determinations about what techniques will best help in "maximizing life" and protecting the race

(Foucault, 1976/1990, p. 123). Foucault (1999/2003a) contends, "Almost from the outset, the field of abnormality is very quickly taken up with the problem of sexuality" (p. 167). It is ultimately the biotechnology of the repressive hypothesis that allows psychoanalysis to frame both abnormality and sexuality in a space where they can truly be grafted onto one another.

One of the countless ways that this biotechnology of psychoanalysis regulates and normalizes sex is in its prioritization of heterosexuality and, somewhat paradoxically, its denigration of "female" sexuality below "male" sexuality, largely through Oedipal theory. Among others, feminist philosopher Sokthan Yeng (2010) explains,

> The conceptual framework of psychoanalysis did not offer any cures but only techniques to reify standards of normalcy. Applied to female sexuality, this means that its techniques are aimed at controlling the individual body as well as the greater population. Psychoanalysis does not offer a cure. It is, in short, a mechanism of bio-power.
>
> (p. 22)

Psychoanalysis can only ever normalize bodies, rendering them docile to forces of sexual proliferation, which itself reflects the proliferation of public discourse on sex. Psychoanalysis and the modern West may not want to see private sex happening, but they certainly want to see its effects and hear its public discourse to ensure sex is medicalized and regulated to resist death, protect the race, and function in the most "normal" way possible. Foucault's critique of the medicalization of death through sex may thus appear relatively straightforward after this point: Medicalized biopower protects the race by making discourse about sex more publicly regulated, making it easier to normalize sex to productive and heteronormative practices.

Yet this critique of the medicalization of death is complicated by the fact that the modern interrogation of psychology, its reason, and its unreason are, for Foucault, the making of a completely new and problematic understanding of subjectivity. Foucault agrees that the threat of death motivates us to health in the ways a physician might, yet it also provides a contrast for life, meaning that if we have a sense of life as always on the precipice of "death," we might somehow understand ourselves better. The problem, however, is that physicians and psychologists do not really know anything about the experience of death; death hovers mysteriously outside of life, all the while regulating life as a guarded interior space with death on the periphery. Repression, whether of death or sexuality, only makes sense within a framework that generates a private or interior space of the subject from which to expel its repression and consider the prospect of one's many failings.

It is for this reason that the concept of experience and feeling[2] manifests itself in a discourse other than that of the drives, of death, or of transcendence. Foucault (1961/2006) turns away from death and toward madness in his first major work not as a rejection of death's significance for subjectivity, but as a new iteration of the same problem:

> The substitution of the theme of madness for that of death is not the sign of a rupture, but rather of a new twist within the same preoccupation. It is still the nothingness of existence that is at stake, but this nothingness is no longer experienced as an end exterior to being, a threat and a conclusion: it is felt from within, as a continuous and unchanging form of life.
>
> (p. 15)

Here, the very concept of the exterior and the interior is largely eschewed. One sees Foucault's tacit appreciation of the insights of Heidegger (1927/2010, p. 240) and Wittgenstein (1922/1981, 6.4311), that death does not, properly speaking, rupture life because it is not an event in life. But instead of following in the well-worn path of this pursuit, Foucault's response is to completely reconceive of the approach to the "nothingness of existence." Feeling madness "from within" does not mean we "embrace" psychic interiority. Rather, madness provides a substitute for the otherwise transcendental pursuit of death and the impossible task of understanding ourselves in terms of interiority.

It is on this point that Foucault scholar Huffer (2009) explains how keenly Foucault saw the connection between the regimes of psychoanalysis that rely upon moral discourse toward death, and a vision of subjectivity with an interior or internalized space: "The result of this movement of internalization is a moral order that relies on an illusion of psychic interiority to police itself as conscience" (p. 104). Without this psychic interiority, there is no prospect for the biotechnology or its policing. Judith Butler (1990/2006) similarly explains the many ways that, for Foucault and psychoanalysis in equal measure, this

> "inner" and "outer" constitute a binary distinction that stabilizes and consolidates the coherent subject [...] If the "inner world" no longer designates a topos, then the internal fixity of the self and, indeed, the internal locale of gender identity, become similarly suspect.
>
> (pp. 182–183)

But by not giving in to the allure of interiority and psychoanalysis, Foucault's analytics of power offer a potentially more viable interpretation of the prospects for thinking subjectivity, one that does not fall into the trap of interiority that comes out of psychoanalysis, or the banal empiricism that emerges as behaviorism and cultural materialism in the twentieth century. Strozier (2002) affirms that "Foucault's turning of the subject toward its historical constitution may be the most striking and productive reconception of the subject since the ancient world ... Foucault's subject is real without being merely empirical; it has being" (p. 269). While it is true that Foucault's understanding of modern subjectivity does not have the so-called "depth" that is characteristic of most post-Kantian continental thought and post-Freudian theory, this metric of depth is predicated on a false ideal of what proper subjectivity looks like: something requiring deep introspective interrogation. The turn to madness and to the genealogical account of modern thought is a turn to the ways that subjectivity has been shaped by political regimes staking their claims on bodies, their sex, and their reason or unreason. The substance or being of Foucault's subject is seen in these analytics of power and in the bodies that resist biopower. This may not appeal to the grand visions of interiority and subjectivity championed by the likes of Freud and other late moderns, but at least Foucault's pursuits are not duped by false ideals of liberation.

The psychoanalytic resistance to Foucault on sexuality and madness

Given the force and weight of Foucault's indictments against psychoanalysis, it might seem questionable to generously consider a psychoanalytic response to him. Why give voice to a regime that so fantastically silences and confines others in their sex, madness, and subjectivity? Does this gesture not invite the silencing of Foucault and all of his efforts to resist malicious uses of biopower?

Because his critique is rooted in a fundamental rejection of psychoanalysis' key concepts and premises, developing a psychoanalytic response to

Foucault is complicated. As both a sympathizer with and critic of Foucault's project, philosopher and psychoanalyst Joel Whitebook underscores the close connection between Foucault's critique of psychoanalysis and his critique of psychic interiority. Whitebook's (2005) analysis contends that Foucault not only assumes that "self-observation is, by its very nature, violent," but also that

> there is no possibility of a non-objectionable split between an observing and an observed part of the self and a form of benign self-exploration. There is no place in Foucault's thinking for the distinction between an observing ego … the necessary precondition for a psychoanalytic process.
>
> (p. 320)

In other words, Foucault believes that, by turning to introspection and interiority, psychoanalysis necessarily silences the voice of human sexuality and madness because of the inherent hostility and objectification implied in the subject exploring itself.

This unstated assumption, as Whitebook puts it, makes it difficult to dialogue with Foucault's polemics on psychoanalysis. Yet with it comes a series of subsequent questions about the *modus operandi* of Foucault's attack on interiority, particularly in *History of Madness*. Most central is the issue of what exactly concerns Foucault in legitimating the inward gaze of introspection into interiority. Specifically, given Foucault's substitution of madness in the place of death in his project, what is it about the interior space of the psyche that might problematize these proprietary efforts? Is there something about the conversation with interiority that undermines his analytics of power? Or, worse, does doing so reveal a silence behind a silence, an omission of voice in Foucault while alleging to offer an *histoire* of madness?

Through a series of exchanges with Foucault and continuing reflections on Foucault after his death, Jacques Derrida has become an enduring resister of Foucault in his attacks on psychoanalysis. Taking special issue with the contention that psychoanalysis is incapable of hearing madness, Derrida turns the tables on Foucault, asking whether his treatment of madness is capable of hearing madness. In his earliest response to Foucault in 1963, Derrida (1968/1978) questions,

> Now, is not the concept of madness—never submitted to a thematic scrutiny by Foucault—today a false and disintegrated concept, outside current and popular language which always lags longer than it should behind its subversion by science and philosophy? Foucault, in rejecting the psychiatric or philosophical material that has always emprisoned the mad, winds up employing—inevitably—a popular and equivocal notion of madness, taken from an unverifiable source. This would not be serious if Foucault used the word only in quotation marks, as if it were the language of others, of those who, during the period under study, used it as a historical instrument. But everything transpires as if Foucault knew what "madness" means. Everything transpires as if, in a continuous and underlying way, an assured and rigorous precomprehension of the concept of madness, or at least of its nominal definition, were possible and acquired. In fact, however, it could be demonstrated that as Foucault intends it, if not as intended by the historical current he is studying, the concept of madness overlaps everything that can be put under the rubric of negativity.
>
> (p. 41)

At first glance, Derrida's critique seems to be that Foucault succumbs to a form of confirmation bias: He comes to his massive history already having a vision of what would count as "madness," and systematically discredits all psychiatric and philosophical approaches that do not agree with it. If this were the case, then resolving the conflict between Foucault and psychoanalysis would merely be a matter of clarifying those differing models of "madness" and getting on the same page.

Yet the problem, as Derrida sees it, is that Foucault refuses to submit madness to any form of understanding—psychological, philosophical, or otherwise. Derrida's commentary is a more critical interpretation of Foucault's classic statement that madness is nothing other than the absence of an *oeuvre:* The best strategy Foucault can develop to work against the powers that silence madness is to make madness fundamentally incomprehensible, a negative or apophatic concept in the highest. Just as with Meno, virtue can be pursued only on the basis of a cursory and therefore paradoxical "precomprehension" of virtue,[3] so Derrida contends that for Foucault, "Only when the totality of this content will have become manifest in its meaning for me (but this is impossible) will I rigorously be able to situate it in its total historical form" (ibid., p. 44).

This strategy simultaneously allows Foucault to denigrate the psychoanalytic engagement with madness as allegedly normalizing subjectivity in its effort to communicate madness within itself, while also allowing him to circumvent any real engagement with madness, even when dictating the discourse in his own terms. Derrida's resistance to Foucault might be succinctly stated in this way: You, Foucault, succeed in preventing madness from being silenced, but only by ensuring that it is never heard to begin with.

In tandem with Derrida, scholars such as Whitebook (2005) have argued more trenchantly that Foucault's methodological approach to madness does not transform madness from something that is silenced to something that is heard, but rather into something that is rendered unquestionable, sacrosanct, or even something that is to be coddled: "Furthermore, just as, psychologically, Foucault never put the patient/madman's position into question, so, using radical-sounding anti-foundationalist rhetoric, he stubbornly refused to reflect on his own theoretical position throughout his career" (p. 316). In his attempt to push back against the forces that normalize madness and render all its forms—sexual and otherwise—docile, the consequence of Foucault's analysis is the insulation of madness in a theoretical place without interiority and without dialogue of any kind. Because his analytics of power consider any encounter with the interiority of madness a hostile interrogation, Foucault insulates madness in a place that may not be "confined," but that is also without a voice.

Even with Freud's at times restrictive and detached attitude toward countertransference in the therapeutic dyad,[4] Whitebook contends that one can only defend Foucault's caricature of the authoritarian attitude of psychoanalysis with a profound distance from the practice of therapy. An analyst himself, Whitebook notes that "analysts wouldn't see challenges from their patients—which question their competence, their mastery of the countertransference, their own psychopathology, indeed their very humanity—negatively" (ibid., p. 136). Analysts understand the importance of affective self-awareness and bias in interpretation, which is why they are required to go through their own analysis during training. This also helps analysts to appreciate the plight of being analyzed and to know what it is to experience the inevitable empathic failures and misunderstandings they will offer to their own analysands.

Whitebook also goes to great lengths to nuance the way that Foucault's clinical training in the 1950s and his *Diplôme de Psycho-*

pathologie positions him, in fact, *within* the tradition of psychology and by no means outside of it (ibid., pp. 313–314). It is worth considering whether Foucault is able to shirk psychoanalysis or interiority given his embeddedness within it. He is, unabashedly, a *modern* thinker, even if at times a utopian one, as some contend (ibid., p. 338). Furthermore, one should hold in view the following question when considering Foucault's corpus on sexuality and subjectivity: If Foucault is capable of so grossly misreading—or intentionally misconstruing—the psychoanalytic tradition even with his deep conversancy with it, then what prospect does this hold for Foucault's engagement with madness as something that, unlike psychoanalysis, fundamentally resists language and discourse? At the very least, this warrants some circumspection or resistance to Foucault's treatment of psychoanalysis on interiority and sexuality.

The Foucauldian may reply to Derrida's rebuttals by conceding that Foucault criticizes modern understandings of madness without a constructive replacement, but pointing out that psychoanalysis has the opposite problem of co-opting power without critical awareness of what it is doing to sexed bodies. Yet even Butler (1990/2006), whose work ambulates between appropriations of Foucauldian analytics of power and resources in Freud and psychoanalysis, takes issue with the contention that psychoanalysis does not have a mechanism to critique the forms of power over sexuality and gender that are manifested in public discourse on sex. "Clearly," Butler contends with regard to the specific sexual theory on incest and heteronormativity in psychoanalysis,

> psychoanalytic theory has always recognized the productive function of the incest taboo; it is what creates heterosexual desire and discrete gender identity. Psychoanalysis has also been clear that the incest taboo does not always operate to produce gender and desire in the ways intended.
>
> (ibid., p. 104)

Not only can these resources for cultural analyses of power be found in Freud's later work on *Civilization and Its Discontents*, *Totem and Taboo*, and *Moses and Monotheism*—texts that Foucault seems to neglect in his treatment of Freud. More still, the psychoanalytic tradition between Freud's death and Foucault's writing generated profound criticisms of the politics of psychoanalytic experience from within itself.

Psychologist of religion Jeremy Carrette (2007), who typically sides with Foucault in his scholarship, similarly argues that psychoanalysis is capable of thinking the limits of discourse: "To think economy inside the psychoanalytic theory of religion is to move towards the limits of what can be said inside those discourses of the *same* and to stumble into the unknown of the *other*" (p. 136, emphasis in original). This can be found in object relations theory, which speaks quite closely to the advent of critical theory. Given that he sought feedback from R. D. Laing on his manuscript of *Folie et déraison*, Foucault was clearly conversant with the anti-psychiatric movement and its profoundly critical and anti-totalitarian analyses of normality. Laing's (1967) use of psychoanalysis in works such as *The Politics of Experience* appeared contemporaneously with *History of Madness,* but prior to Foucault's later and more sustained criticisms of psychoanalysis and its apparent futility in speaking to madness, power, and unreason.[5] When it comes to sexuality and psychic interiority in particular, Foucault may simplify the psychoanalytic project and the ways it is able to think beyond the mere repetition of repression and liberation through talk therapy. Psychoanalysis' resistance to Foucault is as multiplicitous as the power that Foucault himself characterizes. Even if imperfectly, psychoanalysis possesses mechanisms to critique itself and how discourses of sex manifest in power relations.

Thus for Derrida, even 30 years after the dust had settled on their original exchange, Foucault's caricature of psychoanalysis and its reception to madness and unreason neglects its most basic potential. While Foucault (1961/2006) insists time and time again that psychoanalysis "does not even condescend to language" in madness (p. 510), Derrida (1992/1994) insists that

> [p]sychoanalysis, on the contrary, breaks with psychology by speaking with the Unreason that speaks within madness and, thus, by returning through this exchange of words not to the classical age itself – which also determined madness as unreason, but, unlike psychology, did so only in order to exclude or confine it – but toward this eve of the classical age that still haunted it.
>
> (pp. 237–238)

Foucault's approach to psychoanalysis involves more than a resistance to this haunting of the classical age, but a negligence—or, if one must, a repression—of the only way that madness might actually speak: within and through philosophy and the interiority of the subject it invokes.

Prospects of synthesizing psychoanalysis and Foucauldianism

One of the more sobering features of the conflict between Foucault and psychoanalysis is the prospect that each potentially offers for analyzing subjectivity. Given the complex structures of madness and sexuality, it would seem that theorists should draw from as many resources as possible to track the ways that subjectivity might be understood as both repressed and regulated. Yet synthesizing the perspectives of Foucault and psychoanalysis into a unified or even complementary system is a complex and deeply contested task.

Noting the traps of modern subjectivism and biological reductionism facing Foucault, sociocultural anthropologist P. Steven Sangren (2002) insists that failing to consult both psychoanalytic and Foucauldian perspectives would effectively blind theories of sexuality and madness from essential features of modern identity. At the root of the claims fortifying the division, Sangren suggests, are appeals to methodological purity when it comes to matters of individualism and constructivism:

> One need not suppose, indeed it would be a mistake to do so, that one must choose between discursive productivity or romantic subjectivism, between biological or individualist reductionism and hopelessly decentered subject-positionality, between "the subject" and "agency," when it comes to understanding individuality and desire. Our personhood, desire, or "subjectivity," in other words, is a complex process, not so much "split" or "shifting" as simultaneously both authentic and inauthentic, encompassing contradictory and paradoxical tendencies, perhaps most fundamentally revolving around an existential imperative that insists on resisting that which might define us as pure effects or objects, a resistance put into motion by the same disciplining constraints against whose limitations we rebel.
>
> (ibid., p. 117)

Sangren even goes so far as to argue that "we might take some inspiration from Foucault, and, even more, from psychoanalysis" on simplistic forms of modern subjective theory, including unrestrained cultural constructionism (ibid., p. 118). Alternative analyses of sexuality in the social sciences tend to rely on some form of cultural constructionism. Yet these strategies neglect experiences of sexuality that are subject to discipline and various forms of psychic cathexis. For Sangren, while it would be convenient to align oneself wholly with psychoanalytic or Foucauldian analyses of sexuality, doing so forfeits features of sexual experience.

Other theorists in philosophy and the social sciences have made similar cases to Sangren, though perhaps less optimistically on the possibility of mitigating the hostility between Foucault and psychoanalysis. Sociologist Mauro Basaure (2009) contends,

> All the attempts to forge links between Freud and Foucault – as for instance in feminism and queer-theory – do not doubt at all the possibility of remaining equally faithful to both of them, above all by reinterpreting Freud both within and against the conceptual framework of his understanding of science.
>
> (p. 357)

Basaure offers the caveat that succeeding in this venture requires a "competent critical perspective" to discern what methods are appropriate in forging these links—which remains poorly defined in his analysis—but does not foreclose on this as a possibility (ibid., p. 357). Social psychologist and Foucault scholar Derek Hook (2007) has also argued with modest ambition that despite "bring[ing] with it a series of prospective benefits and dangers," the task of bridging psychoanalysis with Foucauldianism on technologies of subjectivity "provides a rich set of terms" that might be essential for thinking through "a political rationality *that is not always rational*" (p. 272, emphasis in original). That is, the silence that imposes itself on sexuality and madness does not inherently translate into any particular analysis better than any other; even given their tradeoffs and deficiencies in thinking sexuality, Foucauldianism and psychoanalysis might be the only theoretical pairing that is different and complementary enough to fully consider what madness and sexuality bring in modern subjectivity.

Despite the momentum of these synthetic, dialectical, or complementary approaches to Foucault and psychoanalysis, such efforts have been met with profound opposition. Notably in queer theory, where psychoanalysis and Foucauldianism have remarkably functioned as compatible resources for thinking subjectivity, Huffer (2009) has offered acerbic criticism of what she repeatedly terms the rampant "Freudo-Foucauldianism" of scholarship in theories of sexuality (p. 131). Taking ownership of what might be read as an obscurantism in queer theory, Huffer offers the following explanation: "In my view, this strangely American twinning of Freud and Foucault has produced the odd, distorted, infamously ungraspable conception of sexuality that has become the common fare of queer theory" (ibid., p. 36). Not only do synthetic approaches to Foucault and Freud lead to a potentially insurmountable wall of jargon-laden theory when it comes to thinking subjectivity, but this synthetic or dialectical approach neglects the core content of these figures, particularly Foucault. Huffer argues, "Foucault's critique of psychoanalysis in *Madness* is categorical" (ibid., p. 36). As such, attempts to reconcile Foucault's analytics on the biopower of sexuality with psychoanalysis miss the intention of Foucault's project.[6] Huffer insists that "[s]uch readings of the psyche don't ignore Foucault completely, but are based on an incomplete engagement with his work" (ibid., p. 129). The force of Foucault's *histoires* cannot be approached in a piecemeal way that decides the moments at which one wants to use concepts of psychic interiority and the language of repression to understand how it is that the nineteenth and twentieth centuries have deployed regimes of eugenics and biopolitics on sexual discourse.

It is on this basis that Huffer turns directly to Derrida's engagement with Foucault. The danger of Derrida, she contends, is not that he critiques Foucault head on, but that he deliberately tries to blur the boundaries between psychoanalysis and the analytics of power. Huffer points particularly to Derrida's argument that Foucault's relationship to psychoanalysis and Freud is an ambivalent one that is always including and excluding Freud:

> Exemplifying a middle ground, both/and position is the Derridean deconstruction of any Freud–Foucault antagonism that would reductively pit one against the other in an either/or opposition … Reading Freud as the "doorman" [*huissier*] to the age of psychoanalysis, Derrida discovers *within* Foucault the disavowed psychoanalytic "borderline."
>
> (ibid., pp. 139–140, emphasis in original)

With profound attention to the details of this debate and to the content of their claims made on subjectivity, having entertained numerous attempts to synthesize such a Freudo-Foucauldianism, Huffer argues in the end, "Unlike Derrida, I see Freud as the figure who, mirroring Descartes, functions not as *Madness*'s disavowed borderline but as one of the book's two central targets of critique" (ibid., p. 140). For Huffer, Derrida's allegedly careful and sympathetic reading of Freud, more accurately, conceals the weight of Foucault's critique of Freud.

Though he in many ways aligns more with psychoanalysis than with Foucault, Slavoj Žižek (2014) has similarly stressed this reality for any prospective Freudo-Foucauldianism on the basis of the debate between Derrida and Foucault: "[F]or Foucault, *Cogito* is grounded in the exclusion of madness, while, for Derrida, *Cogito* itself can only emerge through a 'mad' hyperbole (universalized doubt), and remains marked by this excess" (p. 28). Even Whitebook (2005), in large part a critic of Foucault's treatment of psychoanalysis, contends that "[u]nderlying their disagreement is the fact that Foucault and Derrida operate with different conceptions of madness" (p. 327). Whitebook subsequently notes that, given Derrida's obvious criticisms of essentialism, Foucault's desire for the "*acute fragmentary psychosis*" of subjectivity simply extends Derrida's work in deconstruction further than Derrida envisioned (ibid., p. 328, emphasis in original). Though scholars like Whitebook desire a more moderate resolution of the dispute between Foucault and psychoanalysis on psychic interiority, even they concede that these positions cannot be synthesized—certainly not without profound scrutiny on which features of subjectivity are under analysis from moment to moment.

Whether or not Huffer's precise critique of Freudo-Foucauldianism fully captures Derrida's project, she unquestionably succeeds in clarifying that the potential gains to be made by uniting Foucault and psychoanalysis do not justify gerrymandering their analyses for the sake of convenience. More work needs to be done to plunge into the differences that characterize their understandings of sexuality and madness, particularly on how subjectivity understood therein operates within or beyond those limits.

Conclusion: the limits of sexuality, madness, and psychic interiority in Foucault and psychoanalysis

Given the obstacles facing these more contemporary attempts to synthesize their positions, it should not come as a surprise just how extreme

Derrida and Foucault considered their own theoretical and ethical differences to be. On numerous occasions, Foucault (1999/2003a) draws parallels between the technology of psychoanalysis and the eugenics of Hitler's politics, claiming, "We should not be surprised that German psychiatry functioned so spontaneously within Nazism" (p. 133). Derrida (1968/1978) makes an equally grand accusation about the restrictive determinism of Foucault's project in *History of Madness*:

> I am not saying that Foucault's book is totalitarian, for at least at its outset it poses the question of the origin of historicity *in general*, thereby freeing itself of historicism; I am saying, however, that by virtue of the construction of his project he sometimes runs the risk of being totalitarian.
>
> (p. 57, emphasis in original)

These accusations between Foucault and those representing psychoanalysis are, I would contend, overstatements. It is a bit of an affront to associate either Freud, a Jew displaced from his home by the violent activities of the Shoah, or Foucault, a scholar-activist who resisted oppression in every way he could in both his writing and the way he lived, with Nazism or totalitarianism.

The intention of this moderated reading of Foucault and Derrida's disagreements at this juncture is not to trivialize their difference, nor is it to suggest that one cannot oppose the effects of totalitarianism and biopower while also being complicit in their propagation. On the contrary, the weight of their resentment for one another is evidence that there are methodological limits in discourse that Foucault and Derrida profoundly disagree about. In a moment of clarity on method, Derrida (1992/1994) offers a rather generous reading of Foucault's approach to psychoanalysis and where the two of them may diverge:

> But let us not oversimplify things. What Foucault generously grants psychoanalytic experience is now nothing other than what is denied it; more precisely, it is the being able to see what is denied it. Indeed, the only privilege that is here granted to psychoanalysis is that of the experience that accedes to that to which it can never accede. If Foucault here mentions, under the name of madness, only schizophrenia and psychosis, it is because psychoanalysis most often approaches

> these only in order to acknowledge its own limit: a forbidden or impossible access. *This limit defines psychoanalysis.*
>
> (p. 257, emphasis in original)

One thing that Foucault understands perfectly well about psychoanalysis is this sense of limit or methodological propriety in analysis. To think madness requires that one think within the confines of the method itself. For Derrida, Foucault's (1961/2006) foundational assertion that madness is "[i]n all probability, nothing other than *the absence of an oeuvre*" is nothing other than Foucault's admission that he has abandoned the project of thinking madness altogether, that Foucault has in some sense given up (p. xxxi, emphasis in original). This negation is, at best, a form of psychic apophaticism, an attempt to reconstruct madness on the basis of its erasure and negativity.

Yet for Foucault, it is precisely this confinement to tradition that ultimately damns the psychoanalytic project. He appreciates the struggle that Freud had with the methodological and scientific limits of psychoanalysis, that Freud

> concentrated its powers, stretched them to the limit, and placed them in the hands of the doctor. He created the psychoanalytic situation, where, in the short circuit of a stroke of genius, alienation became disalienating because, in the doctor, it became subject.
>
> (ibid., p. 510)

To suggest that Foucault is out of touch with tradition or that his archival work is not grounded in history would be indefensible slander. The problem for Foucault is that these limits have already failed sexuality and subjectivity in modernity, manifesting in countless forms of confinement in and through even psychoanalysis. Perhaps the greatest point of agreement one can expect between Foucault and psychoanalysis is on the existence of this limit in method, discourse, and silence. The point of disagreement, however, is on whether and when to transgress this limit in theory and comprehension.

While her engagement with both Foucault and Freud may suggest she falls prey to the Freudo-Foucauldianism characterized by Huffer, Butler's careful and consistent evaluation of her own project reveals that she understands this issue of methodological limit well. Reflecting in a

1999 preface on her own relation to the concept of interiority and its implication in the work of Freud, Foucault, and psychoanalysis, Butler (1990/2006) describes her 1990 attempt to subvert gender identity in *Gender Trouble* as having understated the importance of thinking sex and gender in terms of interiority:

> Although I would deny that all of the internal world of the psyche is but an effect of a stylized set of acts, I continue to think that it is a significant theoretical mistake to take the "internality" of the psychic world for granted.
>
> (p. xvi)

Butler's recalibration of her project toward psychoanalysis is not restricted to *Gender Trouble*, but also finds footing in *The Psychic Life of Power* (1997), where she admits that she is "in part moving toward a psychoanalytic criticism of Foucault" and remarks, subsequently, that in "describing the body in Foucault, [she has] clearly wandered into a psychoanalytic vocabulary of sublimation" (p. 87; p. 92). Butler's decision to embrace psychoanalysis further is complex, and is motivated at least in part by the issue of cathexis and mourning that is thinkable primarily in terms of selfobject relationships and psychic interiority. Yet her decision is just that: a decision of terms and of method, no more so than is the case for Foucault.

For Derrida as early as 1963, what is said of the distinction between reason and unreason can also be said of the relation between Foucault and psychoanalysis itself. "The issue is therefore to reach the point at which the dialogue was broken off, dividing itself into two soliloquies – what Foucault calls, using a very strong word, the *Decision*," Derrida argues (1968/1978, p. 38, emphasis in original).

> The Decision, through a single act, links and separates reason and madness, and it must be understood at once both as the original act of an order, a fiat, a decree, and as a schism, a caesura, a separation, a dissection.
>
> (ibid., p. 38)

For psychoanalysis as much as Cartesianism and transcendental phenomenology, Foucault's decision fundamentally concerns this limit of method and of reason. The foundation of Foucault's project, as mad as it seems, already goes beyond the limit of what might be permissible in Descartes, Husserl, and Freud: namely, an analysis that rejects the prospects of introspection, phenomenological reduction, and self-analysis. Derrida (1996/1998) tracks Foucault's treatment of Descartes in *History of Madness* at least in part to reveal the direction of Foucault's analysis at the roots of modern subjectivity, which finds iterations in Kant and Husserl. Derrida sees as much in 1963 as in 1994 that if the interiority of consciousness is rejected on the grounds of a "theme of normality" that is endemic to phenomenology and psychoanalysis, then the decision over dialogue and silence between Foucault and psychoanalysis has already been determined (ibid., p. 60).

Derrida contends,

> If, in an absurd hypothesis, there were one and only one deconstruction, a sole *thesis* of "Deconstruction," it would pose divisibility: differance as divisibility. Paradoxically, this amounts to raising the analytical stakes for a thinking that is very careful to take account of what always rejects analysis.
>
> (ibid., p. 33)

For Foucault, it is not divisibility itself that he feels so compelled to reject, but rather the prospect of what madness might become if it is ever understood strictly in terms of a divisible psychic interiority. Yet it is this attention to difference, to its divisibility and to its resistances, that grants psychoanalysis the means of parsing out and deciding its own relation to theoretical and methodological dissent. That is, by transgressing the boundaries of the tradition, Foucault relocates madness and psychoanalysis to a place where he is unable to adjudicate any of the claims made by either the analytics of power or by psychoanalysis. Whereas Derrida employs a double strategy that operates within and outside the limits of reason, phenomenality, and decidability, Foucault transgresses the limits of madness altogether. Properly speaking, with this one reaches the impasse with Foucault: One can neither indict nor criticize him for his willful decision to transgress the limits of discourse and method in his analyses of sex, madness, and biopower. It is because of this decision that Foucault is so profoundly successful in his efforts to "share the experience" of modern identity in its many vectors (1981/1991, p. 223). Yet it is this same decision that limits his discourses on sex, madness, and psychic interiority to this sharing, but nothing more.

Notes

1 Already in Foucault one sees the complex theoretical territory of the pleasure that comes from confinement both in therapy and in sex. For an excellent analysis of the implication of pleasure, desire, and confinement both within the therapeutic alliance and sexual encounters, see Jessica Benjamin's *The Bonds of Love: Psychoanalysis, Feminism, and the Problem of Domination* (1998).

2 Commenting specifically on *The History of Sexuality, Volume I*, literary theorist Robert Strozier (2002) thus observes, "The deployment of sexuality entails the production of human interiority and the tendency to construct that interiority as individual identity; this interiority is the locus of our sexuality or desire, or, more generically, 'feeling,' as Foucault sometimes puts it" (p. 209).

3 Meno presents the paradox to Socrates, "How will you look for [virtue], Socrates, when you do not know at all what it is? How will you aim to search for something you do not know at all? If you should meet with it, how will you know that this is the thing that you did not know?" (Plato, 1980, 80d).

4 Freud (1912/1953) belies his resoluteness toward the direction of transference in noting, "The peculiarity of the transference to the physician lies in its excess, in both character and degree, over what is rational and justifiable—a peculiarity which becomes comprehensible when we consider that in this situation the transference is effected not merely by the conscious ideas and expectations of the patient, but also by those that are under suppression, or unconscious" (p. 314).

5 In the few moments that Foucault (1997/2003b) acknowledges these self-critical strands within psychoanalysis, he discounts their efforts as empty by asking, "Look: ever since the very beginnings of anti-psychiatry or of the genealogies of psychiatric institutions … has a single Marxist, psychoanalyst, or psychiatrist ever attempted to redo it in their own terms or demonstrated that these genealogies were wrong, badly elaborated, badly articulated, or ill-founded? The way things stand, the fragments of genealogy that have been done are in fact still there, surrounded by a wary silence" (p. 12).

6 Huffer's appeal to authorial intent in her reading of Foucault may be considered odd given Foucault's attitude toward authorship and the death of the author. See Foucault's (1969/1984) criticism of conventional notions of authorial intent and individualization in "What is an author?"

References

Basaure, M. (2009). Foucault and the "anti-Oedipus movement": Psychoanalysis as disciplinary power. *History of Psychiatry*, *20*(3), 340–359.

Benjamin, J. (1998). *The bonds of love: Psychoanalysis, feminism, and the problem of domination.* New York: Pantheon.

Butler, J. (1997). *The psychic life of power: Theories in subjection*. Stanford, CA: Stanford University Press.

Butler, J. (2006). *Gender trouble: Feminism and the subversion of identity*. New York: Routledge. (Original work published 1990.)

Carrette, J. (2007). *Religion and critical psychology: Religious experience in the knowledge economy*. New York: Routledge.

Derrida, J. (1978). Cogito and the history of madness (A. Bass, Ed. & Trans.). In *Writing and difference* (pp. 31–63). Chicago, IL: University of Chicago Press. (Original work published 1968.)

Derrida, J. (1994). "To do justice to Freud": The history of madness in the age of psychoanalysis (P. A. Brault & M. Naas, Trans.). *Critical Inquiry*, *20*(2), 227–266. (Original work published 1992.)

Derrida, J. (1998). *Resistances of psychoanalysis* (P. Kamuf, P. A. Brault, & M. Naas, Trans.). Stanford, CA: Stanford University Press. (Original work published 1996.)

Foucault, M. (1984). What is an author? In P. Rabinow (Ed.), *The Foucault reader* (pp. 101–120). New York: Pantheon Books. (Original work published 1969.)

Foucault, M. (1990). *The history of sexuality, Volume I: An introduction* (R. Hurley, Trans.). New York: Vintage Books. (Original work published 1976.)

Foucault, M. (1991). *Remarks on Marx* (R. J. Goldstein & J. Cascaito, Trans.). New York: Semiotext(e). (Original work published 1981.)

Foucault, M. (2003a). *Abnormal: Lectures at the Collège de France, 1974–1975* (G. Burchell, Trans.). New York: Picador. (Original work published 1999.)

Foucault, M. (2003b). *Society must be defended: Lectures at the Collège de France, 1975–1976* (D. Macey, Trans.). New York: Picador. (Original work published 1997.)

Foucault, M. (2006). *History of madness* (J. Khalfa, Trans.). New York: Routledge. (Original work published 1961.)

Freud, S. (1953). The dynamics of transference (J. Riviere, Trans.). In E. Jones (Ed.), *The collected papers of Sigmund Freud, Vol. II* (pp. 312–322). London: Hogarth Press. (Original work published 1912.)

Heidegger, M. (2010). *Being and time* (J. Stambaugh, Trans.). Albany, NY: SUNY Press. (Original work published 1927.)

Hook, D. (2007). *Foucault, psychology and the analytics of power*. New York: Palgrave Macmillan.

Huffer, L. (2009). *Mad for Foucault: Rethinking the foundations of queer theory*. New York: Columbia University Press.

Laing, R. D. (1967). *The politics of experience*. New York: Ballantine Books.

Plato (1980). *Meno* (G. M. A. Grube, Trans.). Indianapolis, IN: Hackett Publishing Company. (Original work published 4th century BCE.)

Sangren, P. S. (2004). Psychoanalysis and its resistances in Michel Foucault's *The history of sexuality*: Lessons from anthropology. *Ethos, American Anthropological Association*, *32*(1), 110–122.

Strozier, R. M. (2002). *Foucault, subjectivity, and identity: Historical constructions of subject and self.* Detroit, MI: Wayne State University Press.

Whitebook, J. (2005). Against interiority: Foucault's struggle with psychoanalysis. In G. Gutting (Ed.), *The Cambridge companion to Foucault* (2nd ed., pp. 312–347). New York: Cambridge University Press.

Wittgenstein, L. (1981). *Tractatus logico-philosophicus*. (C. K. Odgen, Trans.) New York: Routledge. (Original work published 1922.)

Yeng, S. (2010). Foucault's critique of the science of sexuality: The function of science within bio-power. *Journal of French and Francophone Philosophy, 18*(1), 9–26.

Žižek, S. (2014). Cogito, madness and religion: Derrida, Foucault and then Lacan. In C. Davis, M. Pound, & C. Crockett (Eds.), *Theology after Lacan: The passion for the real* (pp. 19–33). Eugene, OR: Cascade Books.

Chapter 13

Beautiful troubling alterity

An intersubjective response to Nabokov's *Lolita*

Steven Huett and George Horton

We have this intense belief and hope that the greatness of a great book will announce itself in the power of its opening lines, so that one would find oneself standing long after, rapt and besotted, as though against one's own will, by the forcible allure of the narrator's voice. This expectation—that the greatness of great books will be immediately perceptible—is, of course, manifestly untrue, except when it is not. As an eminent instance of such an exception, we offer Humbert Humbert's opening seduction in *Lolita*[1]: "Lolita, light of my life, fire of my loins. My sin, my soul. Lo-lee-ta: the tip of the tongue taking a trip of three steps down the palate to tap, at three, on the teeth. Lo. Lee. Ta" (Nabokov, 1955, p. 9). Note the immediate alliteration and assonance of 'light' and 'life' with the second syllable of her name and of her name's first syllable with 'loins.' Note the tragically juxtaposed doublet of 'my sin' and 'my soul.' Note the individual syllables of 'Lolita' spoken with incantation-like diction, followed by much, much longer alliteration echoing the 't' of her name's final syllable. Note the voice that intermingles veneration and profanity, reverence and vulgarity with impeccable rhythm and euphony. We are three sentences in and already the deviant pedohebephile's seduction has started to take hold. Are you aware that you are being groomed? After all, later in this passage he does warn us: "You can always count on a murderer for a fancy prose style" (Nabokov, 1955, p. 9).

Within the still controversial preoccupations of *Lolita*—the confession of a 37-year-old man's love affair with a 12-year-old girl—lies a jeering challenge to the psychoanalytic tradition; a challenge made by the author, Nabokov himself, who called psychoanalysis "voodooism" (Nabokov, 1956, p. 314) and Freud "the Viennese witch doctor," and who proclaimed unequivocally that he "reject[ed] completely the vulgar, shabby, fundamentally medieval world of Freud, with its crankish quest for sexual symbols … and its bitter little embryos, spying, from their natural nooks, upon the love life of their parents" (Berman, 1985, p. 211; Nabokov, 1967c, p. 10). So confident is Nabokov that the siren song of his novel will tempt just the sort of analytic interpretation he despises that he begins the book with a satiric foreword by one John Ray, Jr., Ph.D., a psychologist who makes an impassioned case that, "As a case history, *Lolita* will become, no doubt, a classic in psychiatric circles" and highlights the "ethical impact the book should have on the serious reader" to help create a "safer world" (Nabokov, 1955, pp. 5–6). This, of course, is first-rate parody.

In this think-piece, we argue that the folly of a psychoanalytic reading of *Lolita* inheres in the paradox of Nabokov's prose, which overtly tempts the literary psychoanalyst with the putative confession of the eloquent and loquacious pedohebephile, Humbert Humbert. This confession simultaneously leaves the reader enthralled by his storytelling and disturbed at deriving subjective pleasure from a story with such manifestly deplorable content. Furthermore, we argue that any putatively 'neutral' analytic interpretation is destined to reproduce a significant aspect of Humbert's own manipulative violence whereby the reader fails to recognize the irreducible alterity and ambivalence of Humbert and the alterity of oneself as simultaneously disgusted-and-enthralled witness to the story he tells. We then break from Nabokov's formalist assertions to propose a potential 'meaning behind' (or 'alongside,' or 'between') *Lolita*, located in the troubling cavern of alterity within oneself, where one cannot honestly analyze or access *Lolita* without, ironically, confessing as the reader the multiplicity of stirrings aroused by the book. We draw upon intersubjective theories to perform this reader-response approach, to express our own ambivalence, to better approach Humbert, and to explore the delicate and often problematic terrain between aesthetic enjoyment and moral complicity.

Nabokov's objections to psychoanalytic literary interpretations were manifold. However, an especially sore point for Nabokov was Freud's habit, in his incessant search for unconscious patterns, of stripping the formal and narrative particulars and filching them as reinforcing material for the analytic paradigm and project, and of assigning a defensive function to the creativity of the individual mind—effectively marking the text as little more than an apologia for psychoanalysis (Berman, 1985; De la

Durantaye, 2005, 2007; Ingham, 2002). Freud's analytic proclivity for subsuming fine details into mythologized configurations in order to 'reveal' and 'explain' what really occurs within the text hazards radical revisionism, substitutions of meaning, and artistic disfiguration. The first and most renowned instance, of course, was Freud's (1908/1953b) analytic interpretation of Sophocles' *Oedipus Rex*, a composition held up by Aristotle in his *Poetics* as a near perfect rendering of the poetics of tragedy (Barstow, 1912). In Freud's hands, it was treated as though it were waiting two and a half millennia for its mythical sexual triangle to be unearthed and identified as the more fundamental human condition. For Nabokov, such hermeneutic motives were more than suspect, they were absurd: "Let the credulous and the vulgar continue to believe that all mental woes can be cured by a daily application of old Greek myths to their private parts" (Nabokov, 1967b, para. 19). The result of Freud's literary revisionism is to reorient and divert the story away from the reader's ability to *perceive, feel,* and *apprehend* the tragic, while the excised and fetishized Oedipal triangle reproduces itself with fractal-like prolificacy, urging resolution of the complex rather than purgation of passions, so that whatever story one thought one was experiencing appears, in the end, as a changeling.

This method was diametrically opposed to Nabokov's, who sought to inlay his work with the story's theme with ever finer intricacy, so in the end "[t]hat which is revealed is not another story, but a deeper interconnection of elements in the same story—all its hidden winks, nods, clues, and codes tell the same story more finely perceived" (De la Durantaye, 2006, p. 318). True, Nabokov masterfully concealed these patterns but "what is hidden is not another meaning, but that same meaning more artfully *signed*"—that is, an artwork that bears the author's "watermark," which, rather than conveying a ciphered message, "signs and seals [the work's] authenticity and provenance" (De la Durantaye, 2006, pp. 317, 321, emphasis in original).

And so, Nabokov invites and anticipates the analyst's critical, scouring eye and, with acumen, accordingly baits the text throughout with parody: Freudian symbols and a saturated portrayal of psychopathology, a "mocking invitation to read allegorically" (De la Durantaye, 2006, p. 311). Just what are some of these inscriptions? We already noted the faux Forward by Dr. Ray. At the book's start, Humbert Humbert intimates an origin story of his pedohebephilia (or love of nymphets, as he terms it) starting with his summer romance with a girl, Annabel Leigh, when both were 13. He describes her and their romance in magical terms, and laments their failure to consummate their love when her parents interrupt a fondling tryst, followed four months later by her sudden death "of typhus in Corfu" (Nabokov, 1955, p. 13). Humbert avers of the magical tryst that,

> the haze of stars, the tingle, the flame, the honeydew, and the ache remained with me, and that little girl with her seaside limbs and ardent tongue haunted me ever since—until at last, twenty-four years later, I broke her spell by incarnating her in another.
>
> (Nabokov, 1955, p. 13)

Then there is the Oedipal stymieing treatment of his parentage, of which very little is conveyed. About his mother, he says little more than: "My very photogenic mother died in a freak accident (picnic, lightning) when I was three, and, save for a pocket of warmth in the darkest past, nothing of her subsists within the hollows and dells of memory" (Nabokov, 1955, p. 10). He provides an uncomplicated description of his father as "a gentle, easy-going person" whom he loves unequivocally: "He, *mon cher petit papa,* took me out boating and biking, taught me to swim and dive and water-ski, read to me *Don Quixote* and *Les Miserables*, and I adored and respected him" (Nabokov, 1955, p. 10).

He also describes being hospitalized for melancholy and taking pleasure in deceiving his psychiatrists, "never letting them see that you know all the tricks of the trade" and "teasing them with fake 'primal scenes'" to disallow "the slightest glimpse of one's real sexual predicament" (Nabokov, 1955, p. 34). He teases the analytic concepts of idealization and projection as he expounds on the very special, uncanny qualities that distinguish a nymphet from an ordinary girl: "not human, but nymphic (that is, demoniac)," with their "ineffable signs" such as "insidious charm," the "slightly feline outline of a cheekbone, the slenderness of a downy limb," discernable only to "an artist and a madman" (Nabokov, 1955, p. 17). He reveals omnipotent, grandiose fantasies by claiming his physical love of Lolita is not about sex, but rather "to fix once for all the perilous magic of nymphets" (Nabokov, 1955, p. 134). And he seems to justify his overall project with a rescue fantasy, as he seeks to save and avenge Lolita from the encroachment by his rival double—the other pedophilic adult male whom he murders in the end (insert narcissistic projective identification of the loathed bad object).

Yes, Humbert Humbert seems an id-creature apparently lacking any semblance of superego, with an ego consorting brilliantly to satisfy his whims, seemingly obsessed beyond cure by regressive sexualized fantasies for his idealized Lolita. We could go on and on. So, how fares Humbert Humbert and his creator under the attentive care of the analyst-critic?

As it happens, Nabokov's wry prediction for how Freudian acolytes would manhandle his story was not without merit. A psychoanalytic study by Friedman (1999) makes the case that Humbert is secretly a homosexual, and gives "consideration … that Lolita is, unconsciously, a boy" (p. 252). Friedman notes: "It is remarkable that Lolita never menstruates," and further states, "it is also noteworthy that at no point is it clear that Lolita even has a vagina," and finally, "When Lolita is sick: [Humbert says] 'her brown rose tasted of blood.' Does this imply a familiarity with analingus?" (p. 252). In a second analytic interpretation entitled "Vladimir Nabokov: A Case Study in Pedophilia," Centerwall's (1992) abstract reads:

> The author of *Lolita*, Vladimir Nabokov, was himself consciously a pedophile who acted out his desires vicariously through his writing. Drawing upon his literary works and biography, the manifest and genetic origins of Nabokov's pedophilia are traced back to an unresolved oedipal conflict complicated by childhood sexual abuse. The raw power of *Lolita* derives from the abreactive discharge of a libidinal cathexis denied any other mode of expression.

The article then goes on to pursue this indicting thesis. Both essays adduce circumstantial evidence to make their respective inferences, both are reductive in their treatment of text and character, both fall for the novel's trap, and both fail to realize they are the butt of Nabokov's parody.

Such literary-analytic interpretations are unsurprising, as Freud (1908/1953b) himself reductively postulated the creative writer's pursuits to be an extension of childhood play, a form of "build[ing] castles in the air" from "daydreams" as a form of wish fulfillment, replete with characters who were split "into many part-egos" (pp. 145, 151). Correspondingly, the reader experiences a reduction in psychic tension by projecting his/her own shameful fantasies onto the book's characters. Triumphantly, Freud concludes that psychoanalysis has given us the keys to fiction's hidden meanings.

Psychoanalytic criticisms such as these fulfill precisely Nabokov's concern about "getting it wrong" by treating the text like a cipher and the reading experience as a cold investigation and not an affecting encounter with art, with the product being at the very least wrong-headed and at worst disingenuous and hypocritical (and, in the case of Centerwall, arguably libelous). These are not cases of psychoanalysis finding a Nabokovian secret, but, as Derrida (1987) has observed, of psychoanalysis always rediscovering itself in its revealed objects, always another repetition, just one more, ever recursive, ever and ever seeing its reflection within the *mise en abyme*. Psychoanalytic responses such as these provide an apt punch-line for Nabokov's joke.

But all joking aside, these interpretive gestures also reproduce some very unfunny dynamics, for *Lolita*, at bottom, is a story about complicity. Nabokov's foremost commentators have remarked that in reading "we have come virtually to condone the violation it represents ... [w]e have been seduced into conniving in the violation, because we have permitted our fantasies to accept what we know to be revolting" (Trilling, 1982). It has been said that "the rhetoric of *Lolita* is the rhetoric of reader entrapment" (Toker, 1989, p. 199). Most disturbingly, Humbert's confessional tends to beget confessions from its readers and critics, much like the one presently unfolding (Whiting, 1998).

But these claims remain on the level of reaction to the representation of Humbert's crimes, and we maintain the complicity goes a layer deeper to the level of reader reenactment, insofar as you or I as reader become an accessory to Humbert's character. The most troubling aspect of Humbert Humbert, beyond his groveling and aggrandizing criminal confession, is his deeper violence, which threatens to infect and reproduce in the reader: Other Blindness. Throughout the story, Humbert's inability or refusal to recognize Lolita's subjectivity and alterity results in the constant sacrifice of Dolores, the girl, to his gratifying ideal of her as Lolita, the fetishized object. Relatively early in the novel, during a pivotal scene where Humbert would have us believe that he unexpectedly masturbated against Lolita as she sat in his lap, he says afterward that:

> Lolita had been safely solipsized ... What I had madly possessed was not she, but my own creation, another, fanciful Lolita – perhaps, more real than Lolita; overlapping, encasing her; floating between me and her, and having no will, no consciousness – indeed, no life of her own.
> (Nabokov, 1955, p. 62)

Nabokov believed that great writers are storytellers and enchanters, a quality with which he endows his "creature Humbert" (Nabokov, 1956,

p. 315). So beguiling is Humbert Humbert that in the numerous instances where, as readers, we are aware of his efforts to seduce, cajole, manipulate, collude, rationalize, and convince us—and though we know he perverts, exploits, and abuses—we nod skeptically and continue reading. All this because we wish to hear what he will say next. And so, he depicts a reenactment of the Fall with Lolita on his lap holding her "beautiful, banal, Eden-red apple," alone with Humbert while her mother is at church. "Her legs twitched a little as they lay across my live lap," he says,

> Lola the bobby-soxer, devouring her immemorial fruit, singing through its juice, losing her slipper, rubbing the heel of her slipperless foot in its sloppy anklet ... every movement she made, every shuffle and ripple, helped me to conceal and to improve the secret system of tactile correspondence between beast and beauty—between my gagged, bursting beast and the beauty of her dimpled body in its innocent cotton frock.
>
> (Nabokov, 1955, p. 59)

He consummates this entire episode by saying, "I crushed out against her left buttock the last throb of the longest ecstasy man or monster had ever known" (Nabokov, 1955, p. 61). Of this passage, one commentator says that Lolita "ceases, in Humbert's description, to be an *ethical subject*, and becomes an *aesthetic object*" (De la Durantaye, 2007, p. 71, emphasis in original). And what about us? What has become of us through the transpiring of this scene?

Reading *Lolita*, we submit, is a profound encounter with ambivalence arising from the dissonance created between enjoyment, disgust, and empathy. Humbert lulls us ever deeper into his gratifying view of Lolita—Lolita as carnal iconography, Lolita as aesthetic refuge—so persuasively rendered in his sublime marriage of aesthetics and metaphysics that he would certainly lull us hopelessly were it not for the one fact of her that tethers us to reality: her age. We realize much too late that Humbert's putative confession is a Trojan horse. In reaction, readers wish to castigate or redeem Humbert—to justify or disclaim a meaningful reading of *Lolita*.

We readers glimpse with astonishment and horror the cavern of alterity opened within ourselves—this experience of revulsion and desire, of horror at troubling literary beauty. Nabokov (1956) denied that *Lolita* has any "moral in tow" (p. 314), denied that literature had or was meant to have any practical value, cared little for readers or their responses, and distanced himself from the strong moral overtones of the book. However, if we as readers fail to produce a phenomenology and hermeneutic to traverse the unassailable complicity produced by the reading, we are bound to either reproduce Humbert's reductive violence or unjustly exonerate him for self-justifying purposes. But if we are to understand the morality of *Lolita,* we must think of it in terms other than normative and prescriptive. We must be emotionally open to the plenitude of ambivalence in the story's tragic element evoked in the lives presented on the page—of joy and pathos, discomfort and horror, disgust and sorrow. As readers, we can wish to castigate or to redeem Humbert, we can deny him personhood for his abuse or stand in solidarity with his aesthetic project of rendering his Lolita as art. But if Nabokov's approach is not didactic, nor prescriptive, nor moral in the normative sense, just how should we think of the ethics of *Lolita*? Precisely, we propose, as an aesthetico-ethical work—that is, one that does not enjoin but rather is morally sensitizing by virtue of encounter. The brilliant post-modern writer Donald Barthelme (1997) ingeniously showed in his essay on fiction, "Not-Knowing," that literature is ethical not as a reflection of the world, but as a meditation upon it, in that it accomplishes imaginative possibilities of other realities, that artistic style reconfigures our taken-for-granted realities, so that "art's project is fundamentally meliorative. The aim of meditating about the world is finally to change the world" (p. 24). Taken as such, Humbert is a koan, his protracted confession an aporia, and our meditation on him an opportunity for enlightenment and a deeper understanding of ourselves as well as a deeper affective encounter with ambivalence. Let us begin by recalling that Humbert and his Lolita are not people but language, and that the complicity is not in pedophilia and child abuse, but in their representation in reading itself; the crime is not the fictionalized perpetration, but the story itself and the seduced receiving mind (Mount, 2009). So also are we the victims who approximate a near dissociative experience of confusion about what has happened to us.

To bring comprehensibility to this confusingly pleasurable and rending experience, we believe that a formalist understanding of *Lolita* in line with Nabokov's intentions also requires an intersubjectively-informed reader-response because, despite Nabokov's claim, the ambivalence of *Lolita* has always belonged to the reading of it, and because, we believe, the moral anxieties evoked by *Lolita* occur in the generation of an intersubjective space that raises important doubts about oneself. It is not our intention to describe, develop, and adjudicate between existing intersubjective theories and comb through the text with them, nor to specify which concepts lend themselves best to a felicitous rather than reductive reading. We recognize the valuable potentiality afforded by reading *Lolita* through multiple intersubjective lenses—to better articulate the reader's phenomenological experience toward hermeneutic ends.

Within intersubjective systems theory, one can conceive of *Lolita* as a field of differently organized and operating subjectivities between reader and text, where the story itself functions to overcome the reader's negative organizing principle, a story that enacts disorienting inverted conjunctions with Humbert where disjunctions are expected (Atwood and Stolorow, 2014). Or within a relational psychoanalytic approach we could also speak, as readers, of encountering *Lolita* as an instance of binary impasse that demands the hard work of developing a third position from which to more ably respond (Aron, 2006); or of *Lolita* as an encounter with dissociated self-states, such as the hated reading-self who is moved by Humbert's character, who manages, per Nabokov, to appear "'touching,'" but whom we know to be "a vain and cruel wretch" (Nabokov, 1967a, para. 14); or, complementarily, of reading shame, evil, and pathology safely into Humbert in order to perpetuate one's own sense of innocence and magnanimity (Davies, 2004). These approaches would aid us greatly in meeting literary critic Peter Brooks' (1987) proposal to conceive of reading as transference, as a mind's passage through the text's "systematic discourse," which bears a resemblance to "the structure of mind," and "the dynamic organization of the psyche" (p. 337).

But rather than delineate and expound an intersubjective reader-response, we wish to perform one. To return momentarily to Freud's misreading, the point, we maintain, is to be open and receptive enough to experience the tragic element of *Lolita,* just as in Aristotle's experience of *Oedipus Rex.* Just as with Oedipus we pity the "great-souled man, endowed with all the gifts of nature" (Barstow, 1912, p. 4), whose frailties and flaws bring him to ruin, so with Humbert we pity not the monstrous character he incessantly (and disingenuously) ascribes to himself, but the man whose unparalleled gifts of language and insight enable him to compose masterful "articulate art" (Nabokov, 1955, p. 283), but never lead him to change his course, nor be empathically transformed through the encountered alterity of Lolita, nor be broken by the fracturing pain he inflicts. *We* know that *Humbert* has been safely solipsized; Lolita has not. Nor have we. *We* feel the sorrow he is unable to feel. *We* feel the ego dystonic otherness arising in both the perpetration and remorse so assiduously denied by Humbert.

Consider the beauty and sorrow of this passage—importantly, the penultimate passage of the book. Lolita has managed to escape from Humbert with Humbert's rival double, and he describes his moment of agony where, grieving, he pulls off the highway onto a remote mountain pass. He gets out of his car. He vomits on the roadside. He talks about the sun and the clouds and the asters overlooking a river-cut valley. And there he registers a distinct sound. Here are his words:

> That vapory vibration of accumulated sounds … never ceased for a moment, as it rose to the lip of granite where I stood wiping my foul mouth. And soon I realized that all these sounds were of one nature, that no other sounds but these came from the streets of the transparent town … Reader! What I heard was but the melody of children at play, nothing but that, and so limpid was the air that within this vapor of blended voices, majestic and minute, remote and magically near … one could hear now and then, as if released, an almost articulate spurt of vivid laughter, or the crack of a bat, or the clatter of a toy wagon … all really too far for the eye to distinguish any movement in the lightly etched streets … And then I knew that the hopelessly poignant thing was not Lolita's absence from my side, but the absence of her voice from that concord.
>
> (Nabokov, 1955, pp. 307–308)

Here, at last, it seems Humbert has experienced redemption. Here is his expression of true remorse. But this passage takes place two years prior to the final chronological events of the novel (Boyd, 1991), during which time Humbert spends two sullen years searching or waiting for Lolita, and, finally locating her, visits and finds her married and pregnant at 17, learns the name of the man—Humbert's double—whom she ran off with, meets Lolita's new husband, and then, realizing he still loves her, furtively asks her to run away with him. "No," she says, "No, honey, no" (Nabokov, 1955, p. 279). Here is where Lolita overcomes him, with a clear 'no' and a casual 'honey' (Wood, 1994; Quayle, 2009). But it does not last long. A moment later, Lolita vanishes after accepting $6000 of monetary support from him. Humbert then leaves, seeks out his double, and, in a scene of farcical and ineffectual vengeance, barely manages to murder him. To further this tragic trajectory, we know from the book's opening by John Ray, Jr. that both Humbert and Lolita have already died (of heart failure and in childbirth, respectively).

This is the final challenge of *Lolita*, to hold in one's own body, to the point of breaking, all the unredemptive truth: disgust at Humbert's deeds, his manipulative violence, his Other Blindness; ecstasy at his soaring prose, his "articulate art," his incomparable ability to render beauty and enliven a world both immanent and transcendent; compassion for the dead girl whose ordinary childhood was rapaciously stolen; admiration for the dead girl who, to the bitter end, never abandoned the pursuit of her own path and kept her subjectivity alive amidst incessant efforts to exploit and objectify her; sorrow for the man whose brilliance enabled him to create a lasting masterpiece of art but whose gift could not redeem his soul, nor morally transform his mind. Nabokov described art as "beauty plus pity" (De la Durantaye, 2006, p. 317; Mount, 2009). In *Lolita*, he offers us both, from the first down to the last word:

> I wish this memoir to be published only when Lolita is no longer alive. Thus, neither of us is alive when the reader opens this book. But while the blood still throbs through my writing hand, you are still as much part of blessed matter as I am … I am thinking of aurochs and angels, the secret of durable pigments, prophetic sonnets, the refuge of art. And this is the only immortality you and I may share, my Lolita.
>
> (Nabokov, 1955, p. 309)

Listen. Listen to the dissembler in the midst of his aesthetically evocative abuse. Let your ears be opened to all his deafened registers. When we listen to and feel our way through this story closely, we are the ones who might hope to be humanly formed, reformed, and transformed.

Note

1 Excerpts featured in this chapter are taken from *Lolita* by Vladimir Nabokov, copyright © 1955 by Vladimir Nabokov, copyright renewed 1983 by the Estate of Vladimir Nabokov. Used by permission of Vintage Books, an imprint of the Knopf Doubleday Publishing Group, a division of Penguin Random House LLC. All rights reserved.

References

Aron, L. (2006). Analytic impasse and the third: Clinical implications of intersubjectivity theory. *International Journal of Psycho-Analysis*, *87*, 349–368.

Atwood, G. E. & Stolorow, R. D. (2014). *Structures of subjectivity: Explorations in psychoanalytic phenomenology and contextualism* (Second Ed.). New York, NY: Routledge.

Barstow, M. (1912). Oedipus Rex as the ideal tragic hero of Aristotle. *The Classical Weekly*, *6*(1), 2–4. Retrieved from www.jstor.org/stable/4386601.

Barthelme, D. (1997). Not-knowing. In K. Herzinger (Ed.), *The essays and interviews of Donald Barthelme* (pp. 11–24). New York, NY: Random House.

Berman, J. (1985). *The talking cure: Literary representations of psychoanalysis*. New York, NY: New York University Press.

Boyd, B, (1991). *Vladimir Nabokov: The American years*. Princeton, NJ: Princeton University Press.

Brooks, P. (1987). The idea of a psychoanalytic literary criticism. *Critical Inquiry*, *13*(2), 334–348.

Centerwall, B. S. (1992). Vladimir Nabokov: A case study in pedophilia. *Psychoanalysis and Contemporary Thought*, *15*(2), 199–240.

Davies, J. M. (2004). Whose bad objects are we anyway? Repetition and our elusive love affair with evil. *Psychoanalytic Dialogues*, *14*(6), 711–732.

de la Durantaye, L. (2005). Vladimir Nabokov and Sigmund Freud, or a particular problem. *American Imago*, *62*(1), 59–74.

de la Durantaye, L. (2006). The pattern of cruelty and the cruelty of pattern in Vladimir Nabokov. *The Cambridge Quarterly*, *35*(4), 301–326.

de la Durantaye, L. (2007). *Style is matter: The moral art of Vladimir Nabokov.* Ithaca, NY: Cornell University Press.

Derrida, J. (1987). *The post card: From Socrates to Freud and beyond.* Chicago, IL: University of Chicago Press.

Freud, S. (1953a). *The interpretation of dreams*. In J. Strachey (Ed. & Trans.), in collaboration with A. Freud, assisted by A. Strachey & A. Tyson, *The standard edition of the complete psychological works of Sigmund Freud* (Vols. 4 & 5, pp. 1–627). London: Hogarth Press. (Original work published 1900.)

Freud, S. (1953b). Creative writers and day-dreaming. In J. Strachey (Ed. & Trans.), in collaboration with A. Freud, assisted by A. Strachey & A. Tyson, *The standard edition of the complete psychological works of Sigmund Freud* (Vol. 9, pp. 142–153). London: Hogarth Press. (Original work published 1908.)

Friedman, S. M. (1999). Nabokov's *Lolita*: A psychoanalytic study. *The Annual of Psychoanalysis*, *26–27*, 245–259.

Ingham, J. M. (2002). Primal scene and misreading in Nabokov's *Lolita*. *American Imago*, *59*(1), 27–52.

Mount, N. (2009, February 12). Nick Mount on Nabokov's *Lolita*. Innis Town Hall, University of Toronto. Podcast retrieved from http://podbay.fm/show/129166905/e/1344659400?autostart=1.

Nabokov, V. (1955). *Lolita.* New York, NY: Vintage International.

Nabokov, V. (1956). On a book entitled *Lolita,* in *Lolita* (pp. 311–317). New York, NY: Vintage International.

Nabokov, V. (1967a). Interviews. Vladimir Nabokov: The art of fiction No. 40. *The Paris Review, 41.* Retrieved from www.theparisreview.org/interviews/4310/vladimir-nabokov-the-art-of-fiction-no-40-vladimir-nabokov.

Nabokov, V. (1967b). Nabokov's interview. *Wisconsin Studies in Contemporary Literature, 8(*2). Retrieved from http://lib.ru/NABOKOW/Inter06.txt-with-big-pictures.html.

Nabokov, V. (1967c). *Speak, memory.* New York, NY: Alfred A. Knopf, Inc.

Quayle, A. S. (2009). Lolita *is* Dolores Haze: The "real" child and the "real" body in *Lolita. Nabokov Online Journal, 3,* 1–26. Retrieved from www.nabokovonline.com/uploads/2/3/7/7/23779748/v3_07_quayle.pdf.

Toker, L. (1989). *Nabokov: The mystery of literary structures.* Ithaca, NY: Cornell University Press.

Trilling, L. (1982). The last lover: Vladimir Nabokov's *Lolita.* In Harold Bloom (Ed.) (1987), *Vladimir Nabokov's* Lolita*: Modern Critical Interpretations* (pp. 5–12). New York, NY: Chelsea House.

Whiting, F. (1998). "The strange particularity of the lover's preference": Pedophilia, pornography, and the anatomy of monstrosity in *Lolita. American Literature, 70*(4), 833–862.

Wood, M. (1994). *The magician's doubts: Nabokov and the risks of fiction.* Princeton, NJ: Princeton University Press.

Chapter 14

The music knows

Grieving existential trauma in art, music, and psychoanalysis

Malcolm Owen Slavin

We need art so we do not die of the truth.

(Friedrich Nietzsche)

The following chapter was first given as a dynamic presentation, including works of art and music. We encourage readers to follow along with the presentation, found online at: www.psychologyandtheother.com/slavin.

The music knows

A few years before Ethan and I started working together, his sister had suddenly ended her own tormented life, and a very important mentor, a coach, had slowly died. Heart-wrenching new losses, following a childhood rife with rupture and feelings of alienation within his family. A tension, an aloneness had infused his childhood; each family member fled, hid out in his or her own cut-off way. Now, any sense of "at-homeness," of belonging, of connection quickly vanishes almost as soon as it appears. Ongoing sexual encounters and seeming romantic opportunities never evolve into an experience of true connection. Deadened states recur. Ethan longs for someone who can grasp the depth of his despair.

Pretty early on in our work, he's slumped down, despairing that I, or anyone, can ever really understand his struggle: "Maybe … because," I find myself saying, "Maybe, Ethan, because … it's that I'd have to feel it to know it." "Yes,"—looking up, he says, "exactly. Can you? Would you?"

I knew that we were talking about a deeply entangled, lifelong state. I sensed that someday, together with him, I might be able to come much closer to Ethan's experience in a deeper, personally meaningful way—to me and to him.

But, "No," I hear myself saying. "There's no way, Ethan," I said, "that I can really know all that devastation, the loss, the deadness that's with you now. I know it's what you need me to do. I hope I'll get there. But, not now, not nearly as fully as you need it."

Could I have mustered simpler forms of empathy? Sure. And I sensed that Ethan knew it. Mostly, it would be through my words. Sincere, I think. Far from negligible. Maybe even useful. But, by and large, gestures. Maybe, now, I quickly reassured myself (after blurting out that "no"), maybe now he'd know that I knew there was something more, much more—something missing.

And, more or less, it seemed he did. He said he hated and distrusted the distance between us. Yet, I realized, in his way, he was giving me some space, and time.

Because, "Yeah," he says, suddenly, "I'll do now what I've always done: listen to music … it works, it's a good thing … really good … well, sometimes, you know, it's the only thing. When no one really knows, *it* knows," he said, "*the music knows*."

At that moment, I think I simply breathed in the heartfelt, meaningful, and beautiful enigma in Ethan's words. The metaphor was palpably true about music—the ironic mix of resignation and hopefulness in Ethan's use of it. It was true, I knew, well beyond my capacity at that point for words.

How and what does "music know"?

I think it's fair to say that virtually all of us know something about what it means to "use" music, in some way, in order to evoke strong emotion while, simultaneously, processing it—giving it shape, form, and order.

We use music in times of heartache. Especially, crucially, loss, longing, grief. Of course, not only that. Think about it: bodily joy, expressive movement, dance, romance, Eros, nostalgia, mystery, nationalistic identity, pride, resistance to oppression, generational solidarity, inter-generational revulsion, courage, social solidarity—meditative aloneness.

Everywhere, music evokes the sacred, the transcendent. Even when it does so by provoking its own righteous condemnation as evil, a sacrilege, a danger: forbidden in some forms by early Christians as "the call of the devil," still punishable by death by the Taliban and many other Islamic fundamentalists; forbidden in instrumental form as a distraction from God by many Jews in Sabbath services; yet all of them chant, wail, or daven—very musically, in their own, highly ritualized ways.

Uncannily, music seems to know how to get deep inside us. Including, of course, many of us who have not endured as much individual trauma as Ethan. And it gets in deep not only for those of us who are at home in the context of Western culture, but everywhere, musicologists tell us—everywhere that there are human beings. And, as I think we're learning, and I hope to show (in the images and music accompanying this chapter), it goes back further, way further than we realize: it originates at the dawn of our species—at the beginning of the complicated, fraught experience of existing as an evolved human being on this earth.

"We need art so we do not die of the truth." That's Nietzsche's (1872) incredible observation about it. He means *all* art, image, metaphor, drama. Though, perhaps most prominently for Nietzsche, music.

The scope of his comment widens the whole field drastically: life without some form of music and art, the arts—literally unlivable? What could this Nietzschean hyperbole mean?

Beginnings: caves as sacred space

We'll start at, or near, the beginning of the known story—that is to say, my version of what I claim is our human, pre-historic, existential story. It is late-nineteenth-century Spain, the town of Altamira, north of Madrid, quite near the coast. A young girl sees something no one ever noticed before—something that shakes the art and archeological world: cave paintings on the walls and ceilings created tens of thousands of years ago. Many art historians, archeologists, Darwinian evolutionists at that time believed these paintings *must* be forgeries. So-called primitives could never have produced such beautiful, evocative, incredibly well-wrought images (I recommend that readers follow the hyperlink www.psychologyandtheother.com/slavin to see musical and artistic imagery that accompanies these themes).

Soon, more and more cave art is discovered in France and Germany—and eventually many other places in Europe, Asia, and South Africa. A few years later, the paintings are scientifically dated, and it becomes very clear. These magnificent images—usually of animals, very rarely of human forms—are, indeed, quite authentic. Produced by very early, humans 20,000, 30,000, even 50,000 years ago; maybe more (Clottes, 2016).

They did it about as well as the most talented among us could today. But why did they do it? What meaning did cave art have? What functions? Decoration? Magic? Why do we find it almost randomly, it seems, in some spaces within a given cave and not other spaces?

This question of "where," it turns out, leads to a major clue. Recently, some French archeologists decided to go into the caves and, on a hunch, sing. I don't how well those scientists sing, but what they heard is amazing. The chambers where there was art were ones that had, by far, the *best* musical resonance. Generally, only where there is the best acoustics do we see paintings on the walls.[1]

Moreover, there is virtually no evidence of human habitation deep in those caves. So-called cave men (and women) did not live in them. But soon in those painted chambers, hollowed-out bone flutes, pipes, and percussion instruments were discovered. And we begin to realize these art-filled chambers were probably, in good part, also musical spaces. Though skin drums probably existed, they would be more perishable—easily lost. But all the other elements of resonant, rhythmic, melodious sound are there. Most likely (to imagine it now all together) singing, dancing, flutes, pipes, and percussion. In torchlight, beneath vivid, stirring images.

So, our best guess from these, and other surviving, aboriginal cave paintings is that 40,000–50,000 or more years ago, humans came to use the caves as art-filled, musical, and—probably from everything we know about ritual and myth in human groups—*sacred* spaces. Sacred places.

Sacred images were combined with music—song and likely dance. An atmosphere of communal enchantment was created that was probably infused with the supernatural. In every known culture, music has been, and still is, seen as a way of communicating with God (the gods)—however variably (He, She, They, It, We) are defined.

Were these spaces, then, something we could call "Winnicottean caves," so to speak—collective "transitional," or "potential," spaces? Spaces where they (we) "dream up" meanings—as Bion (1962), Ogden (2010), Ferro (2009) might say. Are the caves—through the medium of art—early temples: meaning-making, meaning-reinforcing, spiritual homes?

Whatever our varied beliefs about the nature of human spirituality and religion (and, for me, these are very open questions), I think that some crucial clues to our need for and expression of the spiritual through the arts lie in our evolutionary history. By which I mean that what emerged in visual art and music—and, I'm suggesting, accompanying myth and ritual—was rooted in the existential core of human needs and anxieties. Anxieties that arose, as I hope to show, in the very basic, complex identity of being human. An identity that emerged in the earliest moments of our species' life on this planet (Erikson, 1963). The caves testify to the sacred meaning-making functions of the arts. Here is my relatively naturalistic view of *how* and *why* this powerful, existential, and spiritual set of needs emerged. Although I will come to focus specifically on the art of music, I will try to show how the overall proclivity to create art evolved as a crucial way of addressing this core set of emergent human needs.

The familiar story: the evolution of abstract thought and language

Not long (in evolutionary time) before we painted and sang in the caves, we humans had become transformed into a distinctly new species—a species with, on the whole, a relatively unique way of knowing and relating to reality.

For a long time (a few million years) we had been an earlier, ape-like primate—a mammal adapted to our universe (like all the other non-human animals), primarily through a huge amount of innate (and innately unfolding) knowledge of, and responsiveness to, the world.

But then, around 150,000 years ago, we shifted pretty radically. A radical but by no means total shift (remember this: it's a partial, not a total shift, because this "incompleteness," as it were, will turn out to be crucial to the nature of human identity). We shifted toward the need and the capacity to construct our experience—to construct and narrate our experience of the world. Human language had begun to develop. We began to be heavily shaped by, and to shape, our world through everyday language, as well as through an immense amount of learning. We began to know the world in good part by taking in (identifying with) aspects of the minds—the now complex, constructed subjectivities—of others including the group's collective, historical institutionalized mind that we call culture (Mayr, 1974; Slavin & Kriegman, 1992; Trivers, 1985).

Imagine it. Bit by bit over evolutionary time, as human infants we came into the world with much less innately organized, less directly usable knowledge (less knowing of the world, knowing others, and being known by them and the world). We then start to use—to need to use—the minds, the experiences, the subjectivities of others, to know the world as well as continuously to create—to sustain and modify—our very sense of self. We begin to experience a vastly expanded and reflected-upon sense of time. Language, a distinctly human language, evolves with the recursive, self-reflective, layered structure for generating metaphor—for, as Robert Frost quipped, "saying one thing while meaning another." And we begin to live largely within the stories that we and our culture create (Hrdy, 2010; Konner, 2011).

"God made humans," quotes Elie Wiesel (1995), "because He loves stories" (p. 10). Of course, some of us might say, "humans made God because we love (and need) stories." God being, for some of us, one of those vital stories. The point is, here, though, as Joan Didion put it simply, as humans, "We tell ourselves stories in order to live" (Didion, 1979, p. 11).

So far, this is not a terribly unfamiliar human, evolutionary story. But my point today is that in this form of the evolutionary story—the so-called "natural history"—something absolutely crucial is left out. Left in the shadows of this "evolutionary story" is the recognition that there was also for us, along with these cognitive, linguistic, instrumental gains, a very significant loss.

In the evolutionary shadows: "original loss" and existential anxiety

What do I mean by significant loss? I mean that in order to open ourselves, our minds—literally, our brains—to these vast new cognitive capacities, we needed to open up more and different interior space, as it were (neural space, if you will)—space for a whole new neural system. In order to allow language and increasingly complex cognition to shape us, we needed, simultaneously, to radically diminish our ready access to—and reliance on—our existing mammalian, primate, psychological organization. In evolving into a distinctly human way of "Being-in-the world," as Heidegger might put it, we needed, bit by bit, to lose a good deal (certainly not all) of our formerly pervasive, visceral way of knowing of the world—knowing who and what we are. We lost an innate, internally cohesive animal embeddedness in nature. We lost the unmediated immediacy of a coherent, ordered net of evolved strategies about what to eat and what to fear, where we belong and where we don't. We lost clear imperatives about who we are—about what "in our blood" defines us, and, what, as the poet Stephen Dunn wrote, "needs to be done"(Dunn, 2009, p. 30).

Put simply, as a result of the combination of both what we gained (in awareness) and lost (in instinctual connectedness), we came to live in a universe relatively emptied of firmly inherited, innate, instinctual meanings. A background sense of relative aloneness emerged in what had become a relatively silent universe.

Pascal's (1662) haunting phrase "le silence éternel de ces espaces infinis m'effraie" ("the eternal silence of these infinite spaces terrifies me") (p. 4) puts it quite chillingly: the silent, empty world we sense is always already right there behind, I believe, any of the dense, compelling meaning frames, the beliefs, the worldviews (religious or otherwise) that we need and cherish. "God made the world out of nothing," wrote Paul Valéry (1941), "but the nothingness shows through" (p. 168).

What I'm saying is that an evolutionary, so-called pre-historic,[2] perspective puts this existential worldview into a context that highlights not simply the element of *absence* (that is already fundamental in Kierkegaard, Nietzsche, Heidegger, Sartre, Camus, Becker) but also the process by which that absence may have arisen—a process that, over time, also entailed substantial loss.

This new precariousness, this edge of uncertainty, evolved very early (at the dawn of homo sapiens, in the time of primitive hunter-gatherers). It became a fundamental background part of the human experience of self and reality. Our sense of our fallibility, our finiteness—our subjectivity—emerged hand in hand, as it were, with a substantial loss of our former implicit, animal oneness. We became able to know—unable to escape—the certainty of death, the likelihood of future suffering—the inevitable loss of ourselves, of who we are and of what and whom we love. Our self-reflective awareness emerged in the context of loss and impermanence, becoming, in effect, a bodily rooted fact of life.

In analytic language, we can call this inherent, human background dread our potential for annihilation anxiety. It is there, always there, buffered immensely, crucially, by the loving presence of a connected, reasonably attuned other. Yet, as Winnicott (1951) knew, it is "an edge of annihilation" that is there in human children from the beginning. It is not "caused" or created by individual or collective trauma per se. Though certainly it may be ushered into our experience—overwhelmingly, often disastrously—by such trauma. And the loving, recognizing presence of an attuned other is its best, maybe only, ultimate antidote—the only sense that there is something between us and the abyss. But our primal terror does not simply derive from the other's absence. And, of course, as a human universal, it will be constructed and experienced, both individually and culturally, in a huge range of manifestly different ways (Slavin & Klein, 2014).

Cave spaces: grieving "original loss" in art and music

Which brings us back to the subject of art. For if—as the archeological record seems to indicate—the caves were a site for "dreaming up," representing, and performing re-embodied meanings (as Bion (1962), Ogden (2010), Ferro (2009), Winnicott (1951) might refer to this process), the appearance of very early human cave art suggests that the very capacity to create metaphorical meaning probably evolved—in my view, had to evolve—virtually simultaneously with the emergence of human existential anxiety. And that, put simply, our metaphor-generating, symbol-forming capacities (in visual, musical, poetic, and narrative forms) provided a kind of antidote—or, better, a vitally needed complement—to the otherwise sometimes silent, perhaps newly terrifying world into which we were evolving.

In short, the arts—the basic capacity for metaphor—may have given a needed aliveness, a connectedness (or *re*-connectedness) to an otherwise always-about-to-be-empty universe. Art enabled us to create—in effect, *re-create in a distinctly human way*—a sense of deep, visceral connection to others. It also enabled us to re-connect with a natural world that had lost large chunks of its immediate and automatic meanings.

It was thus in the challenge of facing this universal sense of a void—as if longing to re-connect with a former, visceral, instinctual way of knowing—that our voracious need for art emerged. "Suffering," said Nietzsche (1872), "is universal."

"Survival," he said, "lies in making meaning of it." Art, the arts—in their own transient, ritualized, here-for-a-moment-then-gone ways (the ways of beauty)—create the momentary, visceral experience of such re-connection. They carry and, as my patient Ethan said, "know" such meaning.

Serving as temples—distinct, bounded, part and apart from the world—and "transitional" or "potential" space (Winnicott, 1951), the caves became symbolically transformed physical spaces in which the "original loss" of our instinctual embeddedness could be grieved through the creative use of our new cognitive capacities. By "grieved" through art and ritual,

I imply a distinctly new, paradoxical, human form of both remembering and forgetting loss; of bearing it, enduring it by re-connecting with what is lost (even, in the caves, killed) in a fashion that does not deny the loss but transforms and, in some sense, deepens the experience of it.

Grieving "original loss" through myth: the lost garden, the Fall, blame, sin

The mythologies of all cultures provide crucial vehicles for such grieving—stories, conveyed with images, sounds: narratives of human origins. Stories that build meaning around the universal human trauma entailed in the loss—and ongoing absence—of our earlier visceral primate interconnectedness. All cultures in their myths of human origins try to grieve and heal what I call that "original loss."

For example, consider a very familiar Near Eastern myth that has endured in the consciousness of Judaism, Christianity, and Islam and that has distinct parallels in many of the major African, Australian, and Asian religious cultures (Mulhall, 2005).

Adam and Eve's exile from the Garden of Eden is sometimes a very beautiful (and in many ways a very troublesome) story—a metaphorical narrative—that, as I see it, serves to capture in symbolic story form the evolutionary narrative, and to address precisely these existential anxieties. Think of it like this: Eating the fruit of the tree of knowledge stands for having gained an immense capacity for a reflective, language-mediated awareness of self and the world. A need to navigate the incredible tensions of self-love and love for others—the knowledge of good and evil. The expulsion and the Fall then depict the evolved, psychological reality of our awareness of our precarious, finite, mortal condition in terms of the loss of the innocent, immortal harmony of life in Eden.

The overall story symbolically depicts both our evolutionary gains—the extraordinary human capacity to know, to learn, and to manipulate the world—and our loss: the separation from an earlier, wordless unity with the natural world in which we were unselfconsciously free from the haunting awareness of our mortality.

Then, as in most traumatic loss narratives, the story is defensively turned to blame, both self and other blame. Human capacities are re-cast as a transgressive desire to overreach—to want to know, to try to know too much. Knowledge beyond what God ordains becomes transgressive, destructive knowledge. The cause of the Fall becomes focused on our desire—rather, Eve's desire, woman's desire, erotic desire. It becomes a matter of having been influenced by her and thus not accommodating to God's rules.

The metaphor, the myth, transforms our sense of "original loss"—the vague human sense of a void where there was once a fuller, more seamless, embedded connectedness to nature—into a narrative of blame and sin, especially female sin. She did it. Women did it. Inherently, still do it. A core, natural, evolved psychological state is transformed into an ancient transgressive choice. It is as if our "original loss" is brilliantly, implicitly grasped; and, then, through the lens of a patriarchal, historically misogynistic culture, depicted as an "original sin."

As Fairbairn (1952) put it so well in terms of individual trauma, self-blame and a sense of one's own evil is preferable to facing a godless, thus empty, universe. The narrative of blame, of sin, replaces the greater psychological danger of the experience of utter loss—the loss on the individual level of all "good objects" (Fairbairn, 1952). As a shared, cultural experience, it is represented as a collective loss of a former, blissful existence in a paradise free from existential anxiety.

In one sense, viewing things in these terms is like acknowledging, with Nietzsche, that at some point in the evolution of a distinctly human awareness "God died." By which I mean that a few hundred thousand years earlier than Nietzsche realized the experience of a certain overarching, instinctual, automatic embeddedness in nature was no longer an innately given aspect of human experience. The various deities we imagine and worship are thus creative, human attempts to capture (re-capture) that connectedness and coherence of Being-in-the-world. In this very open and broad sense, God—as Winnicott (1951) said of the object—is always waiting to be both "found and created"; in a fully human sense to be known.[3]

So, if the caves were, in fact, such sacred spaces of worship, they were then, perhaps, the space in which, in a certain sense, we humans celebrated the birth of God. A sacred space in which, early on, we began the vital process of creating the "transitional illusion" (in its broad, adaptive, Winnicottean sense) of profound reconnection with the world. Grieving, in a broad sense, the trauma of our original loss. Not our original sin—that's a defensive, substitute story—but our "original loss." Our need is to continuously find, create, re-find, and re-create a world of forms, beauty, morality, connection. To experience immediate visceral, beyond-words meanings that in some measure retrieve and order the embeddedness in nature that we lost. Finding God in this human way restores viscerally a sense of being "at home" in this world. God, in this view, is a continuing creative human process of grieving.

Music as an evolved capacity in the brain and the mind

Now, moving back towards Ethan's, "the music knows," I'll look a bit more closely at the art of music.

Recent as well as traditional, historical work on music gives us a close look inside musical form.[4] We can look inside the form as it lives within the patterning of sound itself and, simultaneously, we know now, inside the neural machinery of the mind. How fully and uniquely music connects itself with our being. How, in this wordless medium, complex, human, existential realities and interactional themes can be reached, evoked, processed—known.

We know that music is basically humanly organized sound. And, as all musicians know, just as important are the spaces between sounds. The rhythmic timing of sound and silence. Not enough silence, and music is intrusion.

We know now, from fMRIs, that when music evolved—literally, organically—into our bodies, it became a form of experience (the one form of experience) that lights up more brain areas (cortical and sub-cortical) simultaneously than any other. The whole team, as it were: the limbic system (the amygdala), the executive functions of the pre-frontal cortex, memory circuits (the hippocampus), the motor system (the cerebellum), and, of course, the auditory cortex. Musicality evolved into more of the brain, *simultaneously*, and in more complex interconnections than any other direct experience. Music, in other words (and without words), reaches deep, reaches everywhere—in a holistic, not left- or right-brain, way.

And it's essentially a human universal. Although musical styles, conceptions of beauty, and preferences vary enormously around the world and throughout history, there seems to be, roughly, basic universal agreement that certain emotions are evoked by the same basic musical tropes: joy, sadness, terror, Eros, disgust, rage, triumph.[5]

So, it's universal. It taps everything in the multiplicity of the brain. And, take my dad, for example, who, like people you probably know, was in his mid-90s when a simple, slowing-down kind of dementia crept in. Many bits of memory are lost. Yet musical memories, including thousands of beautiful lyrics, are the last to go (Sacks, 2007). They don't go. And, in my father's case, an incredible, creative capacity actually emerges for producing new melodies, new lyrics—especially love songs to my mother, who had just died.

At the other end, from fetal life onward, human children are designed to learn crucial aspects of relating, essentially tonally and musically (Trevarthan, 1998; Beebe & Lachmann, 2014; Sander, 2008), calling and responding, playing, making relational and even moral meaning are learned through what are essentially "proto-conversations" (Trevarthan, 1998). These are games with predictable harmonies and pauses—distinctive melodies and rhyming cadences. The sympathetic sharing of musicality in these natural movements defines the human biology that motivates companionship and learning. All of this inherent musicality echoes Jessica Benjamin's (1995) conception of the "rhythmic third" as an inherent dimension of both early and later intersubjective communication.

Music became entwined with our being (as did other art forms) because its very structure can echo aspects of the deep structure of the human condition. I'm suggesting that as music evolved its complex links to every interconnected region of our brain, it was literally "selected for," favored, and shaped as a human need through natural selection—because, in its preverbal fashion, it momentarily restores us to experiences of a connectedness that we lost (and need).

Musical repetition, variation, newness and conflict: self and other

Specifically, but very broadly, music is, at its core, about setting up expectations, violating them, renewing them, and re-affirming them. All music is about remembering and repetition—crucial. And variation—equally crucial. Remembering, repeating and … creating something new.

My brother (a musicologist and my closest consultant as well as my musician friends and patients) tells me that truly effective music must end in a paradoxically expected and unexpected place—in its essence both affirming and surprising.

Thus, minor keys shift to major keys, to minor. Harmony to threatened disharmony. And back. Timing shifts. Consonance, dissonance, consonance.

Tiny shifts that mean a lot in the larger picture. Or huge shifts that turn out to be restorative. Ordered ritual and deviating spontaneity—both, as Hoffman (1998) says, in a dialectical (crucial) relationship to each other and to the greater whole.

The point is the means by which music engenders an experience of breakdown of expectation—followed in some way each time by some effort at a genuine "restoration-with-variation." This entails a kind of deeply structured "destruction/creation" pattern within the form itself, akin to where Benjamin (1995) (following Winnicott (1969)) finds the deep structure of our basic sense of intersubjective realness.

But there is also a second, basic dialectical tension in musical form that links it to a fundamental, human, existential dynamic: being alone and being with an other. Being capable of being alone while being *with* another—others. Reconciling the separateness of the agendas of self and other.

We are very alone, internally, with music and also, often, more intensely connected with others (listening, dancing) than at any time except, maybe, occasionally, sex. Getting inside musical experience itself—the rhythms, notes, melodies and harmonies, and timing and tonal interplays in all forms of music—we experience in bodily form the tensions, the natural oppositions (and the equally natural and necessary accommodations and interconnections) between the individual and others. Musical elements themselves (not to mention the performers) are constantly creating their own dynamic inner world that parallels (reflects and organizes) the universal human tensions between self and other. The music sets them up, resolves them, and re-creates them. Consider an incredible example (a very un-familiar one to our ears) of this lived "individual–otherness" tension in music.

The Congo Pygmies. They say that their incredible music (what we call "asynchronous polyphony") does two things for them:

1 They say that their music lets individuals go off on their own, do their own thing, shout, pray, dance, and express individuality. Something, they say, we all want and need to do. While at the same time each of us is actually staying with, fitting in with others, the group, the band (Turnbull, 1962).
2 They say (in a way that brings us directly back to the theme with which we started) that their music connects them with the wider, ancestral world—the world in and of the forest. A world, they say, their ancestors long ago used to be part of, and in living memory no longer are. In

> short, it sounds strikingly like their version of evoking and addressing the experience I called "original loss." The music, they say, gives meaning to the now silent separateness of Nature—imbues it with a sense of a recognizable, god-like, spiritual presence.

Might we say that effective music somehow "knows" that, in the process of creating and conveying its larger meanings, it needs to address this deep, primal longing for lost connection as well as these universal, self–other, individual–group tensions? Operating in its immediate, wordless, visceral way, must effective musical form—like form in all the arts—encompass our experience of differing, sometimes clashing, subjectivities? Does music thus work as an antidote to our existential aloneness, momentarily restoring a sense of human connectedness as well as a lost sense of oneness with the world?

We may tell ourselves that tribal hunter-gatherers like the pygmies are so close to nature (in our eyes) that somehow they would not experience what I've called our universal, human "original loss." But pretty openly they tell us that they do, and that they are using this form of art to share—not to negate, not override—their loss, their aloneness with others.

This is best expressed experienced through the ears, and I hope readers will listen along to the audio that accompanies this section of the chapter.[6] The music knows. It seems to "understand" our human condition. It is beauty that at the same time *hurts*, says Carson McCullers, describing her heroine, Mick, in her 1940 classic, *The Heart Is a Lonely Hunter*: "Wonderful music was the worst hurt there could be … [T]he whole world was this symphony and Mick felt there was not enough of her to listen" (p. 131).

Not enough of her. Not enough of us. The power of something that hurts because it is stretching us. Recognizing us *and* stretching us, to something missing, absent, lost—bigger.

"Beauty is nothing," as Rilke (1955) put it, "but our first glimpse at a terror that we can barely endure" (First Duino Elegy).[7]

Coda: What Ethan and I know

"No. There, no way, Ethan, that I can really know all that devastation, the loss, the deadness that's with you now …" As you remember, that's what I heard myself saying to my patient, Ethan. And, then, his reply: "Yeah, I'll do now what I've always done: listen to music … the music knows." In those moments, I violated a certain expectation of Ethan's: that he would be, could be, known. And simultaneously, of course, I fulfilled an old one: that he won't be.

Yet, something had told me that I needed to risk disappointing a certain expectation because, perhaps, I sensed the deeper nature of what Ethan needed. And if we were ever to inch nearer to what, for me, might become authentically knowing him, I might have to violate the expectation of a kind of hoped-for, more immediate connection right now.

I don't mean deliberately frustrating his need for empathic connection. And I certainly listened to the particular music by the particular groups he sometimes sent to me. Rather, his bringing in music's mysterious "capacity to know" signaled to me—probably to both of us—something more profound than I realized concerning the level of experience he needed to deal with in himself: the primal resonances of loss, of grieving to which he needed to go. A level to which I would somehow need to become closer, not only in him, but, somehow with him, in myself. A level of recognition that—far from moving away from the personal, or away from the specific relational moment between us—paradoxically deepens and amplifies my grasp of the particular emotional meanings of the moment.

Why? How do things move from the universal to the immediate, the personal, including the personal history of trauma? Well, as I've come to see it, in part, because the deadening, alienating, unreal states that plague someone who has known deep trauma actually also grant them exceptional access to, capacity to see the darkest edges of experiences we all share. Patients like Ethan (whose experience may be hard to reach) very often see only too plainly, as it were, the existentially precarious and conflictual context of all attachments. They have seen and known the existential void, the precarious and illusory dimension of all meaning—the inevitable clashes of their needs, their reality, and that of the very people they must turn to for love. The reality they've seen about the human heart has had too few buffers, too little shared experience of love and recognition to contextualize it, to render it more bearable. But it is real.

My capacity to recognize this level of what his trauma "knows" about life will ultimately become a profound source of connection between us. By which I mean opening myself anew to my only real way of feeling it with him. That is, coming to feel it anew and struggle in some form with my own versions of what are, in effect, the same shared, existential human issues that Ethan faces. Different versions of, frankly, what are, for all of us, the same human conflicts around our own needs and those of the needed other—set precariously in the shadow of the often haunting existential abyss.

Ethan's trauma "knows" that we must, somehow, enter that shared abyss. As I have come to understand it, the trauma won't loosen its grip until he's taught enough about it to me, to us—together. Until the underlying deeper meanings of both his individual trauma and the universal trauma that it illuminates find some better form of expression.

Trauma repeats, often, in order to compel us to remember what must not be forgotten—not only in one's individual history but in the crucial glimpses of the shared, existential trauma that individual trauma has painfully unveiled. The realities of loss and conflict that, when recognized, actually create the essential background, the bracing foundation of our vital capacity to find and create beauty, hope, meaning, nobility, and loving connection.

Clinically, this translates into an incredibly complex, personal, internal, and intersubjective process. Opening ourselves around the evocation of our own deeper annihilation fears as well as to the here-and-now lived conflicts around the ways our own needs and agendas will inevitably clash with those of our patients. Ethan probed my personal capacity to respond differently enough from lifelong efforts to engage others in this way. Failing this challenge, we intensify what are the worst aspects of our patient's trauma—that their experience separates them continuously from the world. Very few of us can, or want to, grasp the unbearable truths in what they have seen and known (Slavin, 2005; Slavin & Kriegman, 1998).

For me, an evolutionary-existential perspective calls us to a kind of radical empathy and recognition: a challenging openness to being seen and felt struggling with our patients to re-enter the process of making meaning around the same human issues that torment them, calls us to what I think is a radical level of empathy, based in a universally shared ancient trauma and ancient human vulnerability. Linked, deep down, to the ongoing experience of the shared loss of a greater embeddedness in nature that, as I've told it, we all partially lost when we became human. Linked, ironically, to our common suffering—to our shared, enduring "original loss"—there may well emerge the most poignant, yet reassuring and potentially creative, human bonds.

Notes

1 On my own visits to the caves, the guides affirm this correlation over and over.
2 That term is a pejorative othering of our early ancestors because it is, actually, simply more deeply historical.
3 On my own visits to many caves, I could easily imagine how early humans probably crawled along and found, in the actual cracks, convex mounds, and holes in the wall, the "presence" of the animal in its spirit. Then, only then, would they represent it in paint. The animals were what they needed, worshiped, killed, and loved. Many were wounded animals—in essence, wounded gods.
4 Like Daniel Levitin's *This Is Your Brain on Music* (2007) and *The World in Six Songs,* (2010), Oliver Sacks' *Musicophilia* (2007) and Steven Mithen's *The Singing Neanderthals* (2007) built upon centuries of brilliant musical theorizing from Plato though Schopenhauer, Nietzsche, and the work of Leonard Meyer, John Blacking, and Ethan Huron.
5 I wish I could illustrate and you could directly experience these links between sound and emotion.
6 Please go to www.psychologyandtheother.com/slavin to experience the music that accompanies this section of the chapter. In my experience, certain Western polyphonic music composed for church liturgies—especially when sung and heard in cathedral settings—stirs a profoundly "spiritual" response from even the most secular non- (even anti-) religious audiences. This capacity to pull at what I believe are unconscious existential chords embedded in the created, musical forms occurs in many types of music of many different eras. Listen to the French Renaissance piece "Nasciens Mater"" by Mouton, illustrated on the link. In it, there are eight voices, only four written parts, in ordered canonical tension—all notably separate yet all exquisitely together.
7 Translated from the original German by the author.

References

Beebe, B. & Lachmann, F. (Eds.) (2014). *The Origins of Attachment: Infant Research and Adult Treatment.* New York: Routledge.

Benjamin, J. (1995). *Like Subjects, Love Objects: Essays on Recognition and Sexual Difference.* New Haven, CT: Yale University Press.

Bion, W. R. (1962). *Learning from Experience.* New York: Basic Books.

Clottes, J. (2016). *What Is Paleolithic Art? Cave Paintings and the Dawn of Human Creativity.* Chicago, IL: University of Chicago Press.

Didion, J. (1979). *The White Album.* New York: Simon & Schuster.

Dunn, S. (2009). *What Goes On: New and Selected Poems, 1995–2009.* New York: W.W. Norton Co.

Erikson, E. (1963). *Childhood and Society.* New York: W. W. Norton.

Fairbairn, W. R. D. (1952). *An Object Relations Theory of Personality.* New York: Basic Books.

Ferro, A. (2009). Transformations in dreaming and characters in the psychoanalytic field. *The International Journal of Psychoanalysis*, *90*(2): 209–230.

Hoffman, I. Z. (1998). *Ritual and Spontaneity in the Psychoanalytic Process: A Dialectical-Constructivist View.* Hillsdale, NJ: The Analytic Press.

Hrdy, S. (2010). *Mothers and Others: The Evolutionary Origins of Mutual Understanding.* Cambridge, MA: Harvard University Press.

Konner, M. (2011). *The Evolution of Childhood: Relationships, Emotion, Mind.* Cambridge, MA: Belknap Press of Harvard University Press.

Levitin, D. (2007). *This Is Your Brain on Music: The Science of a Human Obsession.* New York: Penguin.

Levitin, D. (2010). *The World in Six Songs*. London: Aurum Press.

Mayr, E. (1974). Behavior programs and evolutionary strategies. *American Scientist*, *62*: 650–659.

McCullers, C. (1940). *The Heart Is a Lonely Hunter.* New York: Mariner, Houghton Mifflin.

Mithen, S. (2007). *The Singing Neanderthals: The Origins of Music, Language, Mind, and Body*. Cambridge, MA: Harvard University Press.

Mulhall, S. (2005). *Philosophical Myths of the Fall.* Princeton, NJ: Princeton University Press.

Nietzsche, F. (1872). The birth of tragedy. In Kaufmann, W. (Ed. & Trans.), *Basic Writings of Nietzsche* (pp. 1–144). New York: Random House, 2000.

Ogden, T. H. (2010). On three forms of thinking: Magical thinking, dream thinking, and transformative thinking. *Psychoanalytic Quarterly*, *79*(2): 317–347.

Pascal, B. (1662). *Pensées* (A. J. Krailsheimer, Trans.). New York: Penguin Classics, 1995.

Rilke, R. M. (1955). *Rilke: Sämtliche Werke. Band 1–6, Band 1.* Wiesbaden und Frankfurt: Insel Presse.

Sacks, O. (2007). *Musicophilia: Tales of Music and the Brain.* New York: Random House.

Sander, L. (2008). Recognition process: Context and experience of being known. In Sander, L., Amadei, G., & Bianchi, I. (Eds.), *Living Systems, Evolving Consciousness and the Emerging Person: A Selection of Papers from the Life Work of Louis Sander* (pp. 177–204). New York: The Analytic Press.

Slavin, M. O. (2005). Afterword, Why the analyst needs to change. In Aron, L. & Harris, A. (Eds.), *Relational Psychoanalysis II* (pp. 211–219). Hillsdale, NJ: The Analytic Press.

Slavin, M. O. & Klein, E. J. (2014). Probing to know and be known: Existential and evolutionary perspectives on the "disorganized" patient's relationship with the analyst. In Beebe, B. & Lachmann, F. (Eds.), *The Origins of Attachment: Infant Research and Adult Treatment* (pp. 163–171). New York: Routledge.

Slavin, M. O. & Kriegman, D. (1992). *The Adaptive Design of the Human Psyche: Psychoanalysis, Evolutionary Biology, and the Therapeutic Process.* New York: Guilford Press.

Slavin, M. O. & Kriegman, D. (1998). Why the analyst needs to change: Toward a theory of conflict, negotiation and mutual influence in the therapeutic process. *Psychoanalytic Dialogues*, *8*(2): 247–284.

Trevarthan, C. (1998). The concept and foundations of infant intersubjectivity. In Braten, S. (Ed.), *Intersubjective Communication and Emotion in Early Ontogeny* (pp. 15–46). Cambridge, MA: Cambridge University Press.

Trivers, R. (1985). *Social Evolution.* Menlo Park, NJ: Benjamin Cummings.

Turnbull, C. M. (1962). *The Forest People*. New York: Simon & Schuster.

Valéry, P. (1941). *Mauvaises pensées et autres.* Paris: Gallimard.

Wiesel, E. (1995). *The Gates of the Forest: A Novel.* New York: Schocken.

Winnicott, D. W. (1951). Transitional objects and transitional phenomena. In *Collected Papers: Through Pediatrics to Psychoanalysis* (pp. 229–243). New York: Basic Books, 1975.

Winnicott, D. W. (1969). The use of an object and relating through identifications. In *Playing and Reality* (pp. 101–112). London: Penguin.

Index